In your role as a parent, have you occasionally wondered if you're doing the right thing? You need wonder no longer. The Paradox Principle of Parenting *will address this and many more issues, and you will learn how to parent great kids God's way.*

BOB AND YVONNE TURNBULL
Marriage & family speakers and authors

Oh, how I wish I would have read this book 22 years ago when I first became a parent! It is the most compelling and transformational training manual on parenting I have ever read, masterfully written for parents who are prayerfully rearing the next generation. Author James Lucas captures in print the mind of God on parenting.

MARTY CUTRONE
National Campaign Director of 40 Days of Purpose, Saddleback Church

Too often parents feel they don't have the tools or the expertise to be effective parents. James Lucas promises to help all parents gain a greater mastery of the demanding ministry of parenting. By showing us how God himself relates to us as a parent, Lucas has illuminated a long-overlooked example for us to emulate. Lucas's grasp of Scripture and its application to the all-important task we have as parents is certain to help everyone who reads this book to become a more effective parent.

DR. RICHARD D. LAND
Host of *For Faith and Family* and *Richard Land Live*

Have you ever experienced a sense of confusion about the task of parenting? Have you felt trapped between seemingly contradictory expectations of what it means to be a good parent? Take heart! James Lucas slices through the "How-to" thinking of our day to take us directly to the foundation of good parenting: the example of God, our heavenly parent.

WARREN SCHUH
Executive Pastor of Calvary Community Church, CA

Good parenting is often survival; great parenting is much, much more. If you've never processed the counterintuitive nature of great parenting—as modeled by the One who calls Himself "Heavenly Father"—you owe it to yourself (and your kids) to read this powerful manual for positive molding!

BOB SHANK
Founder/Coach of The Masters Program

James Lucas gives us tremendous insights not only about parenting but about life. As a father of six grown children, I can verify the value of Lucas's insights about parenting. As a follower of Christ, I can verify Lucas's insights about the Master Parent's relationship with us. [Lucas] shows us how to practically apply seemingly paradoxical principles to our most treasured relationships.

LINUS J. MORRIS
President of Christian Associates International

The

PARADOX PRINCIPLE

—➤ *of* ◄—

PARENTING

How to parent your child
like God parents you

JAMES R. LUCAS

Tyndale House Publishers, Inc.
WHEATON, ILLINOIS

Visit Tyndale's exciting Web site at www.tyndale.com

Visit the Relationship Development Center at www.relationshipdevelopmentonline.com

Edited by Lisa A. Jackson

Designed by Ron Kaufmann

Library of Congress Cataloging-in-Publication Data

Lucas, J. R. (James Raymond), date.
   The paradox principle of parenting : how to parent your child like God parents you / James R. Lucas
     p. cm.
   ISBN 0-8423-6105-7
   1. Parenting—Religious aspects—Christianity.   I. Title

BV4529 .L83 2003
248.8′45—dc21   2002152941

Printed in the United States of America

06   05   04   03
  7   6   5   4   3   2   1

For

PETER BARRETT

Table of Contents

Acknowledgments

This is my twelfth book, and I am always awed when I sit down to write the acknowledgments page, because there are so many kind and caring people involved in a project like this.

From the beginning, Dave Hoover at Tyndale House believed in this project and its vision for parenting. Jan Long Harris, in her shepherding of the book and her substantive editing, has been an author's dream—open, honest, encouraging, visionary, and pragmatic. Lisa Jackson has edited this book with a care that can only be hoped for and has gently but firmly challenged me to make the whole book, every line of it, the best it can possibly be. Jan and Lisa, you're the best. I want to thank the rest of the team at Tyndale House, including a very fine marketing and publicity group, for your contributions to this effort.

Members of my staff, who are also my dear friends, have put their hearts and prayers and ideas into this book. This is the real Dream Team. I want to give special thanks to Priscilla Buchanan, who has been a tremendous supporter and encourager all the way through, and to Maryl Janson, who has supplied insight and examples. Thanks to all for your understanding, and for reminding me that I really do enjoy being a writer!

I want to give a special thanks to Dr. Les Parrott for his insight and encouragement. Les, few have been as devoted to developing effective relationships as you.

When you write a book about parenting, you can't dodge the contributions of your children: the ideas and insights that have grown out of a thousand individual and group conversations, the development of great character as they've trusted the principles, and their forgiveness for my mistakes and willingness to put up with me. They are a special group of human beings who have bonded remarkably well with each other—despite a lot of teasing and banter. Many and deep thanks to you, Laura, Peter, David, and Bethany—and, of course, to Pam.

And I want to acknowledge the many parents and young people who have shared their agonies, joys, problems, and victories in this inescapable relationship called "family." Through our work at the Relationship Development Center, an organization dedicated to helping people enhance their crucial life relationships, we have seen the whole range of emotions and situations that family life can bring. The depths of all of those experiences are somehow built into the soul of this book.

Finally, my thanks to L. L. for your inspiration and encouragement.

Foreword

When Woodrow Wilson was president of Princeton University, he spoke these words to a group of parents: "I get many letters from you parents about your children. You want to know why we people up here in Princeton can't make more out of them and do more for them. Let me tell you the reason we can't. It may shock you just a little, but I am not trying to be rude. The reason is that they are your sons and daughters, reared in your homes, blood of your blood, bone of your bone. They have absorbed the ideals of your homes. You have formed and fashioned them. They are yours. In those malleable, moldable years of their lives you have forever left your imprint upon them."

As a college professor for more than a dozen years, I know a bit about what President Wilson was getting at when he spoke to these parents. And now as the father of two little boys who haven't even begun kindergarten, it sometimes scares me to death. I look at these little lives God has entrusted my wife and me to care for and I am jolted into the vivid awareness of my responsibility. What I do, say, and think over the next two decades will be one of the most important influences in shaping the kind of men these boys will grow up to be. As a psychologist, I've had plenty of opportunity to assess other people's homes and analyze why they might be the way they are, but as a new parent, the tables have turned. I'm staring into the proverbial mirror and praying that God will show me the pathway to take in nurturing these little ones in a way that will bring deep and meaningful blessing to their lives.

That's why when James Lucas gave me a sneak peek at the book you hold in your hands I was thrilled. James has zeroed in on a revolutionary parenting model that is both simple and profound. Its paradoxical principles will turn your parenting perceptions inside out and upside down, but I'm certain they will help your kids turn out right. How can I be so sure? Because James goes straight to the source by showing us how our heavenly Father parents us. He brings us to the ultimate biblical example and reminds us that the birth of a baby in a manger once caused midnight to become midday as the glory of the Lord came to this planet and forever inverted the way life can be lived. And through *The Paradox Principle of Parenting*, James Lucas is showing us exactly how that inverted life can powerfully impact our parenting—and ultimately the children we parent.

Dr. Les Parrott III
Seattle Pacific University

Introduction

It hit me one day, like a lightning bolt from a relational storm: The way to parent great kids is right there in front of us.

It struck me that imitating God, our Parent, should be the central theme of any parent's efforts if he or she wants to raise great kids. I was stunned by what now seems obvious: God should be used as a model in all respects, right down to the level of daily family life. He's our *Father*. We're made in his image. Why not copy him, including his parenting techniques?

I saw that this modeling involved looking at the "both/and" nature of God—how he blends apparent opposites (or contradictions) into a deep, rich, complex whole. For instance, he tells us over and over that he will punish us for our sins. And yet at the same time, he wipes the whole slate clean! Only by understanding these parenting paradoxes and following God in practicing them can we hope to have a solid and effective parenting life.

It was this idea that led to this book. I wanted to show you something other than a human scheme or "style" of parenting. I wanted to help you see that the best way to parent is displayed clearly in the relationship that God has with us—or wants to have with us, if we'll allow it. And we're not just talking about the parenting relationship that God displays in the Bible but also what is displayed in the reality of our own lives, our own experiences, and our own relationships with a very personal God.

There are books that talk about God as our Father and what this means about his relationship with us, but these books usually don't make the connection to the way we should parent our children. There are also numerous books on parenting. Many aren't based on biblical principles, much less on using the God described in the Bible as the model for parents. Using God, in all of his majestic complexity, as the model, this book will help you think about parenting in a way you may never have imagined, no matter how much you've already read on the topic.

Who is this book for? People who are serious about understanding God's plan for their families. Some might say, "Most parents aren't deep enough or smart enough to read a really serious book on parenting." I have more respect for you than that. I believe you want real help to do a fabulous piece of work raising fabulous kids, and I believe you know that only a serious book can help you make this happen.

This book is written for *all* parents. It is written for parents of children in all age groups (toddlers, teens, adults, etc.), for parents in all situations (two-parent households; single, divorced, foster parents, etc.), and for parents who are having success as well as parents who are struggling. This book is aimed at any parent who wants to eliminate the guesswork and do it like God. It applies to all of us, because God is the Father of all who believe.

This book is also for those in a position to positively impact parents and children: grandparents, who can also apply these principles very directly; relatives of parents or prospective parents; friends of people who have (or are expecting) children; and pastors, priests, rabbis, and counselors, for use in sermons, small-group studies, Bible studies or classes, or in individual counseling. Kids are complex, and since most parents are not armed with a guidebook, they need all the guidance they can get.

In my work as the executive director of the Relationship Development Center, an organization devoted to helping people develop and enhance their crucial life relationships, I have interfaced with a great many parents, including adoptive parents and foster parents. In my earlier work as a pastor, youth pastor, and director of youth education, I saw so many parents—and their children—colliding with each other in a clash of emotions and a battle of wills. Through those experiences, I've come to believe that most of these parents are struggling, with earnestness and even agony, to do the right thing. This guidebook is humbly offered to you.

I am the father of four—two young women and two young men—so I know where you are and what you are experiencing. The approach you'll read about in this book is not just theory, although the theory is sound because it is God's. It's also a very real-world application. I haven't always done these things; sometimes I've missed the mark with my own children. But I intend to keep trying to do these things, from now until forever.

As parents, we're constantly bombarded with advice on raising our kids. But it's tough to tell which way, if any, is better than all the rest. In this journey that I invite you to take with me, we'll see that there is indeed a "best way." It's not a mystery, and it's not something I've made up. It's laid out before us in the way that God parents us. It's not a course of study but a way of life. It's not about God's *advice* on parenting but about his *example.*

This book will help you to do the right thing. As you follow God, the Master Parent, you will see a dramatic difference in your kids. As a side benefit, your relationship with God will reach new levels of richness.

Why? Because master-parenting resonates with the longings we have in our own hearts to have an intimate connection with our own children *and* an intimate connection with our Father-God. Because from the highest perspective, parenting isn't a job or a profession. Parenting is a *relationship.*

With this book, you can become a master parent. You can do it just like God. No one will be happier than you.

Except, perhaps, your children.

MASTER-PARENTING
AND
THE PARADOX PRINCIPLE

———————

YOU want to raise good kids.

On your really hopeful days, you want to do even better. You want to raise *great* kids. The best. Kids who aren't just taking up space but who are really going somewhere. You want to raise not just decent kids but kids who will have an impact in life—kids who will make a difference.

I've got some wonderful news for you: *You can have what you want.*

You can have good kids. You can even have *great* kids. All you have to do is ask the right question.

It's not one that most of us are ever taught to ask, but it makes all the difference when it comes to raising great kids.

What is this question? Well, it's not about systems and approaches and tools and techniques. It's about a way of life. The most critical question you can ask as a parent is this: "Who or what is the perfect model for parenting?" To answer this question, we have to look first at the complicated role we've been called to play as parents.

THE ULTIMATE PARENTING PARADOX

"Listen, buddy, I'm your parent. Whether you like it or not, I'm in charge around here. Got it? You can complain all you want, but I'm not going to overlook your disobedience. And I'm not going to put up with your laziness and irresponsibility. God didn't put me here to be your friend. I'm the boss and don't you forget it. If you challenge me, you'll be sorry."

What kind of parent would say such things? Well, we would. You and I. If we're honest, most of us would have to admit that we've thought or said something like this at some point, to at least one of our children. Maybe even today.

What causes us to think or say such things? There are a lot of reasons, and not all of them are bad.

First, as parents, we have this *sense of responsibility,* this anxious feeling that if we don't do this "parenting thing" well, our kids will fail and we'll feel like jerks. And there's a lot of truth to this. We *do* have responsibility, and if we don't parent well, it *will* affect our children and we *will* feel rotten about it. The Bible says, "To have a fool for a son brings grief; there is no joy for the father of a fool."*

For most parents, our first goal is to *not* mess up our kids. "Do thy patient no harm," as the saying goes.

Second, we are accountable for the way our children turn out. It's going to sound pretty weak, later in life and on into the next, if we say, "But it wasn't my fault," or "That wasn't in any job description that *I* ever agreed to," or "Hey, I just wanted *babies.*" We can't duck it. Somehow, we all know in our souls that parenting Judgment Day is coming.

The third reason we assert our authority is that we *do* have authority over these children—an authority straight from God. We are the parents. We *are* in charge . . . well, sort of. We *are* the boss . . . well, kind of. We have the authority . . . whatever *that* means.

---

* References for Scripture quotations and sources for other material referenced in this book are located in the sources section in the back of the book.

Fourth, we speak this way because we think we don't have the resources that can make us great parents. We think we have to fall back on our own force or strategies. But it's not true. We can't say, "But I didn't know how to be a parent." We've got the truth straight from God. He didn't destine us to fail. In one sense, continuing in failure means that we simply didn't access the resources.

Fifth, these little collection points of tortured irrationalities—our kids—can be very, very frustrating. Yes, it's true that we're flawed as parents—not patient enough, not understanding enough, not mature enough—but our kids are also chock-full of flaws as well: problems, laziness, and irresponsibility (among many other things). We finally get past our youth and being treated badly by other kids, and then we have our own kids to carry on the work of making us feel inferior! If you really stop and think about it, you might come to the conclusion that your kids were sent here with a top-secret mission from God: to test your ability to withstand major doses of annoyance and aggravation. In fact, some days you *know* that's why your children are here.

And finally, we tend to get tough with our kids because these children are positively brilliant. They know how to play the "friend" dimension of our relationship like a fine fiddle. They know how to mess with the part of our hearts that really longs to have a terrific relationship with them. And they take advantage of it, deploying words and facial expressions and tears and body language in a guerrilla war of emotional blackmail. You might have thought they were napping in the other room all those years, but they were actually sneaking out to attend preschool classes like "How to Use 'I Hate You' as an Effective Means of Getting Your Way" and "Manipulate Your Way to Teenage Happiness."

Oh, yes. There is one final problem with the tirade at the beginning of this section. We are, indeed, supposed to be our children's friends.

Parenting really is a paradox. How is it possible to train our kids and mold them and discipline them and be in authority over them and still end up being their friends? Talk about a tough proposition! It feels as if God has given us dual assignments, each one working against the other.

As parents, we must be the masters of our children. Not "master" in the evil sense of boss, ruler, or dominator, but "master" in the historic sense of "one whose teachings others accept and follow." Another good definition is this: "A master is a worker qualified to teach apprentices." As masters, we are to be teachers, discipliners, mentors, spiritual leaders, and ultimately, the *authority*.

Not only are we to be masters, we are also to be lovers of our children. Not "lover" in the romantic sense but lover in the biblical sense of "one who treasures the soul of another." As lovers of our children, we are to be nurturers, partners, collaborators, fellow pilgrims, and ultimately, their friends.

The inescapable truth is that God put us here to be both master and lover, both authority and friend. It is one of the mind-boggling paradoxes of parenting, but it is at the center. It is the Ultimate Parenting Paradox. It not only affects our role as parents; it also affects our *identity* as parents.

How can God expect us to be both master and friend? It seems so contradictory. But this very idea is modeled in our own relationship with God, which is overflowing with this dual principle. God lives out the parenting paradox every day with you and me: "You are my friends if you do what I command." Wait a minute! What did that say? If we want to be God's friends, we must respect his authority. He has tied the master/authority thing together with the lover/friend thing.

As long as we're not living in rebellion, God can focus on the "friend" side, as Jesus does in this verse: "I no longer call you servants, because a servant does not know his master's business. Instead, I have called you friends, for everything that I learned from my Father I have made known to you."

Every one of us needs God, the Master Parent, to live out this dual assignment in his relationship with us. In the same way, our children need us to be both master and friend in our relationship with them. And believe it or not, you can be both!

You can live out this dual assignment fully with your own children, because God does it with you and he will gladly show you the Way. And if you learn the Way, something remarkable will happen. If you follow God's lead in this, becoming an apprentice to the Master Parent, you will end up with more than good kids—and more than great kids.

Because you're parenting your children like God parents you, you will end up with *godly* kids. They'll know what God is like, because you'll be showing them in the way you interact with them every day. As you become a master parent, fully trained by the Master Parent, master-parenting will transform your family.

MASTER-PARENTING

This book is about being a master parent. A parent who parents her children like God parents her. A parent who parents his children by following God's perfect model.

At the beginning of this chapter, we suggested that the most critical question of your parenting life could be, "Who or what is the perfect model for parenting?"

The answer we're looking for is a person, not a program. "Be imitators of God," Paul advised the Ephesian church. Does this include God's role as a parent? Yes! "In everything set them an example," Paul told Titus. God wouldn't ask something of us that he himself was not able and willing to do.

The general rule of master-parenting is this: If God does it, we will do it; if he doesn't do it, we won't either. God is our model and example. As we follow his lead, we become the best—because we've learned from the best.

And here's the best news of all: If we follow him in this, we will be a smashing success as parents. As we become master parents, our kids will make it all the way past good, eventually arriving at something truly great and godly.

SO WHAT DOES MASTER-PARENTING LOOK LIKE?

Master-parenting is based on the classic model of master and apprentice. An apprentice doesn't spend the day sitting in lectures or being told what to do. An apprentice learns by word, by example, and by practice. An apprentice listens to what the master says in order to lock the principle clearly in her mind. Then she watches the master do the work. She sees how to implement the principle, how to avoid mistakes and wasted effort. And then the apprentice tries to do the work herself—stumbling at first, asking the master for help, and growing in confidence as she sees her work improve.

Master-parenting follows this classic model of the apprentice and master. We listen to the word, the principles of the Master Parent, as presented in the Bible. We study it in order to lock the principles in our minds. Then we watch how the Master Parent parents his children. We see in detail how to implement the principles well, by looking at the Bible and at how God actually works with us every day. We learn how to stop making parenting mistakes and to avoid unhelpful practices. And then we put it into practice. We stumble, but we ask the Master Parent for help and we try again.

If we keep working at it—listening, learning, watching, practicing—we will indeed become master parents.

MASTER-PARENTING IS EFFECTIVE AND RADICAL

Master-parenting is very different from any other approach to parenting. Master-parenting is effective because it relates to humans—in this case, our children—as the beings they were designed to be. God didn't create people to be domesticated like cattle, trained like dogs, or whipped like horses. When we are treated this way, we often rebel—not because we are evil but because we were created to be respected and free: "It is for freedom that Christ has set us free."

This principle carries over into parenting as well. When treated like animals, our children are bound to rebel. But this reaction isn't really rebellion at all. Although our children are smaller than we are, they are of no less value or importance in God's sight. In their souls, they know it. In fact, rebelling against unfair or disrespectful treatment is actually a much better response than choosing to follow orders blindly or cower before demands. As our children get older, we *want* them to be strong enough to rebel against the unreasonable demands and orders of their peers.

We do indeed have a responsibility to set the rules, but that is not the whole of parenting, nor is it the best part. We need to offer our children the best relationship they will ever have. We need to be a model for all of their relationships for the rest of their lives.

Every parent, and every home, is perfectly designed to produce the results it is now getting. If you don't like the results you're getting, you need to change the design. Doing more of what you're already doing won't produce different results, just more of the same.

So here's the deal: If we don't like the results we're getting from our parenting techniques, then we must not be doing it like God does. We've got some other design or plan going and it just isn't working.

The good news is, of course, that we are free to change the design. And with God's help, we *can* change. It is possible for us to become proactive parents who take action now in order to make a difference later.

Maybe your children are young, and things seem to be going okay right now. Does it really make a difference if you apply these principles? Yes. You can be fooled by apparent success in the early years. What looks okay now could look terrible in ten years.

Master-parenting is *radical,* a word that means "to get back to the root." The root of parenting is God. He invented parenting. Then he invented the first parents. He gave them the ability to have children and the wisdom to parent well—and also the opportunity to do it badly if they didn't follow his lead.

When Jesus taught us to pray, he started off with the address, "Our Father." Not Savior or Lord or Master (although God is all of these), but "Father." God is interested in having us relate to him as his children, not as distant slaves or preprogrammed robots.

The concept of master-parenting frees us from schemes and programs and methods. It even frees us from focusing on results. When we ask, "How should I parent my child?" we need to ask, "How does God parent me?" in order to find the answer. Master-parenting is not a new approach to parenting. It is *the* approach to parenting. If we get this right, all of the rest will fall into place. We can throw out the old ways and "put on the new self, created to be like God in true righteousness and holiness."

A master parent is a beautiful being to behold. She resists doing it "just like Mom" (or just the opposite of Mom) and takes up the challenge of parenting her child like God parents her. And she takes comfort from the idea that she can learn it all from a person who loves her: her Father, her Master Parent.

HOW DOES GOD PARENT YOU?

If we're honest, we must admit that we want some things from our parenting that seem contradictory. We want a deep relationship with our children, something special that will last till the end of our lives. And we also have expectations and plans and directions for our children.

God is in the same "predicament" as we are. He is our Father, and he wants deep relationship with us. He is also our authority, so he has expectations and plans and directions for our lives. But there is no conflict between these roles in God's parenting of us because our relationship with him grows as we learn to trust his leading in our lives. The same thing happens as we parent our children.

If we agree that we want to parent our children like God parents us, we're ready for that next question: *How, indeed, does God parent us?* What does he do? What does he *not* do?

If we can figure this out, and go and do likewise, we will be able to raise kids who are the very best they can be, who form healthy relationships, and who lead godly lives that really count.

To do this, you first have to make sure that you are looking at your children like your Master Parent looks at you. You can ask yourself, *How does God look at me?* Your answer to this question is very important to your parenting. If, when you look at yourself through God's eyes, you see only failure—a messy loser—it's also easy to think of your children as worse than they really are.

On the other hand, if you look at yourself through God's eyes and see only success—a real godly star—it's also easy to think of your children as better than they really are.

The key is to look at your children *exactly as your Master Parent looks at you.* You've had failure, you've been a mess, you've lost— but he still loves you and blesses you and brings you back from defeat. And you've had success, you've done some godly things, you've had some moments of being a star for the kingdom—but he still disciplines you and punishes you and brings you down from your pedestal. A large part of this book is designed to help you discover how your Master Parent looks at you and parents you, so you can pass that accurate picture along to those eager young souls that so desperately need a master parent.

THE PARADOX PRINCIPLE

Master-parenting is simple but not simplistic. In this book, we'll look at eight great elements of master-parenting—eight paradoxical truths that make it all work. Understanding and practicing these truths are the keys to fully experiencing the Ultimate Parenting Paradox: that we can be both master and friend to our children.

Mediocre parenting results from an either/or attitude. *Either* we have high standards *or* we allow for sloppiness and mistakes. *Either* we take charge *or* we let our kids make their own decisions. *Either* we get them to respect us *or* we connect as friends. Mediocre parenting is easier than master-parenting, but the results are miserable. At the end of the day both parents and children wind up very unsatisfied.

Parenting books are often very incomplete because they talk about only half of the many gifts that God offers to us as his children. One book might emphasize relationship but miss emphasizing respect; another might focus on inherent personality but not see the power to change; still others address unconditional love while losing sight of justice and discipline and punishment. Ineffective parenting very often results from taking a one-sided view of a two-sided truth.

Master-parenting considers both sides; it's a both/and proposition.

In chapters three through ten, we will look at the eight great paradoxes that are at the heart of master-parenting. In my experience, most of the really great parenting blunders have been made by missing one, two, three, or more of these crucial paradoxes. "Great blunders are often made like large ropes, of a multitude of fibers," said novelist Victor Hugo. A wrong or incomplete emphasis in our approach to parenting can produce many negative, unintended results—the fibers of parenting disaster.

THE DIFFERENCE

There may be some who think that parenting is actually pretty clear-cut: run a tight ship, teach children some "absolute values," give them a good education, take meals and vacations together, be part of a good church, and discipline your kids when they miss the mark. Hit the beaches, take no prisoners or guff, and deliver the goods.

But although these ideas aren't necessarily wrong, they really don't get at the heart of what it means to be a parent.

Being a parent of great kids—what most parents want—means we must learn how to parent really well. It means that we know it isn't going to be easy. Parenting is a complex undertaking, full of richly textured paradoxes.

The paradoxes are there, at the center of parenting reality, whether we believe in them or not. Perception is not reality. Reality is reality. Believing an illusion—that there are schemes and formulas that will work better than godly principles—is just a way station on the path to being disillusioned. Adopting an illusion involves accepting a false or overly simplistic view of reality. But reality is a powerful force that demolishes those tempting views. Ultimately, we become disillusioned as the illusion crumbles under the relentless pressure of reality. By following schemes and formulas in our parenting, we believe an illusion. And that illusion feels good— right up to the moment when our home comes apart at the seams.

If we get these paradoxes right, we win. If we get them wrong, we . . . don't win.

But no one likes to lose, especially when it means losing our kids. That's why it's important to understand the inadequate alternatives to master-parenting. That will be the subject of the next chapter.

Two

INADEQUATE ALTERNATIVES
TO
MASTER-PARENTING

IT WAS a lovely fall day, right at the beginning of the new school year. As I passed an elementary school, I saw that it was crowded with cars overflowing with energy and dropping off students. My eye caught a bumper sticker, in bold blue letters, on the back of one car that referred to motherhood as a "proud profession."

Doesn't that bumper sticker sound honorable? What could be better than a woman who is completely devoted to the job of raising her children? Isn't parenting the most important job of our lives?

No.

We can—and should—honor the commitment of anyone who says, "I'm going to pour myself into being a first-class parent." But the problem with this whole line of thinking is that parenting isn't a job at all. It can be thought of as a job, treated as a job, and executed as a job. But parenting isn't a job; it's a *relationship*.

Families are about connecting people at the soul. They bring people together—sometimes in an embrace, sometimes in a collision—so that these assembled souls can learn to live together in this tiny microcosm of the grandest family of all, the forever family of heaven.

But if we think of parenting as a job, we'll start to treat it as a job. We'll focus on things like our job description: provide for their needs, ensure their safety, enroll them in various activities. We'll become the "Marthas" of parenting, scurrying around doing our job and missing the point of the whole show, which is to be the "Marys" of parenting. "You are worried and upset about many things," Jesus said to Martha, "but only one thing is needed. Mary has chosen what is better."

My hope is that we can honor the spirit of the bumper sticker even as we suggest an alternative way to think about how to apply it. In an age of broken homes, tattered relationships, and parents throwing in the towel, it's great when a parent steps up and says, "I'm going to give all I have in order to be the best parent I can be."

My point here is that not only is parenting different from a profession, it's more important and a whole lot more difficult.

Parenting is not simply a job where we have clear and established practices that result in logical and satisfactory outcomes. Consider this:

- **A job has limits.** We can go home from a job. We can leave it "at the office," at least to some extent. But what parent can go "home" from being a parent? How do we get away from it? Even if we could, would that be right? In a profession, we can expect everyone to know and follow the standards, but there is no such luxury in parenting. In a job, we can expect remuneration in accordance with our contribution, but in parenting we have to keep giving regardless of return. We can't demand more pay, take holidays off, or call in sick. We can quit a job, but we can't quit being parents. Even if we abandon our children, they are still our children. Relationships demand a commitment of our whole selves that no profession or job has a right to make.

- **We don't get paid for it.** Professionals, as opposed to amateurs, get paid for doing their work. Parenting is completely upside down from this principle; parents don't get paid, they pay to do it! Who in their right mind would choose a job or a profession they had to pay to do? We don't get paid because it isn't a profession. And we gladly pay, because these children are connected to our hearts. We could be taking nice vacations and buying nice things and building up a nice savings account, and instead we buy dresses and shirts and Happy Meals and Christmas presents and pets. This only makes sense if what we're doing is about love and relationship. A job set up like this would get few sane applicants.

Thinking of parenting as a profession doesn't elevate it. Instead, it lowers it from the majestic relationship that God intends it to be. Think of it this way: Would you say that it's God's *job* to be our Father? Not likely. Instead, it's his joy and his hope, the crowning relationship of them all.

Parenting is like friendship, only harder. With a friend, we develop the relationship as far as it will go. We spend time together, we talk, we find ways to enjoy each other's company. But we generally don't have the responsibility to shape and form and discipline and punish that friend. Intervention even in the best of friendships is rare, but in parenting we're doing it all the time. We have to do things as parents that would kill most friendships, but somehow, with inexplicable and even irrational hope, we would still like to end up being friends with our children. More than friends. Best friends.

SOME OTHER INADEQUATE ALTERNATIVES

There are some ideas out there on parenting that will take you far from your goal if you focus on them as *the* answer. We usually adopt them because we really want to parent great kids and we're willing to spend the time and energy to do it. But we won't achieve our goals if we choose the wrong way to do it. No matter how good our intentions, an inadequate plan will give us inadequate results.

Let me make it clear that these alternatives aren't bad in themselves. On the contrary, they're important components of being a master parent. But when any of these alternatives becomes our primary approach to parenting, we lose sight of the mountaintop and become less able to achieve our goals. "Parent as Professional" is only one really inadequate alternative to master-parenting. Let's make sure we know what other things master-parenting is not:

- **Parent as trainer.** In this popular approach, our primary role is behavior modification. We get our kids to do the proper things and not to do the improper things. It's easy to fall into this way of thinking, because God starts these complex beings off as helpless little people who don't know anything. In this option, discipline and punishment are the main "tools of the trade."

- **Parent as teacher.** Here, our goal is to get all of the things our kids need to know stuffed into their heads and (we hope) their hearts. We say it, and they're supposed to get it. Again, this is a bit of a trap because our kids really don't know anything when they are born, and it's compounded by the fact that God really does tell us to teach our children. In this approach, parents must be the "authority" on a subject and often find it tough to admit confusion, doubts, or mistakes. And there's not much room for the parent to learn from the child, a critical mutuality in any real human relationship.

- **Parent as provider.** This role can really feel like a job. Providing includes earning the money to pay for necessities and desires, as well as doing the work of providing meals, transportation, and necessities. For many parents, this is 90 percent or more of what they call "parenting." But providing food and clothes and shelter—even providing security and opportunity—does not a good parent make. Providing only gets us into the "game" of parenting; it's the minimum that parents are expected to do (even by the government), but it is not parenting. And when we take it too far and provide what our children can and should provide for themselves, we end up creating dependency and crippling them.

- **Parent as protector.** It's a tough world out there, and it's our responsibility to protect our children from it. We can turn much of this role into discerning (or imagining) dangers and then constructing defenses around our children and our homes. Many parents become almost paranoid about this, and it's a key reason why some Christian families decide to homeschool. But even though we need to provide protection for our children, it's just as important that we provide experience and the chance to be "in the world," to become street-smart, to be "shrewd as a serpent." Real relationships don't include one person stunting the other's growth or demanding that he stay in a Christian ghetto.

- **Parent as buddy.** Here, we're zeroing in a bit on the truth, as this starts to sound like relationship. But we can spend a lot of time with our children and still not be master-parenting, still not have a real relationship with them. We can really miss it here, as we confuse being a buddy with being a friend. Shopping or playing catch or going on field trips together can begin to seem like parenting. But this approach leaves out a critical aspect of parenting: knowing when to keep your distance. All great relationships grow in separation as well as togetherness.

- **Parent as CEO.** In this approach, the parent is the big kahuna, the big cheese, the top dog. This assumption of "final authority" orients us to manage and direct our children. We're the boss and they're not. It's our way or the highway. We might "empower" them a bit along the way, but the rope is short and we can always pull them right back in. The problem is that human beings don't need, and usually can't stand having, a personal board of directors.

- **Parent as policy maker.** Too often, parents focus on creating policies and procedures. This focus on "house rules" and "higher standards" can drain the life out of home and relationship, and it's easy to fall into this trap. But even God only had ten commandments. If we wanted an orderly home, we shouldn't have had children (just as God could have had an orderly Earth if he hadn't had children).

- **Parent as enforcer.** When we make rules in the name of heaven (but not necessarily with heaven's approval), we expect those little goobers to follow them! If they don't, we have a whole arsenal at our disposal to get them in line: nagging (parenting by annoyance), bribing (parenting by greasing the wheels), threatening (parenting by ransom), depriving (parenting by elimination). And these kids are so creative! They can find endless loopholes, which we then have to force closed with more rules. When parenting is all about enforcing, your home becomes a prison—and you become the warden.

- **Parent as referee.** As soon as parents have more than one child, a little thing called sibling rivalry (which is like World War II, only louder) turns parents into umpires. Otherwise reasonable people can say, "Stop that" or "Leave her alone" so many times in a single day that even they get sick of hearing themselves say it. At least referees at sporting events get paid.

- **Parent as counselor.** We've learned so much (and much of it the hard way) that all we want to do is pass our hard-earned wisdom along to our children. Fat chance. It doesn't matter how articulately or loudly we dole out advice if they aren't listening to it. If we aren't careful, we can become "Mr. and Ms. Fix-It" parents, with an answer to every question and a solution to every problem.

Many of these alternatives to master-parenting don't work because they're only bits and pieces of what a parent needs to be. A few of them don't work because they aren't even part of being a good parent. Any of them can, if made into the whole of parenting, turn us into cranks and curmudgeons, unpleasant people who must be avoided (and will be). They can take us far from being a parent like God is a parent.

The first and most important responsibility of a parent is to face reality. This can be difficult, because all of us are, to one degree or another, reality impaired. If our theory of parenting has any of the "alternatives" listed above as its centerpiece, we know that it's reality impaired. We need to face the truth that our theories won't get the job done. Only the truth will set our parenting free.

As you try to build a new view of reality, you can't do it until you tear the old building down. Go back over the list of inadequate alternatives and put a check mark by those that might have become your trap. Make a decision right now to tear those rotting old tenements down.

WHY DO WE BUY IN TO THESE IDEAS?

As parents, we search and search to find the best way to raise our children. Pastors, teachers, writers, speakers, and authorities of all varieties have told us that there is in fact a "perfect model," and—further good news—they've developed this model into a practical scheme for us to apply without too much of a hitch in our own homes.

The approaches are many: disciplinary systems, analyses of birth order and personality and temperaments, mentoring, training, coaching, self-esteem boosting, carrot-and-stick strategies, good guy/bad guy (or girl) scenarios.

We're encouraged to manage our homes, control our children, give our children space, spank our children, not spank our children, be the boss, hammer away at values, be a friend, protect our children, and teach them to sink or swim. We're told that homeschooling is the key, Christian schooling is the key, avoiding schooling is the key, the school of hard knocks is the key.

All of these are interesting and some even have value.

At times, these schemes seem wonderful. We want to believe that at least one of them will solve our problems. We don't want to believe that God would plop us down in the middle of "mission impossible" without a plan. So we survey the systems, hoping we can find a winner.

But the fact is, they don't work, not as systems. Why not? Because kids are too complex. In fact, it would be easy to use these schemes effectively if it weren't for the kids.

There is a better way. Following the Master Parent's example in the way you parent your own children is the best way. Learn about his Paradox Principle of Parenting. Apply this principle in everyday life by practicing the eight great paradoxes of master-parenting.

To find out more about what these paradoxes are and how to use them, read on.

Three

MASTER PARENTS
HAVE HIGH EXPECTATIONS
AND
HAVE HIGH TOLERANCE

———————— • ————————

He tells us, "Be holy as I am holy"
~ But ~
"He remembers that we are dust."

WE BEGIN our journey into the eight great elements of master-parenting by turning our boat right into the storm.

Simply put, great parents challenge their children with the highest of expectations while at the same time understanding when their children commit the most miserable of failures.

Why? Because this is what God does with his kids. God's expectations for us are off the charts. "For you made us only a little lower than God, and you crowned us with glory and honor." He made us only a little lower than God himself? How did he do that? Why did he do that? I don't know. I intend to ask him when I see him. But of this I am sure: God wouldn't create us just a *little* lower than himself if he expected us to achieve a *lot* lower than he achieves.

In fact, he expects us to "be like God in true righteousness and holiness." He's not glad that he's righteous and holy even though we aren't. Nor is he glad that each of us is "only a sinner, saved by grace." He expects us—in fact, he created us—to be righteous and holy like he is. The fact that we're sinners saved by grace is only the starting point. He expects us to be much more than that.

Although God has very high expectations for us, his tolerance of our failings is also off the charts. "The Lord is compassionate and gracious, slow to anger, abounding in love. He will not always accuse, nor will he harbor his anger forever. . . . As a father has compassion on his children, so the Lord has compassion on those who fear him." If he didn't have such high tolerance for us we would surely be in trouble, because we all stumble in many ways. We can be pretty sorry children at times. The fact is no one in existence has higher tolerance than God.

Your children are imperfect? Welcome to God's world of parenting. "For all have sinned and fall short of the glory of God." "There is no one who does good, not even one." It's easy to demand of our children what God does not demand of us, but the bottom line is that it isn't godly to be less tolerant as a parent than God is.

Somehow, some way, God holds us to almost incomprehensible expectations while at the same time granting us almost incomprehensible tolerance. Since he does it with us, it must be possible for us to do the same with our children, since we're created in God's image.

It's true that we might not find this balance as often as God does, but we can do it. In this chapter, we'll look closer at how God applies this principle to his relationship with us, and we'll discover how we can do the same with our own children.

HAVING HIGH EXPECTATIONS

If you're going to do anything worthwhile as a master parent, you'd better have some pretty high expectations.

Our Master Parent sets the tone: "Aim for perfection," he tells us without flinching. Perfection? That's pretty high. Just as God has massively high expectations for his children, he wants us to have high expectations as well.

Expectations for whom? For those beautiful, maddening, wonderful, irresponsible beings that we brought into this world. As master parents, what kinds of expectations should we have of our children? We should expect them to:

- **Have a real relationship with God.** This means accepting his gift of salvation and growing in their faith. Master parents want their children to love God and to live their lives according to his principles. They want their children to know that he's close, know that he cares, know that he's committed to them. They want their kids to "think out loud" with God, tell him their complaints and troubles, and thank him continuously for his many kindnesses. They hope that their daughters and sons will meet with God regularly and celebrate him loudly.

- **Have real relationships with others.** Master parents know that loving others and building strong connections is an integral part of living a godly life. The best place for children to learn about connecting with others is through their relationships with us. As we follow the principles of the Master Parent, our children will see what true relationship is all about.

- **Do something meaningful with their lives.** We'd all like to see our children grow up to be someone important. Master parents want more. They want to see their children use their lives to make a difference for God and others.

- **Live a victorious life.** It's natural to want our kids to win. But as master parents, we find that children need to learn to rise above their problems and defeat the enemies of their dreams before they can win the prize.

- **Develop integrity, confidence, humility, and self-control.** These characteristics form the foundation for first-class character.

- **Have high expectations for themselves.** When the late Hall of Fame baseball player Ted Williams was asked what he wanted people to say about him, he responded, "I want people to see me walking down the street and say, 'There goes the greatest hitter who ever played the game.' " Our children also need to pursue excellence and use their gifts in the same way—to be the greatest at something and to do it for God.

What do you want people to say about you as a parent? "He did a so-so job," or "There goes the greatest parent who ever played the game"? Surely, you'd rather hear the latter. And why not? Why wouldn't we go for the gold? Let's set our expectations very, very high—for ourselves and for our kids.

More importantly, what do you want *God* to say about you as a parent? Wouldn't it be great if you were parenting in such a way that the Master was proud of you as his apprentice? Wouldn't it be wonderful to hear, "Well done, good and faithful parent"? Some will hear this. Why not you?

WHAT DO YOU EXPECT?

Having expectations for your children is all about hopes and dreams. Not just any hopes and dreams, but applied hopes and dreams—dreams that we plan and work hard to make come true. And not just any applied hopes and dreams, but those that we believe we will get—that we don't give up when we make mistakes or our children resist.

It comes down to this: What do we really hope for in our parenting? Is it to make it through until our kids are off to college, or in a full-time job, or married—when we'll finally be "done"? Those are some pretty low expectations there, pretty low hopes and dreams. Do you hope that somehow, in some mysterious way, your kids will "succeed"? Nice thought, but pretty low expectation there, as well.

How many really great biblical parents can you name? You can think for a long time about that, but it won't take a long time to say the answer. There's God. And then there's . . . who? Isaac? While he preferred his son Esau, Rebekah (his wife) preferred Esau's twin brother, Jacob, and helped him steal Esau's birthright from under Isaac's nose. How about Jacob? His favoritism toward his son Joseph caused so much hate that his other sons sold Joseph as a slave. (And you thought *you* were dealing with sibling rivalry!) What about David? His absentee approach to fathering contributed to his various children assaulting one another, even killing each other and trying to kill him. You can be a great person and still not be a great parent. But as a master parent, you can be both a great person *and* a great parent.

As parents, where is our target? "In the long run," said Henry David Thoreau, "men hit only what they aim at." We'll never hit the target if we don't aim for it. How high should we aim? How high is too high? "If you think you can or can't," said Henry Ford, "you're right." As we think about what we want for our children, we need to aim high and shoot for the very best. Why spend a first-rate life being a second-rate parent?

As you look into the eyes of that moody young man who is your son, you hope that he will climb out of the pack, break away from the pressures and bogus expectations of his peers. You hope that he will stay away from the dangers of sin, of course, but you long for a lot more than that. You want his life to count, to impact the lives of others. You hope that he will work at something that lets him live large—that he will form solid relationships and some-day raise his own strong family. You want him to be the kind of person that people look to when he is present and miss dearly when he's gone.

But you don't just hope and dream. You apply yourself to

making those things a reality. It's not that you force your vision for his life onto your son. Rather, you help him to find that vision for his life that will lead him to a hundred years of greatheartedness. You help him, inch by inch, to achieve that vision. And you really believe it will be so. You're certain that nothing—rotten peers, corruption, spiritual foes, his own penchant for sin, basic human frailty—will keep him from these glories.

And once you've set your sights on the really high target, you've got to practice your aim or you won't hit it. You've got to think about the high expectations you have, and talk about them, and write them down, and discuss them with your children. You've got to "make it real," stretching yourself before you even try to stretch your kids. And when you don't hit the target, you get back in the game and take another shot. You keep practicing until you hit it, or at least come pretty close.

After you've found your target and taken aim, it's finally time to shoot. As master parents, we have to take action. The good news is this: As we take action in the lives of our kids, we can count on God's promise that "he who sows righteousness reaps a sure reward."

What do we really hope for in our children? Like God does with us, we expect them to "run in such a way as to get the prize." We want them to cover a lot of ground in the very short time they have in this life. We want them to do it in a way that actually accomplishes something. We want them to come in first place, because "in a race all the runners run, but only one gets the prize."

As you look at that exquisite and frustrating young girl who is your daughter, you know she can go anywhere and do anything. Maybe she's always had a tender heart. You watched her with her pets, with little children while playing the part of the teacher, with tears in her eyes as she hears a story about a young girl perishing in a concentration camp long ago and far away. So you encourage that tenderness. You show her how she can use part of her allowance to provide food for children in third-world countries. You sign up to work with her on a Habitat for Humanity home. You go together to visit folks in the hospital or local nursing home. You do all that you can to help her express and develop her gifts of compassion and tenderness.

Because of our high expectations, we'll expect our kids to delete problem areas in their lives and change their ways. We know they won't get the prize by watching television or surfing the Internet 24/7, so we put limits on cyberspace and TV time. We know they won't learn enough by taking the easiest courses in school, so we sit down with them and offer suggestions as they register for next year's classes. We know they'll never develop a solid work ethic if they never go above and beyond around the home, so we don't allow them to slough off on their chores. As master parents, it's our job to point out these basic life realities and insist upon them. It's very difficult for a child to be great if her parents don't expect her to be great—if no one reminds her that greatness is her destiny.

Small expectations will produce small children and, eventually, stunted adults. Great expectations will produce greatness: lives of substance and meaning, wisdom and power, integrity and character, vision and values. We've got to learn the language of greatness. When is the last time you told your son that he had the touch of greatness? When is the last time you told your daughter that, tiny as she might feel at times, she had the power to move and shake the whole world? They need to know that "anything is possible if a person believes. . . . Everything is possible with God." *But they don't look so great,* you might be thinking. That's why they have you as a master parent. You can help them to see and be what isn't there; you can encourage their potential for true greatness.

We also have to guard against wrong or lesser expectations. Do we really want to see social prominence or financial success at the top of their list? Should we really expect them to follow in our career path, go to the same schools, or take over the "family business"? It's too easy to put unhealthy expectations on our children, even without using words. We should not direct the details of their lives when we don't have the wisdom to do it, especially since the Master Parent doesn't do this with us. Our high expectations will motivate our kids to go at life with passion and gusto and to think for themselves. We want them to achieve large goals and to dare to make a difference. Because of our high expectations, we want our kids to dare to make a mark, to make things better because they were here. And above all else, just as God expects us to follow him and obey his commands, we expect our children to be followers of Christ. To lead many out of darkness and into the light. To be great souls with whom the world has to reckon. To "be completely humble and gentle," and to let their "gentleness be evident to all."

Most wildly of all, we should expect our children to "be holy in all you do; for it is written: 'Be holy, because I am holy.' " Now, there's some potential confusion here. Do we expect our children to be holy because God is holy, or because we are holy?

The answers are "yes" and "hopefully." We expect them to fall in line with the clear command of Scripture to "be holy," first because God tells them to, and second because he is their God and he is holy. But we also need to be able to tell our children to "try to be holy, because I am trying to be holy and to show you the Way." This is the "hopefully" part, the example part of parenting. The great diplomats say, "Trust but verify." Master parents say, "Trust me," and they verify their request with their lives.

We can still teach our children about being holy if we're not; we have the right to do it, and it certainly is a good thing to talk about holiness. But we have no right to expect it if we're not in that place of expecting it of ourselves. If we're not modeling holiness, we're reduced to telling them to be holy because God is holy, while we ourselves ignore this command.

HOW HIGH IS TOO HIGH?
It's important to recognize your high expectation "red zone." High expectations, by their very nature, put pressure on our children.

High expectations push them to grow, to become something bigger and better, to do something difficult—all of which can be very uncomfortable, and all of which can put distance between us and them. We have to pay attention and realize when our high expectations in a certain area aren't worth that distance.

Knowing when to back off doesn't make us too lenient; it shows that we're balanced and wise. Master parents know that we can't build a life on policies and rules and regulations. Having high expectations does not allow us to become obsessive-compulsive and always require everything to be "just so." "A foolish consistency," said Ralph Waldo Emerson, "is the hobgoblin of little minds."

We have to know how to stretch our kids without stressing them. In the long run, stress can lead to the same low performance that low expectations can produce. No one can perform at high levels all of the time. At some point, relentlessly high expectations will cause your child to give up. A key element of high expectations is having a rhythm, and knowing when to push and when to back off. Watch your children's responses. If they look overwhelmed and discouraged rather than challenged and inspired, you're probably pressing too hard (or in the wrong direction).

Finally, how we convey our high expectations is key. If they come across as demands, we will only invite resistance in the form of lowered performance. If we're negative or degrading, we are also inviting lower results. Children respond much more to requests, clear visions, and positive challenges. No one ever nagged their children to greatness. You won't be the first.

So, like God, we should expect a lot. We will perhaps never get all of our expectations, but it's certain that we will never get what we don't expect. One of the great truths of master-parenting is that we can only get what we expect—and probably not a penny more.

HAVING HIGH TOLERANCE

If you're going to do anything worthwhile as a master parent, you're going to need some pretty high tolerance.

Why? Because the raw material you're working with—human beings—is pretty fragile stuff. We haven't gotten it right since the early days in Eden, where the first parents sinned and then saw one of their first two sons kill the other. As adults, we're a tangle of motives and intentions, behavior that's both praiseworthy and lamentable. Our children are exactly like that, only less mature and a lot cuter. The most common and ordinary ingredient of humankind is probably imperfection.

So what are you going to do when your kids don't measure up to your necessarily high expectations? Are you going to say, "My way or the highway"? Are you going to raise the bar, watch them more closely, and try to harangue them into world-class behavior? Rest assured that millions of parents throughout the world have tried these and other approaches, but a master parent does not do this. Master parents make room for failure. They don't buy into the myth that parents should never slack off on their standards.

We're not talking about the "sin" stuff here, although our sinful nature is certainly a disability. There's a difference between sin and human weakness. Sin occurs when your son verbally abuses his siblings or when your daughter lies consistently. When your teenager collects and fantasizes about indecent pictures, that's true sin.

But what we're talking about is human imperfection. If your son forgets to do his homework or your daughter breaks a dish because she's horsing around in the kitchen, we're talking about human fragility, not sin.

In the workplace, good leaders try to differentiate between rotten behavior and honest mistakes, between unreasonable and reasonable error. They deal with someone who steals from the company in a completely different way than they deal with someone who accidentally undercharges a customer.

Clear and open sin requires repentance and forgiveness and mercy, which we'll talk about in the next chapter. Human infirmity requires a whole different response. If there is no sin, then no repentance, forgiveness, or mercy is needed. But tolerance is needed by the ton. High tolerance requires that we promote a spirit of honesty, understanding, patience, and contentment in our homes.

HONESTY

Honesty is needed on the part of your children. They need to "fess up" and simply admit the glitch. They can't pretend their way to anything but hypocrisy. In homes led by master parents, bad news quickly makes it to the top. The kids don't hide these mistakes where they can fester and become a stench. They get them out in the open, and master parents help them learn from their mistakes.

Parents have a very important role to play in this honesty business. If our children aren't honest, it could be because they're scared. Maybe we haven't created a safe place for dangerous truths. Maybe we haven't created a mistake-friendly environment. If this is the case, our kids will ultimately become secretive about their mistakes and failures—not because they're scared but because they're *smart*. They've learned not to voluntarily set themselves up to be humiliated or degraded.

The sad fact is that in most homes, honesty is not the best policy. It's a formula for personal disaster. Too many children understand from firsthand experience the meaning of the old Turkish proverb "He who tells the truth will be chased from nine villages." Master parents take great care to make truth-telling, a very hard and dangerous thing to do, a protected right.

UNDERSTANDING

The best way to promote a spirit of honesty in our homes is through understanding. We have to understand that our children have the touch of greatness in flawed receptacles—"treasure in jars of clay." We don't try to be understanding because our children are little. We try to be understanding because they are human.

We also understand that life can be tough. When we as adults are bent down by a thousand pressures, God doesn't come in and pummel us for not responding superbly to all of them. Quite the contrary: "The Lord helps the fallen and lifts up those bent beneath their loads." Just being a kid is enough to knock anyone down; trying to figure out who you are can be a twenty-ton load. We understand, because we've been there, and we're trying hard to remember what it was like.

And we understand because we've laid aside our own egos on this whole parenting business. If God's sense of self were tied up with how well we are doing as his children, he'd have a pretty low sense of self-worth. God is the Parent who sets the standard. But it's the growth he develops in us that's important, not whether anyone thinks he is doing a good job.

Great leaders are always more concerned about the growth of their followers than they are about their own reputation. "Nobody should seek his own good, but the good of others." *Others* surely includes our children. "Love . . . is not self-seeking." We aren't master parents because we want to look good; we look good because we are master parents.

In fact, our understanding as master parents should flow from the command to "do nothing out of selfish ambition . . . but in humility consider others better than yourselves." Our example is Christ himself, who "made himself nothing, taking the very nature of a servant." Master parents concern themselves with what God thinks and with what is best for their children; hang the neighbors' opinions. Someone once said that the two sweetest words ever uttered are "I understand." I think he may have been right.

PATIENCE

Having high tolerance means that, like our Father does with us, we give our children time to grow and room to make mistakes. We know that "patience is better than pride" and we're willing to give our children unfathomable patience even when they make mistakes. This can be tough, especially when others in our lives start questioning our methods: "Why is he dropping out of college?"

our parents ask. "Why is he working only part-time and sleeping his life away?" "Why are you letting her waste her talent?" The answer to all of these questions? Because patience is better than pride.

"Frequently," writes François Fénelon, "a big advantage can be gained by knowing how to give in at the right moment." Master parents watch for that advantage. They aren't going to miss one of the great opportunities offered to savvy moms and dads.

Having high tolerance grows out of honesty and understanding, but then it goes a step further. It grants to others—to our children—the right to be human, the right to be different, the right to be free, and the right to be young.

Tolerating evil is certainly a bad idea. But tolerating human frailty, differences, self-direction, and immaturity is a true mark of greatness in a parent (or anyone else).

God does it all the time with us. "He knows how we are formed, he remembers that we are dust." What can we expect from dust? Well, it can swirl around and annoy us and get on the furniture and, if we add a little moisture, turn into mud. Sort of sounds like kids, doesn't it? We have to remember that our children are dust. There's nothing very perfect about dust. It's aggravating and unattractive and transient. Our kids are just like that. They can't always be on the mark. Nor can you or I. Can we be great enough to extend the graciousness we have received in our dusty condition to the dusty little beings we've brought into the world?

Tolerance is a great virtue that flows from the great heart of a great parent. It doesn't mean "putting up with laziness," "not training," or "accepting mediocrity." It means actively, compassionately, and sympathetically "getting it"—giving other fragile human beings a little breathing room and empathetically (and emphatically) putting ourselves in their shoes.

Here's an example of tolerance: To earn the rest of the money for a CD he wants, your twelve-year-old son promises to do the dishes every night for a week. When you get home one day, you reach into the cabinet for a bowl and are horrified to find something that looks more like a petri dish in use. There's actual alien living matter all over the dish. You check the rest of the dishes and find they're all pretty nasty. Worse, you walk into the family room to find your son watching television while only spasmodically poking at his homework. Everything in you is thinking, "Murder She Wrote."

But you're a master parent, and so the first thing you do is remember, *Oh, yeah. Doing dishes is boring. Doing chores is no fun. Homework, if possible, is even less fun.* And then you remember when you let the dishes pile up last week when you needed that "mental health" day. You still haven't gotten the oven repaired. You've been procrastinating on finishing that mind-numbing report at work. Amazingly, no one has grounded you.

So you sit down and watch the end of an old Dick Van Dyke show with your little fellow pilgrim. You laugh and enjoy the fact that sometimes you can both be sloppy and slow and not get killed for it. When the show is over, you nudge him to finish his homework and say—gently—"You know, we've got a little rendezvous we need to have in the kitchen before the Center for Disease Control quarantines our dishes." As you both start pulling the dishes down from the cabinets, you teach him how to do it well—and fast, so he can have plenty of time for the stuff that isn't so boring.

Tolerance certainly has an aura of acceptance about it. We accept that our kids have weaknesses, just as God accepts that we have weaknesses. Tolerant master parents do try to bring their children's weaknesses up to a level necessary to function effectively, but they don't try to turn their children's weaknesses into strengths, because no one can be strong at everything.

There are some weaknesses you won't work on at all, because you have to give up some ground on something when you're dealing with dust. If you're wise, you'll give up on trying to improve the weaknesses that have little to do with achieving your high expectations.

Perhaps your daughter hates frilly dresses—all dresses, really, but especially the frilly ones—and her hair is always a tangled mess (you know that there's at least one new life-form living in there). And here you are, on another Sunday morning getting ready for church. You have a choice. You can have a war with her—a war that will continue this and every Sunday, for months and years. The result? You might be able to get her to look marginally better, but you've also taught her to really hate going to church. Master parents know better than to make this understandable but terrible mistake. They know that their daughter's appearance isn't as important as getting her to love going to church and worshiping God. Lots of messy people have learned about and loved God. Me, for example. And you.

To try to make everything perfect, to give no ground to imperfection anywhere in our children, is to sow the seeds of oppression—and, eventually, of rejection of us and all of our values. "There is only one thing which gathers people into seditious commissions, and that is oppression," wrote John Locke. "It is not the diversity of opinions (which cannot be avoided), but the refusal of toleration to those that are of different opinions (which might have been granted), that has produced all the bustles and wars that have been in the Christian world upon account of religion."

Locke's insight includes the parenting part of the Christian world. Master parents know that making their children clones of themselves is arrogant nonsense, and that the resulting "treasure" is fool's gold.

CONTENTMENT

High tolerance is about contentment. We have to keep a tension in our thinking with our children. On the one hand, we want to push them to be all that God designed them to be. On the other hand, we want to push them to be content with what they are and have.

Someone once said that "happiness is getting what you want, and satisfaction is wanting what you get." It captures nicely the tension of wanting more while enjoying what we've already got, all at the same time. It's okay to stop along the way and enjoy "what you get."

While we want our children to be content, we want to make sure we're clear on what "contentment" is. Contentment is looking at your child and thinking, "Wow! I can't even believe that I've made it to adulthood, and now I'm raising someone else who is heading in that direction!" It's seeing the shining face and not just the pimples, hearing the wondrous sound of words like *Mom* and *Dad* and not just the annoying music. It's smelling the flowers of new life and not just the stench of leftover food under our kids' beds. It's feeling good that our children are alive and growing up rather than feeling bad that they haven't already made it. Contentment says, "In a life that can be pretty rough, this kid is velvet."

We also need to know what contentment is *not*. I've heard many people say, for example about a fellow employee, "She's happy to be right where she is and doesn't want to do anything more." Perhaps this is true for some.

More often, what is advertised as "contentment" is really giving up. Giving up on hopes and dreams. Giving up because it's too hard to try to change a world encrusted with stupidity and foolishness and wickedness. Giving up because it's too exhausting to deal with the personality conflicts and turf battles and control freaks.

We don't want our children to be content, if contentment means giving up. We can't accept that sort of phony "contentment." We want children who say, "Cold pizza is lots better than no pizza."

THE BLEND

Let's summarize this first parenting principle. You'd better have high expectations, the higher and more clearly defined the better. You'd better have a plan if you want to see those expectations achieved. And you'd better really believe that you can go right up to the top of the parenting mountain. Nothing less than greatness, from you or your children, is acceptable.

And the reason you have such high expectations? Because it's the only way to achieve goals and see those high expectations come to fruition. It's the only way to prevent tolerance from turning into the zone of indifference and into an acceptance of excuses and mediocrity.

If your kids think that you'll accept laziness, that any grade or performance will be given a "That's okay, honey, I know you tried your best," then the simple fact is that they will never try anything significant.

On the other hand, we have to at least give partial credit for attempts to hit those expectations or for hitting only a part of them. Our kids need the chance to pull down some fruit from the lower branches. If success is always just out of reach, if nothing is ever quite "good enough," we'll kill their motivation to success and possibly their love for us. "When we feel that we lack whatever is needed to secure someone else's esteem, we are very close to hating him," warned Francois Duc de La Rochefoucauld.

While you set your high expectations, you'd also better have high tolerance, the higher and more clearly defined the better. You'd better create a mistake-friendly, risk-friendly, dust-friendly environment.

And the reason you have such high tolerance? In part, because it's the only way to achieve your high expectations. It's the only way to come alongside your kids and encourage them after a failure, to remind them that success is never an unbroken chain and that out of this missing of the mark a more accurate aim can grow. It allows you to offer one of the main product offerings of a master parent: hope of a better day to come.

If your kids think that any mistake could be a fatal one, that any failure will lead to relationship issues and disappointment, they will never try anything great—or maybe anything at all. The high wire is too high, and there is no safety net. Master parents know that tolerance is all about safety nets. We must set the high wire super high in order to give them a shot at greatness, but we have to be ready with the unbreakable safety net of tolerance or they won't make the climb in the first place.

In one of the delicious, upside-down truths of parenting, having high tolerance actually gives us the right to have high expectations. Otherwise, our high expectations become a cliff, and our children see clearly that they can fall off the edge and be killed. You've been told that parents can't slack off on their standards, but the surest way to make sure you don't see them met is to never slack off on them.

When you blend high expectations with high tolerance, you gain valuable perspective on the whole issue of parental pressure. When our kids are little, scared, and lacking in confidence, we use a little external "expectation" pressure in order to move them toward their goals. But since we also have high tolerance, we guard ourselves closely to make sure that our external pressure doesn't turn into internal stress.

We want movement, not stress. Movement builds character, while stress tears it apart. For example, while attending a show with you, your daughter expresses an interest in learning to play an instrument. "Maybe the violin," she says, with some enthusiasm. So you take her down to the orchestra pit and start up a three-way conversation with one of the violinists as she puts her music away. You enroll your daughter in music lessons and enjoy shopping for a used violin that will serve a beginner. You agree with her teacher on some practice times. You see some new and unfamiliar confidence in your daughter, some "Wow, I didn't know I could learn to play music" passion lighting up her eyes. She goes overtime on her practices for the first five days.

And then, it's as if she's never heard of music. Doesn't know where the violin is. Doesn't know if it's a string or a wind instrument. Complains about how frustrating it is, that she'll never learn how to do it. She wants to quit. You're thinking, *Are you nuts? I just spent all of this time and money to help you build your future, and you're going to quit after five days? Get in there and play! And I want to see you smiling!* If you follow through with those understandable feelings, you will turn your expectation into stress and her violin-playing into a war.

But you're a master parent, so you don't do it. You remember how many new initiatives you've started and stopped, some within as little as . . . five days. You back off. You talk with her teacher about not pushing or criticizing. You want her to love it more than you want her to do it. You keep the lessons going, but you leave the practicing up to her. If you hear her playing, even for a minute, you find a way to praise her.

There are few areas in which the blend is more important, and less successfully practiced, than in this area of parental pressure. No pressure (low expectation) is a frequent approach, as is too much pressure (low tolerance). Master parents learn to use pressure strategically, and with great care and caution.

It's not tolerance, however, when we give ground to disrespect. "As a father has compassion on his children, so the Lord has compassion on those who fear him." What does "fear him" mean? Are we afraid God will slap us in the face in an angry rage, even when we haven't done anything to deserve it? Not hardly. Fearing God means that we understand his lofty expectations for us and don't make light of them. Then we know we can receive his compassion if we fall short.

It's the same for our children. If we show them compassion where there is no "fear," no understanding of our lofty expectations, we encourage slothfulness and low achievement. This isn't compassion at all. Real compassion, real tolerance, is reserved for those times when our children are trying for the moon and just don't make it.

But if your daughter refuses to spend the evening before an important exam preparing, and belittles your reminding and encouraging, and laughs about the stupid teacher and how easy it will be to get a good grade without studying—and then gets a bad grade—she's on her own. You should discipline her, not because she got a bad grade but because of her attitude. When your children have the potential to go to the moon and beyond but won't try because of a bad attitude and won't listen because of oozing disrespect, they lose their shot at getting tolerance. It's that simple.

Even here, though, we don't declare war. "Minds are conquered not by arms but by love and magnanimity," says Spinoza. We still love the child with the bad attitude. We just don't grant him the grace of tolerance.

If, on the other hand, your child is trying to hit those expectations but simply fails, by all means, give her another chance. And another. When she takes on a project that she doesn't have time to do well, you can help her find the perfect time to do that project again so she'll have the opportunity to experience success. When your son gets a low grade in a course he really does enjoy, you can help him to know when to take it again. We need to push our children gently to try again because we have high expectations.

But we shouldn't push them to try again if it is too soon, if they haven't regrouped, if they're too nervous. The young relief pitcher who failed miserably in game four of the 2001 World Series, by giving up the game-winning home run, needed to be pushed to get out and try again—but probably not in game five in the same situation, where he failed miserably again by giving up another game-winning home run. High tolerance is about timing as well as attitude. We have to know when a tolerant approach can become an intolerable burden.

It's easy for parents to expect too little and demand too much. Master parents don't fall for this trap. Master parents expect a lot and demand very little, because they know the power of high expectations, and they know the power of high tolerance.

LAST THOUGHTS

If we have high expectations without high tolerance, we stress our children until we break them. If we have high tolerance without high expectations, we excuse failure until it becomes a way of life. If we're master parents, we avoid both extremes.

Stephen Ambrose, in discussing his book about the building of the transcontinental railroad, summarized this principle of high expectations and high tolerance: "You could believe that America is the greatest country—and organization—that the world has ever seen," he said, "mostly because it inspires overreaching, and it tolerates failure and messiness."

This is what great parents—master parents—do. They inspire overreaching, and they tolerate failure and messiness.

Four

MASTER PARENTS
DISPENSE JUSTICE
AND
DISPENSE MERCY

He says, "I will make justice the measuring line"

~ But ~

"Mercy triumphs over judgment!"

THE fields of parenting are strewn with the weeds of failure on this most crucial paradox.

Master parents hold before their children at all times an uncompromising sense of justice, while at the same time, master parents let their children "get away" with all sorts of things on a regular basis.

Some of you are probably cringing after reading the first part of the previous sentence, and most of you are probably cringing at the second part. But we can all stop cringing. Why? Because this is exactly how our Master Parent is with us.

Are there times when your kids need some serious justice dealt to them? Are there times when you don't believe your kids even *deserve* any mercy? Welcome again to God's world of parenting. We miss the mark with our Master Parent so easily and so frequently, it should make us think carefully before we ask our children to toe the line. And how often have we not deserved any mercy? If we got what we deserved, we would all be in a world of hurt.

Why? Because God doesn't mess around. God is all about justice. "For the Lord is a God of justice." No question there. If you want loosely interpreted and applied justice, God is not for you. "Follow justice and justice alone" is his unbending declaration.

You want uncompromising? God's justice has no "wiggle room." "If you *fully* obey the Lord your God by keeping *all* the commands I am giving you today, the Lord your God will exalt you above all the nations of the world. . . . But if you refuse to listen to the Lord your God and do not obey *all* the commands and laws I am giving you today, all these curses will come and overwhelm you." The rest of this chapter of the Bible, fifty-three tough verses, is devoted to a detailed listing of the curses. It's not a pleasant read. God is really serious about this justice business.

And, at the same time, God pours out mercy by the bucketful. He's not only *our* Father, he is "the Father of compassion and the God of all comfort." Happily, "he does not treat us as our sins deserve or repay us according to our iniquities." In the wonderful words of George Herbert, "God strikes with his finger, and not with all his arm."

You need someone to give you a break? someone to cut you some slack? God is that someone for you. "For I will forgive their wickedness and will remember their sins no more," Jeremiah records our Master Parent speaking to us. Amazingly, "God has even forgotten some of your sin." We have the best deal imaginable—a Master Parent who is so good that he clears the slate, even though he is so good he has every reason not to.

What is the reaction of God's people, if they're thinking clearly, to this astonishing combination of justice and mercy? "They will celebrate your abundant goodness *and* joyfully sing of your righteousness." One of the best ways we can do this is to pass it along to our children.

DISPENSING JUSTICE

If you're going to do anything worthwhile as a master parent, you'd better dispense some pretty serious justice.

David says to God, "You take no pleasure in wickedness; you cannot tolerate the slightest sin." And as a master parent following God's example, *you* cannot tolerate the slightest sin. What you tolerate today will seem like child's play tomorrow.

When is the right time to start building our homes around justice? Last month. When the children are still tiny. If at all possible, we want to win the battle before our children know there's a war.

It is way too easy to start dispensing justice way too late. Kids are so little and helpless and cute. They belong to us. I heard one mother excusing an array of bad behavior from her little one with a variety of excuses that don't excuse: "He's just tired," "He had a hard day," "He was really sick last week, and he's still getting over it," "He's just a strong-willed child." In the short run, these excuses allowed her to feel better about her son and better about her parenting. In the long run, she was implementing a solid approach to creating a monster.

Our Master Parent is on the job, administering justice, every day. He wants the same from us: "Administer justice every morning . . . or my wrath will break out and burn like fire."

Children need justice. They need it personally because without it, they will have no practical sense of what is right and what is wrong. They can't just hear us talking about it; they have to actually experience justice in the cozy courtroom called "home." They need it so they won't grow up to be rotten apples.

Children also need justice interpersonally. They have to learn, usually through pain to themselves, that it is wrong to hurt others. If your daughter becomes angry and breaks her brother's favorite toy, she doesn't need a lecture as much as she needs to pay for the toy. She can cough up money from her savings, do extra chores, sell something (preferably something as important to her as the broken toy was to her sibling), or give up one of her next "present" times (like a birthday or Christmas) to ask for a present for her sibling instead. As far as lessons in justice go, the more expensive the broken toy was, the better.

Our children also have to see that if others hurt them, justice will be swift to make things right again. If your son breaks his sister's toy, the same rule applies. She shouldn't get injustice because she is older and should "understand" that her sibling didn't mean it. Justice is justice. Even though children can act in absurd ways (and push our sanity to the brink), no one should be declared "not guilty by reason of insanity"—or for any other reason.

Our kids need to see firsthand that the principle of sowing and reaping is, in fact, one of the great principles of life. We tell them, as our Master Parent tells us, "Do not be deceived: God cannot be mocked. A man reaps what he sows." God goes on to make it clear that sowing one way reaps destruction, while sowing another way reaps life. We need to make this point clear to our children as well. We need to warn them, "Don't expect to sow one way and get the opposite result!" Then we follow through on that principle, giving bountiful crops to the good sowers and barren fields to the bad sowers.

So they need justice. What *is* justice? According to the dictionary, it's "the quality of being just; righteousness, equitableness, or moral rightness . . . just conduct, dealing, or treatment. The administering of deserved punishment. . . . The maintenance or administration of what is just by law, as by judicial or other proceedings." It means, "Don't do the crime if you can't do the time."

Justice is first about being right. But it's also about being "equitable"—being fair. And it's not a nitpicky rightness but a moral rightness. It relates not only to the conduct of the children but to other intricately connected ideas: the way we deal with them, the way they deal with us and others, and the way we treat them, including when we administer deserved punishment. It's crucial that we maintain this justice over time. We need to be consistent and persistent in all of our proceedings.

What does this mean for the frazzled mother of three whose home is in disarray and who doesn't know where to begin? She has to say to herself—really *commit* to herself—that justice is too important to get lost in the daily rub and friction of life. When, at the end of a very long day, she walks into a chaotic room to find toys strewn left and right, grape juice spilled on the carpeting, and a broken glass in pieces all over the floor, the easiest thing in the world to do is to say, "Stop! Quiet! Everybody to your room! And don't come out for six months!"

But if one of the children was innocent, that mother has just tossed justice out the window—even though her reaction is entirely understandable. All of her children have just learned that life isn't fair. They've learned that pressure and stress cause justice to melt away like snow under a hot sun, and that equity comes and goes for no apparent reason. They've also learned that it's okay to blame the whole group for the actions of a part of it. Perhaps worse for the parent-child relationship, they've learned that Mom isn't fair.

When you face a situation like this, what's the alternative? Rather than letting the situation get to you, you can realize that, at this very ordinary yet critical moment, the most important thing for you to do is to dispense justice. You can forget about dinner, or the phone call, or a million other important things, and take your seat as a good judge. You can ask the questions, challenge the baloney, get down to the truth, free the innocent, and give out deserved punishment to the guilty. In medicine, prescription without thorough diagnosis is malpractice. The same holds true for parenting.

Whatever else justice is, we are told simply that God "loves justice." I read an article recently that said, "When a child demands a 'just universe,' she is in trouble" and she needs to "adapt to the way things really are." This is not a high view of justice. Our Master Parent very clearly demands a just universe, and he is most certainly not in trouble because of it. He doesn't adapt to injustice; he works against it and, over time, vaporizes it. Master parents take the same approach.

It's important to note right off the bat that justice is not the opposite of mercy. Without justice, there would be no need for
mercy, because any behavior would be considered acceptable. And
justice is not the opposite of love. Justice is a part of love. Without
justice, our homes and our world would be cold, hard places oper-
ating exclusively on the natural principle of survival of the fittest.

Without justice, and its related punishments, we would be
hard-pressed to teach our children anything. Children can't learn
or do anything very useful until they have themselves under control. And it's virtually impossible for our children to learn anything
from us if they don't respect us, listen to us, trust us, or even love us.

The progression is the reverse of what we'd like it to be. It goes
from justice (including punishment), to respect, to a willingness to
listen, to a level of trust, and then finally to an ability to love. Our
Master Parent confirms this: "Whoever has my commands and
obeys them, *he is the one who loves me.* . . . If anyone loves me, he
will obey my teaching." I heard a mother say once about her son, "I
know he doesn't respect me, but I just wish he'd love me." Fat
chance.

And we can't let up. We've got to persist in administering justice. Sin and rotten behavior can, like a bad case of indigestion,
keep coming back. "You may have to fight a battle more than once
to win it," said former British Prime Minister Margaret Thatcher.
"Never think you've seen the last of anything," an old proverb reminds us.

Justice requires rebuke, compliance, restitution, and (often)
punishment.

REBUKE

Rebuke is a word that has lost much of its positive value in common
usage. But a good rebuke can be a stop sign for our children on the
road to ruin. You might be tempted to think, *She's only two years
old! How could she be on the road to ruin?* But here's the problem
with this understandable (but deadly) thought: *Every evil person*

who ever lived was once two years old. Sin is a disease, and bad behavior quickly becomes a habit. "Juvenile delinquency," says James D. C. Murray, "starts in the high chair and ends in the death chair." The sapling of rottenness that you ignore at two can grow into an ugly, twisted tree of death. But you are a master parent and you have the ability to stop it now and save the tree.

I've seen too many parents with out-of-control little children (come to think of it, with out-of-control *big* children as well). They do everything—they hold and hug, bribe with candy, distract with toys, and pass the child back and forth between them in a parental game of Old Maid. They do everything—except the effective thing, which is to hold them tight and whisper in their ear, "Stop being obnoxious! Get yourself under control. I'm not letting you go until you get yourself under control." The emphasis is on *self*-control: "Get your*self* under control." They can do it. I've taken screaming maniacs from parents and won this battle in one sitting. How long do you fight this fight? Ten minutes? Twenty? Thirty? The answer is this: *until you win.*

A rebuke from a master parent is a planned, thought-out, calm attempt to produce a change in underlying attitudes. "Better is open rebuke than hidden love," we are taught. Our hope—and it is a hope, because they may not listen—is that the attitude will change, which will cause the behavior to change, which will cause the resulting events to change.

A good rebuke focuses on big issues, because master parents focus on big issues. We major on the major to avoid majoring on the minor (and *minoring* on the *major*). While we avoid attacking things like messy bedrooms, uncombed hair, and sloppy posture, we do so in order to spend our scarce parental resources on lousy treatment of siblings, persistent rudeness, and repeated lying.

A good rebuke is consistent and persistent. Justice means we take the time to show our children the correct way, to focus on what is right, to encourage them to run on the straight path. We understand that to avoid confrontation is cowardly and is an abdication of our parental role. Justice demands that we don't allow problems to fester or our resentment to build and build. We understand the great truth that if we do not confront, we will end up resenting: resenting their uncorrected behavior, resenting their arrogance, and eventually resenting them.

COMPLIANCE

The purpose of giving a rebuke is to gain compliance from our children, not to hear ourselves talk. This means that they hear what we are saying and align themselves with it. It doesn't include—in fact, it avoids—outward conformity with a resistant inner heart. One little girl sitting in time-out said to her mother defiantly, "I'm still standing up inside!" Compliance doesn't mean brainwashing or being domineering. It simply means that we work with them until they fall in line with the "determination of the court"—the prescribed course of sowing that will reap good things from life (and from you).

You have to watch their reactions closely to know whether you're getting change of heart rather than avoidance of further pain. You have to use spiritual discernment and emotional intelligence to see if they are really getting it. And you're probably going to have to dialogue with them at some length, possibly on several different occasions, to see if the truth is going all the way in—to see if they "own" it. Outward compliance with inward evil intent equals hypocrisy and catastrophe. You'd be better off with outward rebellion, where at least you're dealing with an authentic situation and not breeding a phony.

RESTITUTION

Unlike most legal systems and far too many churches, our Master Parent is very concerned about the topic of restitution. Master parents should be the same with their children. Restitution simply means that our children, as much as possible, need to make things right. If in anger they slam a door, they must go back and do it again the right way. If they take some candy that doesn't belong to them, they must pay for the candy. If they insult someone in front of others, they must apologize in front of those same others. Sin prevents the world from being a perfect place, but restitution helps to heal the imperfection.

PUNISHMENT

What about administering justice? Although most people use the words *discipline* and *punishment* interchangeably, they are two very different activities. Our Master Parent does both with us: "For the Lord disciplines those he loves, and he punishes those he accepts as his children." Our Master Parent gives us two different acts of love, while it's too easy for us to give our children only one. This is a most important distinction.

We will talk about punishment in this chapter and discipline in the next.

The primary purpose of punishment is not to make our children pay their debt or to vent our frustration or to "do our duty." The main reason we punish our children is to get them to *stop*. We want them to stop whatever they're doing that is wrong. *Now*. We don't say, "He's been in the corner for thirty minutes," and let him out if he hasn't changed. Who cares how long he's been there if there is no repentance? We don't punish him for thirty minutes, or until he's "had enough," or until we start feeling guilty. We punish him until he stops.

One question you might have is, "What if staying in the corner longer only makes him more stubborn and rebellious?" Well, it probably *will* make him more stubborn and rebellious—for a while. Of course, the earlier you start winning, the easier it will be to win. But even with older children, you should remember that even though they might be totally obnoxious, they are also *really smart.*

Even if they don't change because they don't think they're that bad, they'll change because what they're doing *isn't working*. What happens when their actions are "working"? They get to do fun things and enjoy their lives. When they lose these privileges, they'll start to make adjustments. This is the way the Master Parent is with us: He'll put us in the corner, make our lives tough, and stick with it until we stop. He knows that if we stop misbehaving ten or twenty or thirty times in a row, we'll probably form a new habit—a new way of acting. Parents don't lose because children are stubborn and rebellious. Parents lose because they give in first.

Making the effort to punish is well worth days and weeks of your precious time, for two reasons: First, you'll save a ton of time later on, time you would have spent dealing with issue after issue that came out of the woodwork because you didn't bring in the exterminator when you first saw the termites. And second, you'll raise a child who really gets it. Many parents have said to their children, "You're going to get it!" They mean their children are going to get a spanking or some other retribution carried out in anger. When master parents say, "You're going to get it," they mean that they're going to keep at this, no breaks, no rest, until their children understand.

Master parents punish effectively and with justice. They make the punishment fit the crime. They use natural consequences, rather than artificially imposed punishments, whenever possible. Their goal is real repentance and, where it fits, restitution. They make no room for the sinful nature to have its way.

Master parents are careful to avoid the "punishment pendulum," where parents can swing from being too tough to feeling guilty and being too soft, back to getting angry that the children are taking advantage of their softness and being too tough again. If there are two parents involved in the master-parenting, they make sure that they're not on independent pendulums, causing children to go back and forth between a "justice" parent and a "mercy" parent.

Master parents don't melt when administering justice. They're willing to "gut it out," because they know it will only get harder later if they let down now. They don't make idle threats, and when they do make a threat, they deliver. They choose a punishment, whenever possible, that doesn't punish other people too (including themselves). Rather than canceling a family dinner out because one child is out of control, they find a sitter for the misbehaving child and go out to dinner without her.

Like Solomon, we'd better ask for "discernment in administering justice." Flawed as we are as parents, this is no small request. We have to make sure that we are not causing, or participating in, the problem. For example, when we see one child hit another, we don't automatically punish only the hitter. We take time to find out if the child we saw being hit actually struck the first blow. Then we don't have to deal with resentment on the part of the child who was punished and a "got away with it" attitude on the part of the other.

Our feeble attempts at justice sometimes produce injustice and all the bad fruit that injustice always brings. Master parents work hard to make sure that justice is *real* justice—that it isn't just skin deep, that it goes all the way to the bone.

We don't take this "justice" thing lightly. We can miss the boat completely when we withhold true justice. "Cursed is the man who withholds justice," we are warned. If we know about the problem, we own the problem. Not wanting to confront, not wanting to rock the boat, not wanting to "deal with it"—all are invalid excuses for withholding justice.

Are we withholding justice when we send all parties to their rooms when we catch them fighting, even if only one of them was the perpetrator? Shouldn't we rather "judge . . . your afflicted ones with justice"? If our children can say, "We look for justice, but find none," we have, in our unwillingness to spend the time and energy to do the right thing, left them looking into a black hole.

Master parents never accept excuses for rotten behavior. They don't use statements like "He threw that tantrum because he was _____" (tired, sick, frustrated, etc.). We see bad behavior for what it is: the sinful nature making a rally.

For example, we don't yield to activities like whining and demanding. We apply the great "more and less" principle: If they complain, they get more of what they don't want and less of what they do. "You're complaining about going to bed at 8:00? Okay, you don't have to; bedtime is now 7:45. Still want to make it an issue? Okay, it's now 7:30." Kids are really, really smart. They might have to go to bed at 7:30 (or 4:30) a few nights, but they'll get it very soon.

And we don't accept bribes to pervert justice. Bribes can be promises not to do it again, or emotional blackmail ("You wouldn't make me pay for that if you loved me"), or trades ("If you won't punish me I'll dust the furniture"). In any case, we have to set our jaws like flint against this devious approach to thwarting justice. "Does God pervert justice?" we are asked. No. Master parents don't either.

If we do it right, justice is not a dark and forbidding concept. Our Master Parent says, "My justice will become a light to the nations." Real justice always brings light, not darkness. Does your parental justice bring light? Can your children see the right way more clearly when your justice has been administered? Or was the light extinguished by your disjointed anger?

We should be able to say to our Master Parent, "Correct me, Lord, but only with justice." If we have even a remote desire to lead a life worthy of something, we will want this type of correction. And we know when we pray this way, God will hear us and correct us only with justice. Can our children say the same of us? Can they count on our correction to be full of justice?

God is serious about justice related to his children. "I will make justice the measuring line," he warns. "Let justice roll on like a river." "The Lord is known by his justice," we are told. So are master parents. Are you known by your justice?

"Blessed are they who maintain justice," we are reminded. May you be blessed in this with your children.

DISPENSING MERCY

If you're going to do anything worthwhile as a master parent, you'd better dispense some pretty serious mercy.

When I was doing a radio call-in show for my book *1001 Ways to Connect with Your Kids,* we'd been talking about this critical aspect of parenting. A parent called in and said that because he agreed with the importance of mercy, he had a "mercy day" for his children once or twice a year. He felt very good about his idea.

Now, I don't know about you, but I'm really glad my Master Parent has more than one or two "mercy days" a year. In fact, I'm glad to say that he has approximately 365 "mercy days" a year—except, occasionally, when he has 366. "There is no man so good," wrote French philosopher Michel de Montaigne, "that if he place all his actions and thoughts under the scrutiny of the laws, he would not deserve hanging ten times in his life."

Isn't being merciful year-round just "being soft" on our children? Yes, just like God is with us. And what might they do if we let them get away with things? Why, they might . . . be grateful, love us, think we're like God, go and do likewise. Master parents don't believe the myth that parents can never let their children "get away" with disobedience.

REMEMBERING THE PAST

Mercy begins with remembering our own deeds. "The line separating good and evil," wrote Aleksandr Solzhenitsyn in *The Gulag Archipelago,* "passes not through states, nor between political parties either—but right through every human heart." It's not that we're good and that our kids can be evil; we all have the potential to be both. We are simply flawed mentors trying to kindly show the Way to flawed apprentices. "Those who are truly humble," said the great spiritual instructor François Fénelon, "are lenient to the faults of others in view of their own."

UNDERSTANDING THE MOTIVATION

Showing mercy means we see the underlying fear, anger, worries, and hurts that sometimes drive sinful behavior. This reminds us that human beings are complex creatures—that seldom do we sin for simple reasons. Master parents listen closely when Jesus says we should stop judging by outward appearance and make a *right* judgment. The chances of accurately judging by outward appearance are slim indeed.

How does this work with the idea we talked about earlier that says master parents don't make excuses for sinful behavior? Well, when you see outward misbehavior—say, a temper tantrum—you simply choose first not to make excuses for it. You don't say he's sick or tired or confused or misunderstood, so it's "okay"; you don't put your own made-up blanket over the ugliness. In other words, you call it what it is: Sin.

But as a master parent, you also don't assume that sin is the whole story. You don't excuse the temper tantrum, but you don't treat it as a single event unconnected to the rest of life. You humbly ask what you might have done to contribute to this disaster, perhaps by excusing earlier tantrums, dispensing unjust punishment, or letting him watch programs that contributed to his aggression. You also look at what other people might be doing to initiate or aggravate the misbehavior: siblings who insult or degrade, neighborhood kids who slaughter his soul, or an oppressive relative who pushes him around.

Jesus is harder on the ones who cause children to sin than he is on the sinning child: "If anyone causes one of these little ones who believe in me to sin, it would be better for him to have a large millstone hung around his neck and to be drowned in the depths of the sea." Look deeply into your child's heart—after the tantrum has passed—to discover what might be driving this overwhelming anger.

Master parents keep in mind that the sin and the sinner are not the same. "Now if I do what I do not want to do," wrote Paul, "it is no longer I who do it, but it is sin living in me that does it." But sin is only part of our story. We are made in the image of God. The sinful nature is an unalterable terrorist living inside of us and our children, plotting to crash our lives into walls. But the sinful nature is not "us." We can lose, but we are not losers.

CLEAN HOUSE

Finally, master parents clean out the debris. They work to reduce or remove everything that makes it easy for a child to sin. They begin to teach him about *self*-control. They explain what will happen if there is a next time: no attention for the tantrum, but a large and growing series of losses of things he enjoys. They do everything they can to put him in a position where it's more difficult to sin.

The outward appearance is only a clue. It's not simply a passing moment to be explained away, but on the other hand, neither is it the whole story. Jesus reminds us that judging by outward appearance will always lead to *wrong* judgments—if not wrong in thinking that the behavior itself is sinful, then wrong in judging why the behavior is happening at all. Like God, a master parent "searches every heart and understands every motive behind the thoughts." We show mercy because we're looking at the outward actions but also looking at the inward heart. "God does not judge by external appearance," and neither should we.

When we look at the heart, our rebukes come from a heart of love rather than anger. They are done with consideration, kindness, and great patience. Rebukes take place in private, never in front of others, including (especially including) siblings. Our rebukes are like an iron fist in a velvet glove. Through mercy, we are able to step on their shoes without messing up their shine. And because mercy is in the mix, our rebukes always end with minimum resentment and maximum hope.

Mercy keeps master parents from having their rebukes turn into negative, self-fulfilling prophecies. We're able to keep the rebuke small ("Well, you missed it this time") instead of expanding it to fill the universe ("You *always* mess up on this"). Mercy keeps us from building defeatist attitudes and negative self-talk into our children. We don't ask questions like "What's the *matter* with you?" because we already know that it's the same thing that's the matter with us.

In this whole matter of mercy, master parents know that they have something to remember and something to forget.

Mary, in her great prayer song, said of her Master Parent, "He has helped his servant Israel, remembering to be merciful." God sees us messing up, violating his laws, demanding judgment, and then he says, "Mercy." When we see our kids messing up, violating our rules, demanding judgment, we need to follow his lead and remember to be merciful.

And we need to forget the "messing up" part. One of the astonishing things about God is that he doesn't keep track of our failings. "If you, O Lord, kept a record of sins, O Lord, who could stand?" The clear implication? God doesn't keep a record. If he did, we'd be goners. The lesson is clear for us. We have to understand that the failings of our children will be many, and we have to resist with our whole wills the temptation and tendency to keep a record of the failings.

The easiest thing in the world is to do the opposite on this remembering and forgetting business—to remember the messing up and to forget to be merciful. When your child doesn't prepare for the big test and performs way below her abilities, it's very easy to remember all of the other times she has slopped her way through life: missed chores, lackadaisical contributions on family efforts, sleeping through three snooze alarms until she's late. It is very hard to remember how little she is—even if she is sixteen—and how you slopped your own way through something just last month.

Sin does require repentance, restitution, and judgment, but it also requires forgiveness and mercy. Sin is a horrible thing, but it is also an opportunity for personal and relational growth as mercy works its magic.

As parents, we are *required* to show mercy to our children. We aren't excused from the lesson of the unmerciful servant who begged for mercy but refused to give it. Mercy is an inheritance, a beautiful gift to be passed from the Master Parent to master parents to their children. "Blessed are the merciful, for they will be shown mercy." The alternative is a loss of mercy from our Master Parent, as he asks, "Shouldn't you have had mercy on your fellow servant just as I had on you?" "I will spare them," he says, "just as in compassion a man spares his son."

Our children are not excused from this mercy transfer. We must teach them that, if they don't show mercy to their siblings or others, they won't receive it from us. We shouldn't cut slack—or at least as much slack—for children who won't cut it for others. It's all part of the deal. It's the way God has set it up. You don't get what you won't give.

How important is mercy for successful parenting? Many parents are willing to sacrifice for their children. They can yield their own desires, give up their time, and spend money on the children while foregoing their own needs. These can certainly be good and wonderful actions. But when we offer them all to God, he's going to cast them aside if mercy is missing from the mix.

Everyone who knew Jennifer considered her to be a totally devoted mother to her two girls. She tried to create the perfect home environment: well-prepared meals, attractive clothes, plenty of books, family projects, lots of activities. She was always running one of her girls to an activity or event (some thought she should claim her van as a home office on her tax return). But Jennifer was a hard woman. She rarely showed understanding or compassion to her children and refused to cut them any slack when they messed up. They quickly learned to toe the line—or else. This brought additional praise from people who knew her: "She has such well-behaved kids!" The only ones who didn't praise her for this were her kids . . . and God. When her kids grew up, both moved away from her city and away from her heart. They struggled with the idea of a merciful God.

"I desire mercy, not sacrifice" is God's clear priority. The only place we can show mercy, as God does with us, is with the people who need it from us—people like our children.

Sacrificing while not showing mercy is a serious failing of human beings. Mercy is not something that we figure out, that we just "get," when we become Christians—or parents. This is why Jesus had to command us to *learn* how to get it right: "Go and learn what this means: 'I desire mercy, not sacrifice.' " Not learning is disastrous: "If you had known what these words mean, 'I desire mercy, not sacrifice,' you would not have condemned the innocent."

Mercy is always needed when our children sin, but there are times and circumstances when we show mercy on the basis of an "I didn't know" rather than an "I knew but did it anyway." Paul was able to say, "I was shown mercy because I acted in ignorance and unbelief." If our children's sin is a result of ignorance, or because they just didn't understand our warnings about a certain situation, we are free to follow our Master Parent's example and show instant mercy.

What if, at the other end of the scale, our kids know better but still mess up big-time? Even here, there is never any room to push them away, just as God never does with us: "In your great mercy you did not put an end to them or abandon them, for you are a gracious and merciful God." There may come a time when we have to put some distance between us, or even ask grown children to leave the home if they are setting a miserable example for our other children, but there is never a time when a gracious and merciful parent says, "You are no longer my child," or acts like it is so. This is where "tough love" can go too far. Thank the Master Parent that *he* never goes that far.

The truth is that a major mess-up creates, if treated properly, an opportunity to increase the love our children have for us. When a sinful woman anointed Jesus' feet, he said, "I tell you, her sins— and they are many—have been forgiven, so she has shown me much love. But a person who is forgiven little shows only little love." When we really know our Master Parent has forgiven us, that's the reaction: We appreciate and love more. How can our own children not be pushed in the same direction? In the midst of parenting trauma, we can receive the gift of much love if we give the gift of great mercy.

Here's a great example of mercy: In spite of all the teaching and encouragement he received to the contrary, a young man got involved with a girl and went way over the line. She got pregnant. They'd only known each other a short time, and she wasn't a Christian. It was a bad match, a bad relationship, a bad mistake. The boy headed home, expecting thunderous judgment—knowing he deserved it—and found understanding, compassion, and support instead. Without excusing the sin, his parents forgave him, showing a true reflection of the Master Parent's response to our mistakes. After many years of friction and frustration with his parents, this young man now felt something different, something like love. Forgiveness did what care and money and gifts hadn't been able to dent.

In everything related to sin we have to remember that this child is our child, now and forever. The story of the Prodigal Son is not primarily a story about salvation, as it is so often used. Rather, it's a story of restoration, *because the Prodigal is already a son when the story begins.* When we receive back a wayward child—our own child—with mercy and kindness and graciousness, we are being just like God.

When all is said and done, we need to go far beyond granting mercy to our children. "Who is a God like you, who pardons sin and forgives the transgression of the remnant of his inheritance? You do not stay angry forever but delight to show mercy." We are given the exceedingly good news that "his anger lasts only a moment, but his favor lasts a lifetime." It's okay to be angry with our children. But not forever. At some point, sooner rather than later, we have to change and move over into the joy, the absolute *delight,* of showing mercy.

Our Master Parent is the God of the second chance. And the third chance. And the fourth. Be a parent of mercy, a master parent of the second chance.

THE BLEND

Blending these two principles is different than "the swing," tough to soft to tough to soft. We have to dispense justice and dispense mercy *at the same time,* not in some sort of swinging-pendulum way.

How can you tell if you're using "the swing" rather than "the blend"? If you're a "pendulum parent," first, you're tough. You make your kids toe the line. No excuses. Then you notice that your children are avoiding you, looking down or away when you talk to them, and performing at no higher a level. Your relationship with them is in tatters. So what do you do? You swing to the other side. You're easy. You erase the line. You start making their excuses for them. Then you notice that they are taking advantage of you, running amok, and performing at no higher a level. That makes you mad. So then you're tough . . . and then you realize you're on the swing.

In earlier generations, there was perhaps too much focus on justice at the expense of mercy, affection, and love. In our day, there is perhaps too much focus on mercy at the expense of justice, discipline, and respect. Either approach works at some level. Focusing mainly on justice produces children with decent values and social graces but with big holes in their hearts. Focusing mainly on mercy produces children with a greater sense of being loved but with big holes in their values. But just think of the success if we do both!

The blend says that we have to dispense both of these, justice and mercy, at the same time. When we're practicing the blend, a typical conversation might go something like this:

"Don't you understand that this stuff you're doing will hurt you? I can't let that happen. I'd never forgive myself if I stood on the sidelines and didn't do anything. So that's why I have to stop you. It's just plain wrong."

"I'm sorry, Mom. It was really, really dumb."

"We're agreed on that. Well, my young friend, we're going to seriously cut back the time you spend hanging out with your friends, all the way to zero with two of them. Your allowance just got cut by two-thirds. And I think we're going to have to knock out any extra activities for a few weeks."

"I know I deserve it."

"I'm not saying that's all," you warn. "I might think up some more restrictions while I'm trying to go to sleep tonight."

The tears come in a flood. You watch closely to see just what kind of tears they are. Are they tears that say, "I'm sorry I got caught and punished" or tears that say, "I'm sorry I messed up so bad and damaged my soul"? You pray that God will give you the discernment to see what kind of tears they are.

"I'm so sorry," the quivering young lady blurts out, her face etched with grief. "I'm so sorry. I didn't want to do it, but then I just did. I feel so awful. I'm sorry. Please forgive me. I won't do it again. I promise. I'll do anything to make it up to you." The tears and moans grow louder but aren't theatrical.

And you know that she's learned her lesson. You walk across the kitchen and sit down next to your wailing daughter, wrapping both arms around her. "Honey," you whisper, "I can see that you're sorry. *Really* sorry. I can see it in your eyes and feel it in your tears. You're making apologies and asking forgiveness. You're talking about changing and making up for what you've done, as much as you can. I think you've got it. *Consider yourself forgiven and the slate erased.* I can't take away the consequences, but I will erase what you've done from my mind and do whatever I can to erase the guilt and shame from your heart."

What if the response from your daughter was different? Let's pick up the conversation midway:

"I'm not saying that's all," you warn. "I might think up some more restrictions while I'm trying to go to sleep tonight."

"I'm sorry, Mom. I won't do it anymore."

"I'm glad to hear it. You need some time to really get your feet on the ground."

"You mean you're still going to do all those things?" she asks, incredulous. "Even after I said I'm sorry?"

"Of course. You earned them."

"You're so mean!" your daughter screams. "I mess up one time and you make such a big deal of it!"

"I'm not doing this because it's fun, or because I don't like you. In fact, I'm doing it because I love you."

"Yeah, right," your daughter says with surprising coldness, flashing anger from her eyes. "Don't give me that love routine. You don't love me. No other parent does all this 'punishment' stuff. Only you." She sags onto a stool and leans on the counter with her face in her hands. "You're a terrible mother," she sobs. "I hate you."

And you know she has not learned the lesson. You walk across the kitchen and lean across the counter to face your bawling daughter squarely in the face. "So you're not really sorry? I can see it in your eyes. You're not saying the right things, or you're saying the right things with the wrong intent. I don't think you've got it. I'm sure you don't. So I think we need to keep going with the consequences and restrictions until you do get it, until you really *stop*. If I forgive you when you're not really sorry, or show you any mercy when you'd use it to continue in a bad direction, I will actually be encouraging you to go and sin some more. I'm sorry that's how you want to play it."

Justice demands that we expect, as a condition of showing mercy, real repentance and a desire to make restitution. God is clear on this point, even though the church has not always been. The alternative is to make a mockery of justice. The Bible makes the distinction between "worldly sorrow" (sorrow that you got caught, sorrow that you have to make good) and "godly sorrow" (sorrow that justice and relationships were violated). Master parents show mercy toward the "godly" variety and continue judgment to the "worldly" kind.

Master parents do not offer forgiveness unconditionally, because their Master Parent doesn't. "If your brother sins, rebuke him, and if he repents, forgive him." Your response to sin should be to rebuke the child. Then you watch. And listen. If he repents, you should forgive him—time after time, seventy times seven times. If you don't forgive him when he repents, if you hold a grudge and say, "Remember when . . . ," then "your Father will not forgive your sins." But if your child doesn't repent, you don't forgive; you continue the rebuke, continue the judgment, and continue the punishment.

The idea that we should forgive even where there is no repentance or true change is one of our day's most popular and insidious lies. It's presented as a way to not be bitter, a way to be a "good person." The only problem is, *this isn't what God does with us.* If we don't repent, he doesn't forgive. We can and should choose not to be bitter, but we can't "forgive them in our hearts," for the simple reason that *forgiveness is a transaction between two people.* We do our children no favors when we forgive a heart that's still as cold as stone.

So to start the transaction, to start both parent and child on the path toward mercy, master parents give good rebukes, godly rebukes. Good rebukes are serious and corrective. And good rebukes are positive and full of care and concern.

Master parents don't let their rebukes turn into nagging criticism or knee-jerk, ongoing commentary that picks at events and external behavior without affecting the child's heart and mind. And they don't let their rebukes deteriorate into begging and pleading that puts the child's sinful nature on the throne. Justice causes us to rebuke strongly to avoid later regrets, and mercy causes us to rebuke gently to avoid later regrets.

It's all right for us to feel righteous indignation when our children have really missed the mark, but only if we, like our Master Parent, "in wrath remember mercy." I once saw a poster that said, "The beatings will continue until morale improves." We know, in our saner moments, that we can't beat people into higher morale. We need to remember this as master parents.

We know that without mercy, we can "turn justice into bitterness." "You have turned justice into poison," the prophet says, not without anger. That's what justice alone becomes: poison. Justice that's not tempered becomes the cyanide of the soul. We must be careful never to do to our children what is hateful to us.

We make the mercy that echoes justice a part of our relationship-building with our children. "Punishment must be combined with crawling inside our children's hearts," I wrote in my book *Walking through the Fire.* "We need to probe to find out what the root of the sin is. While we're doing it, we should acknowledge—to ourselves and to them—that we've faced similar temptations. Always, we need to remind them that they're still loved."

But we don't go to the other extreme and define mercy as "looking the other way." Adonijah, the son of King David, conspired on two occasions to steal his father's throne. And at one point, he declared himself king. About him it was said, "His father had never interfered with him by asking, 'Why do you behave as you do?' " We must be careful not to repeat David's terrible mistake. Who ever heard of a child who was never disciplined? Well, unfortunately, I have. You probably have too. The result is always Adonijahs running amok. In a sense, God is telling us that if we don't discipline our children, we're acting like they aren't our children at all.

We show mercy and we hold back our judgment, but not to the extent of excusing or even encouraging rotten behavior. The driving force behind God's kindness is that it leads us toward repentance. "Do you show contempt for the riches of his kindness, tolerance and patience, not realizing that God's kindness leads you toward repentance?"

What if our mercy—our kindness—leads to contempt from our children rather than repentance? We will not let our generosity be misused to damage our justice. When our kindness is rebuffed, the judgment is no longer held back and justice is fulfilled. If they make light of our mercy, they get the full judgment that mercy was willing to overlook. We remember that "a corrupt witness mocks at justice," and we cut the mocker no slack.

When you find your young teenage daughter listening to truly vulgar music, music you have discussed and forbidden from your home, what do you do? You're full of righteous indignation, and you let her have it—both barrels. You let her know how disappointed you are. Then you confiscate the music (and maybe her stereo), give her some serious consequences (like a two-week grounding), and warn her both about the potential damage of the music to her soul and the potential damage of you to her social life.

What if she repents? admits that she was totally in the wrong? agrees to never do it again? If you believe her—*really* believe her, not just wishful thinking—you could relent. Maybe you let her have her stereo back and cut the grounding back to one weekend. You pitch the CDs.

A week later, you come home earlier than she expected, to find her listening to the same music on the Internet. Your earlier kindness has been abused. You remove the stereo, reinstate the earlier full grounding, and shut down her access to the Internet. For how long? Until she really stops. Until she really understands the purpose of mercy.

There is more than a shred of truth in Shakespeare's strong statement, "Nothing emboldens sin so much as mercy." Like the Master Parent, we are richly merciful. But also like him, we're nobody's fool.

We are told that "mercy triumphs over judgment." What does that mean? We should note that mercy triumphs over *judgment*, not justice. The justice of the situation is always held out clearly before our children. It is only the judgment, the right to *execute* the obvious justice, that can be suspended by mercy.

What is justice without judgment? You got it. Mercy.

In the final analysis, our Master Parent sees no conflict between justice and mercy, and he expects us to see no conflict here either. "What does the Lord require of you? To act justly and to love mercy."

We can see these two great strands coming together in the biblical idea of "covering sins."

James tells us, "Whoever turns a sinner from the error of his way will save him from death and cover over a multitude of sins." There is the justice side. We cover sins by stopping the sinner. Master parents are committed to doing this with their children. You have a teenage driver who is reckless and foolish behind the wheel. You don't play around, telling him, "Naughty, naughty" and giving him a fine so he can conveniently get back on the road and kill someone. You stop him, and you do it effectively. You take away his keys, his driver's license, his car, *your* car. You sell your cars or let the air out of the tires. *Whatever it takes.* He won't like you for it. Tough. It's more important to "save him from death."

Peter tells us to "love each other deeply, because love covers over a multitude of sins." There is the mercy side. We also cover sins by forgiving the sinner. Will we have to do this "covering" business a lot? Yes. Why should we do it? Because our Master Parent gets a lot of work covering our sins, and we desperately need him to do it for us. Master parents are committed to doing this with their children as well. We get over the anguish our son has caused us with his reckless driving. If he really repents and confesses his wrong attitudes and behavior, we forgive him. We empathize with him on the events he's had to miss. But we are *very slow* about letting him back on the road. If he whines and complains and rages about that, we know his repentance was phony. If he accepts it with grace, we plot a strategy to eventually let him drive again.

Let it never be said of us as parents that we've missed these two great intertwined attributes of our Master Parent. We never want to hear from him, "You neglect justice and the love of God." The great prophet Zechariah sums up this single command to dispense justice and mercy: "Administer true justice; show mercy and compassion to one another."

As master parents, we can administer true justice—not arbitrary, not inconsistent, not done out of ignorance or rage—and, as we look into those shining youthful eyes, realize that these children are the "one another" Zechariah was talking about. We can show them mercy and compassion.

LAST THOUGHTS

If we dispense justice without mercy, we build shame into our children and plant the seeds of massive rebellion. If we dispense mercy without justice, we give our children no sense of what it means to "be good."

Master parents dispense justice and mercy evenly, with both hands. They see no conflict between the two, just as their Master Parent doesn't. "Maintain love *and* justice," he says.

Fiorello La Guardia, the longtime mayor of New York, once told a story to the police, whom he thought were being "rather too hard on young offenders." And so he "tried to point out to them the difference between a mischievous prank and true juvenile delinquency."

"When I was a boy," he said, "I used to wander around the streets with my friends until we found a horse tied to a post. We'd unhitch him, ride him around town, then tie him up again."

"Are you trying to tell us," asked one of the policemen, "that the mayor of New York was once a horse thief?"

"No," replied LaGuardia. "I'm trying to tell you that the mayor of New York was once a boy."

Master parents know the difference between delinquency and childishness, between the need for justice and the need for mercy. Master parents know in their souls the difference between being a criminal and being a kid.

Five

MASTER PARENTS
TEACH THROUGH VALUES
AND
TEACH THROUGH RESULTS

——————— ◆ ———————

"He will teach us his ways "

~ But ~

"They must bear the consequences. "

WHEN we teach our children the right things the wrong way it's likely that they'll end up with no lessons learned.

Master parents use every available means to teach their children good values, but at the same time, they force themselves to stand back and let their children learn how these values work through results.

Whether we realize it or not, this is just how God parents us. He is teaching us all of the time. "Since my youth, O God, you have taught me," says Psalm 71:17. And in Isaiah 50:4, we read, "He wakens me morning by morning, wakens my ear to listen like one being taught."

He also uses a variety of resources to teach. Paul says that "faith comes from hearing the message. . . . But I ask: Did they not hear?

Of course they did: Their voice has gone out into all the earth, their words to the ends of the world."

Who is the *they* that Paul refers to? Whose voice is out there, teaching everyone, everywhere?

It's God's Creation. Paul is quoting from Psalms: "The heavens declare the glory of God; the skies proclaim the work of his hands. Day after day they pour forth speech." God uses the very world in which we live to teach his children.

And that's not all. He teaches us his values using many other speakers: his Holy Spirit, pastors, teachers, evangelists, other Christians, little children, and the Bible. Even our own consciences speak to us constantly (unless we pervert or kill them). There is no break from the Master Parent's pervasive teaching of values.

He also teaches us through results. "Don't be misled. Remember that you can't ignore God and get away with it. You will always reap what you sow!" We can ignore the values for a while, but sooner or later life catches up with us and shows that the high cost of ignorance is greater than the high cost of education.

God knows that results are sometimes the best teacher and are often exactly what is needed to bring closure to our understanding of the principle behind the results. Our Master Parent looks at us, shakes his head, and says, "It seems you don't want to learn this the easy way. I have a remedial class for you."

TEACHING THROUGH VALUES

If you're going to do anything worthwhile as a master parent, you'd better teach your children the crucial values of life relentlessly.

Master parents teach their children values that have powerful *content.* They teach using appropriate *methods* at appropriate *times.* They understand that because we're all slow learners, values must be repeated over and over until their children truly understand them. Their teaching is a *balance* between talking and listening. They are always sensitive to the *quantity* of lessons their children can absorb at any one time, pay close attention to *timing,* and make sure that there is real *engagement*. They know that all great teaching is full of *encouragement*. And finally, they know that their teaching can only be effective if they themselves have *credibility*.

Let's look at each of these important master-parenting ideas in more detail.

CONTENT

Master parents focus on the "big values." They don't waste their time on hair length, makeup, clothing styles, most music preferences, or bedroom decoration. They do spend time on the values that God deems important, like:

1. **Worship.** Master parents teach their children the difference between attending church and worshiping the living God. We need to teach the value of real worship, not the kind that is "made up only of rules taught by men." We show our children that worship is not only what you do at church but that it's about using our lives and bodies "as living sacrifices, holy and pleasing to God." Doing this, we are told, is our "spiritual act of worship." Just as our Master Parent modeled sacrifice for us, we need to show our children how to live a life of sacrifice, which is true worship.

2. **Faith.** As they find strength from their Master Parent, master parents make sure their children are "strengthened in the faith as [they] were taught" This means that we start by teaching our children to pray. We can do this a number of ways: by letting them see us pray and listen to our prayers, by showing them that our first response to a crisis is prayer, by praying together as a family, and by talking about prayer and why God doesn't always answer us as we would like. We can teach them the attitude that must join with prayer to make it effective. The Bible calls this attitude faith. "Faith is being sure of what we hope for and certain of what we do not see." We show our children how to offer "prayer and petition, with thanksgiv-

ing," because it's a done deal when we ask. We teach them how to speak the language of faith and of expected answers to prayer. We read them stories of remarkable faith and we teach them how to handle the inevitable assaults on faith that come from so many directions.

3. **Love.** Love is a learned behavior. Master parents "have been taught by God to love each other," and they pass this teaching to their own children. We don't simply teach our children to stop fighting. That target is way too low. We teach them to actually love each other and to find practical ways to show it: "Josh, your brother is going to be tired when he gets home from practice. Why don't we make his favorite lunch for him?" "Melissa, if you help your sister with her math, it would make a big difference in her knowledge and confidence." Sadly, humans seem to know how to fight and insult and hit without any training at all. But we have to *learn* to love.

4. **Decency and holiness.** Our Master Parent says to us, "You were taught, with regard to your former way of life, to put off your old self, which is being corrupted by its deceitful desires; to be made new in the attitude of your minds; and to put on the new self, created to be like God in true righteousness and holiness." Master parents teach their children "the difference between the holy and the common and show them how to distinguish between the unclean and the clean." We talk together at length, for example, about why some comedy movies are funny and uplift our spirits (even with slapstick) and are clean, and why others are twisted and drag our spirits down and are unclean. Master parents take the time to help their children understand and appreciate the difference.

5. **The importance of the invisible.** Master parents teach their children the lesson they have learned that "man does not live on bread alone but on every word that comes from the mouth of the Lord." Young children already appreciate the importance of the invisible. Master parents simply build on that. For

instance, the Bible tells us to invest in others. Jesus goes so far as to say, "Use worldly wealth to gain friends for yourselves, so that when it is gone, you will be welcomed into eternal dwellings." So master parents paint a picture: "If you spend your time and money and resources on others, what you are really doing is investing in them. And in God's world, every investment earns something. You're piling up something really good in a big storage unit in heaven. And part of this treasure is going to be a surprise 'thank-you' party attended by everyone you ever helped. Imagine!"

6. **Warfare.** Our Master Parent allows enemies to test us, "only to teach warfare to the descendants of the Israelites who had not had previous battle experience." Life can be a war at times, and master parents teach their children how to fight battles they have not yet experienced. This means that we practice responses with our children before they face actual temptations. With our teens, we might talk with them about how to stand firm against sexual seduction or peer pressure. With younger children, we might teach them how to handle rejection by others (e.g., older children they want to spend time with or kids at church or in the neighborhood). We might even role-play, just like armies do when they play war games.

7. **Wisdom.** In general, master parents pass along to their children whatever important wisdom God is teaching them at the moment, just like their example, Jesus, did. He once said, "I . . . speak just what the Father has taught me." The source of his words was the written word of God, which is "useful for teaching." For master parents, this means that we talk to our children about the very struggles or lessons we're learning in our own spiritual lives. If we've gossiped about someone and it came back to bite us, we share that. If we've just gotten an insight about how to beat a habitual sin that has plagued us for years, we get our hard-won insight out into the open—even if we do it awkwardly or don't have all the right words.

TIMES AND WAYS

Just as God teaches us values at all times and through every vehicle, so he expects us to teach his values to our children. "Talk about them when you sit at home and when you walk along the road, when you lie down and when you get up. Tie them as symbols on your hands and bind them on your foreheads. Write them on the doorframes of your houses and on your gates."

In this sense, every home is a "home school" and every parent is a teacher. And we're supposed to take this role seriously. Our conversations with our kids can easily become an exercise in the trivial: "Get ready for dinner," and "Pick up your things," and "Turn that music down." Before we know it, the "values" time is gone. Master parents don't allow the petty and mundane to wipe out the important and eternal. They'll leave out some details—even if these details annoy the dickens out of them—in order to bring home a lesson in living.

Master parents overlook small things with their children, because they remember that these things are only a tiny fraction of what the Master Parent has to overlook with them. They don't challenge music, for example, just because it's loud or lacks melody and harmony (and may not technically even be music). Even if the music has words they suspect might have double meanings or creates distance in the family due to the headphones surgically implanted in a teen's ears, master parents talk about the values of courtesy and purity rather than decibel level. They go for the values behind the behavior. I heard someone say once, "They move mountains an inch rather than molehills a mile."

Our Master Parent teaches us his values in at least five ways, and master parents use all of them:

1. **The written Word.** God has given us his truth in words that we can understand. We can follow his example by writing truth to our children—in letters, e-mail messages, on-line cards, notes in lunch sacks, and "quick truths" on pieces of paper slipped

under a bedroom door. Incorporating our Master Parent's words (the Bible) into this process adds a lot of extra "oomph."

2. **The Holy Spirit.** God whispers truth to us in ways that only we can hear. We can do the same with our children, by finding quiet one-on-one times where we can "think out loud," by correcting in ways that no one else ever hears, and by literally whispering truth in their ears. Children often listen the best when they have to strain to hear us.

3. **Our own conscience.** Sometimes, our Master Parent lets us just sit and stew on things with the truth that has already been implanted. Master parents do the same, by knowing when to teach by *not* teaching. They know that there are times when silence is the best teacher.

4. **The Creation.** The world around us is constantly speaking to us about God, from a moon that never shows us two faces to the consistency of the seasons. We can use Creation to teach our children by asking questions that direct their attention to the universal language. We should be like Solomon, who "also taught about animals and birds."

5. **Other people.** God uses all sorts of people, good and bad, to speak truth to us. We can and should do the same. Not all messages can, or should, come straight from us. Master parents welcome an array of teachers, like grandparents and uncles and aunts and older siblings and Sunday school teachers and youth pastors, to help them teach values. And, like Jesus does, they teach "many things by parables," knowing that stories about the successes and failures of others are often the best teachers.

REPETITION

In teaching values, there needs to be *repetition:* "Repeat them again and again to your children." We are told to "impress" the values on our children. Why? It's not that we have to repeat ourselves because our children are stupid, immature, or disrespectful, or because we might be conveying the message poorly. The main reason that master parents repeat the message is to make sure that they say it at just the right moment, *when their children are finally ready to hear it.* It may be the fiftieth time we've said it, but *now* is the perfect time for our children to hear it.

"When the student is ready, the teacher appears," says an old proverb. The teacher may have always been there, but he doesn't "appear" until the student is ready to see.

We're not talking here about simple "house rules," like picking up your toys before bedtime or taking your junk to your room. These are commands that children should follow the first time they hear them. We're on a much deeper level here, talking about values rather than rules. We're talking about teaching concepts that will eventually sink in when the child is ready: "Here's the kind of friend you should be playing with" rather than "Don't play in the street."

BALANCE

As we teach through values, we must find a balance between advocacy and inquiry—between advocating the value because we believe it and inquiring as to how it connects with our children because we want them to internalize it in their own words. In other words, we teach the values with passion and then we stop so we can listen to their doubts and questions and attempts to insert the truth into their own unique personalities.

Advocacy

If we really believe in a value, then we should teach it as though there is no tomorrow. Master parents teach values with enthusiasm and commitment, with power and intensity. There is something very convincing and contagious about passion, whether used by a speaker or a teacher or a parent. If another person believes in something very strongly, we are at least tempted to give it notice. When trying to teach integrity, for example, master parents aren't afraid to ignite the fire.

Integrity means we're whole people. We aren't one person at home, another at school, and another at church. That's phony and sneaky and big-time hypocritical. If we have integrity, we don't say things we don't mean, we don't leave things out that shade the truth into a lie, and we don't use the truth to hurt people. Integrity means we spend our lives becoming more and more the way God designed us to be.

Inquiry
If we really want our children to believe in the value we're teaching, we've got to find out exactly what they are doing with it.

As they teach values, master parents aren't afraid to ask real-world, tough questions. With our example of integrity, these questions might look like this:

"What should you do if a teacher at school wants to know who broke the glass in the trophy case and you know who, but you don't want to get a friend in trouble? What would you *want* to do? Is honesty really always the best policy? What if the only way to tell the truth to someone is to break a confidence with someone else? Should you tell the truth, or should you keep quiet? Is it an act of integrity if we say something that's factually true, even if our purpose is to gossip about someone or slander them?"

We ask, and then we listen—not just for the "correct" answers but for the ideas and sentence fragments and body language that show us there is learning taking place.

QUANTITY
Quantity is an important consideration. We've spent twenty, thirty, forty, or more years accumulating wisdom, knowledge, and experience. We've been taught by many teachers, and we have learned much from our choices, both good and bad. It's normal to want to "download" all of that information into our children. Unfortunately, they're too small to hold all of it. It isn't that they're

stupid, it's just that they don't have enough length or breadth or depth to give our teaching context.

You can't get a college degree in a week—not a real one, anyway. Master parents also know their children can't absorb the sum of their parental knowledge in one sitting.

TIMING

Master parents know it's important to time their teaching.

If it's a matter of life or death—playing in the street, responding to strangers, driving a car—we need to teach in the clearest and strongest of language. *Don't go in the street!* The lesson taught by life in this case—getting hit by a car—is too severe and horrible a result to allow.

The problem is that many parents act like everything is a life-and-death situation, that children should just listen and do what they're told. But there are many teachings that are better learned *after* the results of our children's decisions have hurt them: going out on hot pavement in bare feet, taking a class that's beyond their ability, spending time with a friend who constantly belittles them. Uncomfortable feet, bad grades, and humiliation can present you with a marvelous platform for some concise and well-heard teaching.

Master parents must ask themselves, "Is this lesson best learned early, before my child experiences negative results, or later, after the child has gone through a different 'school' that has gotten their attention?"

Master parents also remember that the learning process takes time. Here's an example: Most parents want their children to come to saving faith at as early an age as possible. Unfortunately, this sense of urgency can backfire. No parent, no matter how loving or serious or knowledgeable about God, can push children into the kingdom of God. They can, however, push them away. It's much better to wait and watch, looking for teachable moments, than to push a child so that he rebels. Master parents pay attention to their children and know when it's okay to push and when to back off.

ENGAGEMENT

Teaching about values is rarely effective when it comes in the form of an extended lecture. You know you've entered the lecture universe when your children aren't engaged in the conversation. Great speakers engage their audiences; great parents do the same. We ask questions, invite questions, welcome disagreements—anything to make the teaching real for our children.

Master parents also take care to make the teaching process a safe one. They aren't insulted and don't become angry when their children ask questions, disagree, or refrain from committing themselves to believing and living the value; quite the contrary, they're concerned when their children *don't* do these things. Our Master Parent isn't thrown off by our questions and disagreements and hesitations, and so neither are we.

Master parents, however, don't let the teaching of values lead to arguments or angry debates. As the "senior members" in the conversation, they make it their responsibility to keep the time positive or to break it off. They know that you can't argue someone into the kingdom of God, or into right thinking, or into true agreement. Their goal is the winning of *hearts,* not the winning of arguments.

ENCOURAGEMENT

The greatest lessons in the world are useless unless the student believes they are doable. Master parents understand this and season their teaching with liberal doses of encouragement. "You can really do this," they exhort. The difference between knowing a truth and applying a truth is often dependent on how encouraged our children feel.

CREDIBILITY

Credibility is vitally important to effective teaching through values. Master parents know they should avoid teaching, at least authoritatively, on areas where they have had no success. They know they shouldn't pontificate on financial responsibility if they can't balance their own checkbook or pay their bills on time. They can still teach on this, but only with the humility and vulnerability of a fellow pilgrim: "Honey, I'm really struggling with this, but here's what I think will work. Maybe you could sit with me and help me, and together we'll see if it works."

Master parents make sure that their practices don't contradict their values. They know that ultimately teaching is about being a living example, that "everyone who is fully trained will be like his teacher." They tremble a bit, because they know that "we who teach will be judged more strictly" and that includes teaching our children.

They don't allow their credibility to be dissipated by a bogus focus on rules and regulations. Like God, they teach "with authority, and not as their teachers of the law," who reduced life-giving principles to life-draining pride.

As their Master Parent has said to them, master parents can say to their children, "See, I have taught you decrees and laws as the Lord my God commanded me, so that you may follow them. . . . Observe them carefully, for this will show your wisdom and understanding." They can say with confidence, "What you heard from me, keep as the pattern of sound teaching. . . . Guard the good deposit that was entrusted to you." Master parents work hard at this business of teaching and warning, and they don't stop with their own children. They know that God has told them to "teach them to your children and to their children after them."

TEACHING THROUGH RESULTS
If you're going to do anything worthwhile as a master parent, you'd better allow your children to learn through the results of their decisions and behaviors.

One of the truly amazing parenting stories is that of the Prodigal Son in Luke 15. One key part of the story is often overlooked because it's about what *didn't* happen. The father—a metaphor for our Master Parent and an example for all master parents—never offers a word of correction or displeasure, either before his son leaves for the wild life or after he returns.

This famous master parent has another interesting "omission." He doesn't go chasing after his son, doesn't check up on him or lecture him, and doesn't say, "I told you so" when he returns. The absence of recrimination is astonishing. What allows this father to do his parenting so quietly? Because he knows where his son will end up. It's as certain as the sun showing up every day; the weakness in the son's character is bound to produce some very definite and inescapable results. The father knows that his son will have a chance to learn from life what he might never learn from lecture.

When we learn the hard way that bad decisions lead to bad results and we come crawling back to our Master Parent, he doesn't have to pound us with his words, *and he doesn't*. He knows that life has already pounded us. We wouldn't be back if we weren't so desperate that we were finally ready to try real values. After the warm and surprising welcome home, we're all ears—but the Master Parent says very little. He doesn't have to say much because we've already learned so much and because every word now has the value of a thousand before.

Mediocre parents often use "I told you so's." Master parents avoid these like the plague. Why? Because the Master Parent has afforded them the same courtesy. Because he's given them the same break. Because he's shown them that pouring on guilt and shame is bad Christianity and bad parenting. Master parents reject the myth that they must always drill their children on every point of truth and every point of failure.

Master parents have learned that character really is destiny. They know that very often the only way to correct bad thinking is to see firsthand that it doesn't work. Immaturity produces frustration, mediocrity, and broken relationships. Our children need to learn from experience that sin doesn't satisfy. In fact, sin only leads to more sin, then worse sin, and then finally slavery and death—

death right here and now, while we're still breathing. There are many ways to be dead, and sin will find them all.

Teaching through results is the equivalent of having hands-on exercises in a seminar or workshop. We can hear the instructor talk about the principle, but until we get our own hands on it, try it out, talk about it, question it, and stumble around with it, we just don't "get it." We can agree with it, but it hasn't become real enough for us to consider actually using it.

Master parents know that results are the great cure for the folly of doing the same thing over and over again and hoping to get a different result. They know that their children will keep getting the same result no matter how much they "hope," and that only through results will they learn that their hope is really an illusion. Master parents can count on results to be their reliable coteacher as they parent their children.

You've told them, but they just don't listen. Your eight-year-old son doesn't want to practice good hygiene? A little ridicule from peers may be more valuable than a hundred "nag sessions." Your daughter laughs when her friends make mistakes? The shaming laughter she hears in response to *her* next mistake may be the remedy. Your child likes to play rough with his friends? Ostracism and loneliness may be the unwelcome result of his actions.

Teaching through results is consistently, even maddeningly, effective. This is clearly true when the behavior is wrong. There is a certain reaping built into the fabric of life. "Those who plow evil and those who sow trouble reap it," we are warned. "If the righteous receive their due on earth, how much more the ungodly and the sinner!"

But teaching through results also works when the behavior is right. We are told that "the wages of the righteous bring them life," that "what the righteous desire will be granted," and that "prosperity is the reward of the righteous." The result of living rightly is "a tree of life." When trouble comes, "the righteous will never be uprooted." Good results affirm and encourage living good values.

Master parents know and teach their children that the results they get will be equal to the values they practice in *kind,* in *degree,* and in *certainty.*

Kind

This means that bad produces bad, and good produces good. "The one who sows to please his sinful nature, from that nature will reap destruction; the one who sows to please the Spirit, from the Spirit will reap eternal life." Master parents remind their children that they can't beat the system. They can't get good reaping from bad sowing. Cheating on a test to get an A, for example, has all sorts of possible returns, like getting caught or getting into a tougher class than they can possibly hope to handle.

Degree

Master parents also remind their children of the great biblical principle that the results they get are proportionate to the decisions they make and the actions they take. Master parents say to their children, as their Master Parent says to them, "Remember this: Whoever sows sparingly will also reap sparingly, and whoever sows generously will also reap generously."

They need to see that they will never get a lot out if they only put a little in. If they rush through their chores in minimum time, never volunteer to help out, and go out of their way to avoid responsibility, they will earn an equivalent return: little or no allowance, no one volunteering to help them when they're in a tight spot, no clean clothes to wear to the party this weekend.

Certainty

Master parents teach their children, as the Master Parent teaches them, not to "become weary in doing good, for at the proper time we will reap a harvest if we do not give up." There is absolutely no doubt about this, since "he who sows righteousness reaps a sure reward" and "he who sows wickedness reaps trouble." There are no loopholes in real life.

If your son, for example, says he wants to organize an event to raise money for the poor and starving, you get behind it. You encourage and exhort, you suggest and brainstorm, you give advice and give money. You do everything you can to encourage him. But if he decides to bail out halfway through, you let the event fall flat and let him deal alone with the frustrated friends and supporters. You don't make it happen in spite of his lack of interest and commitment. It's his deal. You let it rise or fall according to his own actions.

As master parents teach their children these truths, they must distinguish between *natural* and *imposed* results. Both can be effective.

Natural results are the results that are "built in" to life. Ask and you get; don't ask and you don't get. Seek and you find; don't seek and you'll never know it's there. Knock and doors open; don't knock and you can't join the party. If you don't set your alarm, you'll arrive late. Drive carelessly, you'll get tickets (or worse). Exalt yourself and people will knock you down; humble yourself and people will praise your name. Every action gets an equal and opposite reaction.

Imposed results are the results that master parents set, both positive and negative. You don't do your chores, you can't go to the movies. You start a fight with your sister, you go to your room. You leave your toys out, you won't play with them for a week. You come in late, you don't go out the next time. You don't put gas in the car, you turn in your keys for the rest of the month. No words are really even necessary.

Natural results are often the best teachers, for a number of reasons. First, the child can't dismiss the results simply because they were imposed or "artificial"—no one made these results up. Second, it's easy to argue with parents but difficult to argue with reality. Third, complaints about "fairness," so often present with imposed results, are avoided. Fourth, the unexpected, unanticipated nature of natural results makes their impact more forceful and their memory more lasting. Fifth, parents can get sentimental or sloppy on follow-through, but natural results never let up. Sixth, composing a reasonable and effective imposed result is an exceedingly difficult task. And seventh, natural results can help the relationship (we can even empathize), while imposed results—no matter how necessary, reasonable, or fairly administered—almost always take some toll on the relationship.

Because of this, master parents work very hard to make all results natural results. They convert imposed results into natural results whenever possible. For example, instead of saying, "If you don't do your homework, you won't be able to _____" (watch television, talk to your friends, play outside, etc.), they simply let the criticism of the teacher and the embarrassment in front of classmates work their magic. Whenever possible, they make imposed results the backup position. Only if the child is content to live with the natural results should master parents resort to the imposed variety.

DISCIPLINE MAKES DISCIPLES

Master parents know that teaching through results is all about *discipline*. Discipline, to our ears, can sound just like punishment, with very negative overtones. But the root word of *discipline* is *disciple*. We discipline our children to make disciples—followers of "the Way," whatever that "way" is.

We could substitute a word like *training* or *coaching* that has no negative connotations, but I'd rather work with you to resurrect the word *discipline* and give it new life. Think of discipline as "training through results."

Unlike punishment, which has the primary purpose of getting our children to *stop*, discipline's main goal is getting our children to *keep going*. We allow real-world results to challenge them and toughen them, because we want our children to learn what it takes to keep going.

For example, your daughter's piano recital is tomorrow. Unfortunately, she's been goofing off and not practicing. She's embarrassed by the quality of her playing. She approaches you and talks about all of the homework she has, and asks if you would please let her miss the performance. She promises she'll do better next time. You're a master parent, however, and you see that a juicy teaching lesson, a perfect chance for discipline, has just been put into your hands. You tell her she must go to the recital. She ends up practicing into the night and again early the next morning, squeezing her homework in between practice sessions. She goes to school exhausted and still doesn't feel very good about her playing. She's learned that next time she'll need to prepare better.

You might say, "But I want to be there for my children!" Here's the important thing to remember: *Not getting in the way of discipline—even insisting that they face it—is being there for your children.* Will it be hard to follow through? Absolutely. Now you know how our Master Parent feels when he has to discipline us. He does it because he loves us, but it still breaks his heart. When you discipline your children and your heart is torn, take it to the Parent who understands.

Learning to keep going may, of course, include going in a different direction. Your child might end up concluding that the reason she doesn't practice piano is that she really isn't that committed to playing the piano. She'd like to try something new, especially now that she's had more exposure to the range of instruments available. You know that there is great value in pursuing your passions, so you allow her to make a switch after finishing any current commitments.

Although we want our children to modify their approach as necessary when they hit inevitable trials, we also want them to face those trials with "pure joy . . . because you know that the testing of your faith develops perseverance." You don't want your daughter to go to the recital with a bad attitude. You let her know that if she does this hard thing with joy, you'll be a lot more sympathetic about changes she wants to make or other things she wants to do. You want her to persevere, so you teach her that the fruit of perseverance is that "you may be mature and complete, not lacking anything."

Young people are immature and incomplete; they lack so much it makes you hurt to watch them. One of the main reasons they are this way is that we parents don't practice using trials to develop the perseverance that undergirds maturity and completeness. We all too easily fall into the well-intentioned but destructive act of trying to shield them from the results of their own decisions and behavior. It's easy to forget the simple truth that "hot fire makes good steel."

Master parents have the humility to acknowledge and act on this truth. While we could spend hours lecturing on the importance of gratitude and appreciation, we say to ourselves instead, "I've explained the principle, and now I'll let life—including, if necessary, unkind peers—provide the workshop."

And master parents don't let this discipline just happen. "He who loves [his son] is careful to discipline him." This is because we're trying to teach our children values that we as humans generally work very hard to avoid learning, things like responsibility and self-control. We make results a strong part of the curriculum. We let our children experience results, both good and bad, when the impact of these results is as small as possible. It's always better to learn a really important life lesson at a discount. Paying a high price for every lesson could lead them to disastrous personal bankruptcy. If you shield them at age ten, the price might quadruple by age fifteen.

For example, your son isn't doing his homework. Not because it's too hard or too much but because he's simply choosing not to do the work. So you jump in and take over the process. You set times, nag, push, and make demands. When he looks forlorn, you jump in further and start working the problems for him. Every inch of the way, you're the one driving the process. *We're making it,* you think.

His grades hold up for a while, but now he's in middle school or high school and it's much harder to enforce study rules. His grades start sinking, and unfortunately, now is the time his grades really count for his future. You enforce the consequences for low grades, which have now moved from missing bedtime snacks to missing school social events. Rather than grounding him from a favorite television program, you now ground him from using the car. The cost just went way up, and the impact on your relationship just took a more dramatic turn as well. However old your children are, start today before the cost of learning gets even higher.

THE SCHOOL OF HARD KNOCKS

It's okay to let our children attend our alma mater, the "school of hard knocks," beginning as early as preschool. Master parents understand that "no discipline seems pleasant at the time, but painful," and that "later on, however, it produces a harvest of righteousness and peace for those who have been trained by it." Some of the key attributes of the school of hard knocks include:

1. Admission is granted upon birth. No one tests out of this school.
2. Attendance is mandatory. No one gets to drop out and you can't beat the system.
3. There is no grading "on the curve." It doesn't matter how your friends are doing; it only matters how you are doing.
4. The courses are always open and there are no limits on class size. If you want to learn things the hard way, there's a spot for you.
5. All classes are labs rather than lectures. This means that they are harder, messier, and provide more chances to blow yourself up.

6. The supply of teachers is limitless. If you need to learn about relationships, for example, there is a bottomless pit full of people (including some very rotten people) who will be happy to be your tutors.
7. Attending this school will cost you big-time. The fees are high and there are no scholarships. Fees for individual courses go up each time you have to retake them.
8. If you fail a course, you get to keep taking it again and again until you pass or die.

As master parents watch their kids work their way through the school of hard knocks, they learn to replace their natural response with a supernatural one. The natural response when our children are getting knocked about is to protect them and rescue them. In this way, we often protect them from growth and rescue them from wisdom. The supernatural response is to allow the trial to teach its full lesson, so our children won't have to retake the course. We support them, of course, but only by reminding them of the values and assuring them of our love.

After setting the high expectations and teaching the values, master parents let the training come from results, which, while allowing us to act in freedom, also allow us to feel the effects of our own mistakes so we can learn from them. Master parents know that there's much truth to this insight from Luc de Clapiers de Vauvenargues: "The things we know best are things we haven't been taught." They don't shrink back, even though "no discipline seems pleasant at the time, but painful." They don't shrink back because they see the results, the end product of life discipline.

When we intervene, it's often because we don't have the character or guts—or, in the final analysis, the love—to see our children through the discipline to the harvest of righteousness: "Later on, however, it produces a harvest of righteousness and peace for those who have been trained by it."

Part of the problem is that we don't define *blessing* and *cursing* accurately. We often think of blessing as "ease, comfort, happiness, painlessness" and cursing as "challenge, trials, difficulty, pain." But sometimes just the opposite is true. In fact, challenge, trials, difficulty, and pain might very well be the greatest blessing our children could receive at times—the greatest gift we could let them have from life. It can be hard to watch our children struggle, but it's not as hard as watching them lose.

Master parents don't intervene, because they love their children enough to let them get roughed up by results in the context of their love. This means that we have to let our children know that because we love them and because we see the bigger picture, we aren't going to bail them out of their trials.

But to close the learning loop, we have to do more than just say, "I'm not interfering with this lesson because I love you." We have to connect the dots. And we have to let them know what we're expecting them to learn and what will be the long-term effects if they don't learn it. A small pain now is always preferable to major surgery later.

Master parents do this because they know that, like punishment, "discipline is a dimension of love. Love and discipline aren't opposites. Discipline isn't separate from love—it's a part and proof of love. Love expresses itself in discipline. Discipline is one of the voices of love."

"The ultimate result of shielding men from the effects of folly is to fill the world with fools," said Herbert Spencer. The greatest parents—master parents—use the many facets of results to produce outstanding children. They won't let their children be deprived of the powerful, lingering lessons that their Master Parent has designed into the fabric of life. They won't let their children be fools.

THE BLEND

Master parents teach the values and verbally correct their children when the values are violated, but they always remember, "A servant cannot be corrected by mere words; though he understands, he will not respond." Master parents know that their values and the results from the school of hard knocks need to work together and reinforce one another in order to produce a coherent and undeniable lesson. They know that teaching values without results is often simply parenting by annoyance.

We teach through values so that our children can avoid some of the classes in the school of hard knocks. Our children can learn many things without having to experience them firsthand. As master parents, we can help our children change by accepting the softness of values before they're forced to change by the hardness of the results. Don't wait for serious problems before you change.

Master parents often repeat values as they're teaching but are careful not to let the teaching focus only on warnings and reminders. The problem with warnings and reminders is that they turn us into micromanagers (kind of a substitute conscience), and they signal to the children that they have many chances to violate the value before anything happens. The natural outcome is that they *will* violate the value as many times as we're willing to warn and remind. Once the message is clearly understood, master parents let the results do the rest of the talking.

Master parents know that it's time to be quiet and let the results do the talking when they "sow wheat but reap thorns." When they're pouring good stuff in and only bad stuff is coming back out, they know the receptacle is poorly formed and must be reshaped by the results of the thorny behavior. Master parents tell their children, as God tells them, to "break up your unplowed ground" and get a different harvest.

So how do we know when *we're* supposed to do the reminding and when *life* is supposed to do it? We know by *watching*, by *measuring*, and by *listening*.

- **Watching**—We watch and observe our children's reactions to teaching. If they look bored when we're talking, use negative body language, or simply ignore us, we turn them over to results for a while. If they look discouraged by life's school, we enter back into talking and reminding and encouraging. "Logical consequences," said Thomas Henry Huxley, "are the scarecrows of fools and the beacons of wise men."

- **Measuring**—We measure the degree of learning that they are receiving. If they hear us and respond just a little—just enough to get by—we let them experience life. We tell them they need to get ready a little earlier for school so they don't miss the bus, for example, and if they nudge it up just two or three minutes, we let them walk to school in the rain when they miss the bus.

- **Listening**—We listen to hear if they are "getting" what we're saying. You'll know they've "got it" when you hear them talk about it in their own words with you or their siblings or their friends. If there's no sign that they own the value, then you know it's time to let life do the talking. If they complain about the results they're getting but don't seem to be able to connect the dots to their own decisions or actions, it might be time to give them some instruction.

We don't need to worry that they won't get the lessons they need when they are way off base, since "the wages of sin is death." That's the employment agreement our children make when they decide to take the downward path—they agree to be paid, not in dollars but in "death." It's the same agreement we make when we sin. We agree—whether we want to or not—to take payment in death.

We're not necessarily talking here about physical death or death forever in the fires of hell. Although those are the results of the very worst kind of decision making, they're only the final step on a long path. There are many ways to be dead. Losing friends, breaking relationships, destroying other people's respect for you, missing opportunities, suffering from discouragement and depression—all are forms of emotional and spiritual death. When they're dead enough, when the results are bad enough, most children will finally be so desperate that they will be willing to consider listening and changing.

Since master parents have learned that credibility is an important aspect of teaching, they allow their teaching on values to be confirmed by life's teaching through results, and they use those definite results to set the credibility stage for more teaching of values. When real life confirms our teaching and our teaching is related to real life, we know that we have a powerful combination that can have a deep impact on our children.

Master parents know that timing is crucial to learning and that one of the best times to teach values is when children have already received some instruction from results. Children can be all ears after a tough day in the school of hard knocks. Master parents certainly teach values before their children experience results, but they know that the listening/learning factor often goes way up *while* and *after* their children experience those results.

In fact, master parents will often give some teaching of values, then wait for some teaching through results to occur, and then offer some more on the values. Back and forth, looking at the two "schools"—the home school of values and the outside school of hard knocks—as mutually reinforcing teaching units.

Consider this example: You warn your son that his friend is not really a friend at all, since he's constantly putting your son down and making fun of him. But your son doesn't believe you. In fact, he begins to spend even more time with his friend. Instead of saying, "What's the matter with you?" you wait. After a few more life lessons of verbal abuse, you throw in a few Bible verses or personal examples to illustrate your earlier point. He still wants to hang out with his "friend." Instead of saying, "How much abuse are you going to take before you wise up?" you wait.

One day, he comes in angry. He can't believe what his "friend" said to him in front of a group. "I don't want to hang out with him anymore," he says, fuming. "He embarrassed me. Real friends don't say stuff like that." Instead of saying, "I'm glad you finally agree with me," you wait. You acknowledge. You sympathize. Life has taught him. Now it's *his* value too.

Like their Master Parent, master parents know that waiting can take a long time and a lot of patience. For all of us, it often takes a long time before we learn from experience: "Though I taught them again and again, they would not listen or respond to discipline." We can rest assured that our Master Parent has more lessons for us in the school of hard knocks, and we can rest in that same assurance with our own children.

Sometimes our teaching of values is sloppy or mistaken. Clear results can cancel out bad teaching and bad learning. "I never let my schooling interfere with my education," noted novelist Mark Twain. If the values taught are poor or inaccurate, or if the child hears or learns badly, the results will provide the unmistakable correction. And the good news is that the first correction will almost always be a small one.

Master parents know when they've said and taught enough. Some movies require no dialogue to make a point. We need to be willing to let the movie's ending, full of truth and emotion, speak alone. If we add words, we run the risk of deflating the whole experience. Life is, in a sense, a series of movie endings, endings formed as the result of decisions made by the characters. Master parents know which endings need elaboration and which ones need silence.

What master parents really want is for their children to listen to the teaching of values and to *audit* the school of hard knocks. Our Master Parent doesn't require us to learn every lesson the hard way, and master parents don't require this of their children either.

Children can't generally seem to get it all just by listening; some things just have to be learned by experience. But why not learn from other people's experience? "When a mocker is punished, the simple gain wisdom," we are told. "You can observe a lot by just watching," said Hall of Fame baseball catcher Yogi Berra. If our children are "simple"—they haven't lived long enough to understand the value of a value—they can grow in wisdom by watching the bad experiences of others. After that, when they are a little wiser, the second half of the verse can come into play: "When a wise man is instructed, he gets knowledge."

As their Master Parent does with them, master parents always remind their children to remember the lessons of experience, including the things their children have observed: "Only be careful, and watch yourselves closely so that you do not forget the things your eyes have seen or let them slip from your heart as long as you live."

The wisest, sharpest, and shrewdest of God's children are taught through values and are taught through experience—God's values and other people's experience.

LAST THOUGHTS

If we teach our children values but shield them from results, we produce irresponsible, immature, self-righteous hypocrites. If we teach them through results but leave out the values, we produce children who are forever living by trial and error and selecting other wrong answers simply because they might be less painful than the *current* wrong answers.

Master parents teach values, including the value of results, and allow the results to confirm the values. Master parents have a powerful one-two punch, and they use it with wisdom and power.

One young man, after some instruction about the dangers of driving on icy roads, decided to take a short trip on a winter night to meet with friends anyway. The inevitable call came shortly before midnight. "I've had an accident," he said sheepishly. His father said only, "I'll be there in fifteen minutes." He retrieved his son, made arrangements for the car to be towed, and thanked God in his son's presence for the deliverance from harm.

The next day, the young man's friends were amazed to hear that he had been neither lectured nor grounded. "What do you think your dad's up to?" one of them asked. "Nothing," the young man said quietly. "He knew. I thought I knew. And now *I* know what *he* knew."

Master parents know. And they are sure that, with a little teaching through values and a little teaching through results, their children will know too.

Six

MASTER PARENTS
EXERCISE AUTHORITY
AND
SHARE POWER

———— • ————

"The earth is the Lord's, and everything in it"
~ But ~
"The earth he has given to man."

Few issues raise more problems in homes—or the world, for that matter—than the joint issues of authority and power. Get this one right, and parenting will be a lot less like World War III.

Master parents are in charge and exercise divine authority, yet at the same time master parents look the other way while their children make their own decisions and do things their own way.

How does *that* work? We get the "being in charge" part. We're all over that. But why should we have to share power with these immature, inexperienced kids who already have such delusions of grandeur? We should do so because that's what the Master Parent, the ultimate "in charge" person, does with his own immature, inexperienced kids who have those same delusions of grandeur—you and me.

Do you feel like you should be respected because of the authority built into the role of a parent? God knows what you are feeling. You want "divine authority"? He is the *original* Divine Authority. "The heavens are yours, and yours also the earth." The whole kit and caboodle belongs to him, because he "founded the world and all that is in it." We are reminded that "God is the King of all the earth" and that even "the kings of the earth belong to God." God, the Master Parent, has all of the authority that can be had. The truth is, if it *is,* it's *his.*

While it's clear that, as parents, we should model God's authority to our children, we also realize that we should be doing something to develop their sense of responsibility and accountability. It's important to give them some control over their own lives and some input in the decisions that affect them. God has also been there before you. "The highest heavens belong to the Lord," we are told, "but the earth he has given to man."

So which is it? Does the earth belong to the Master Parent, or does it belong to his children? The answer is *yes.* The whole thing belongs to him, and he shares it with us. He doesn't just let us live on it and use its resources; he actually shares ownership. *The earth belongs to us.*

The model is there for master parents. We founded our family, our home, our possessions, the very existence of the whole operation, and these things belong to us. We are in charge and have full authority. We also share the actual ownership of these things with our children. We have to give ownership to our children, because the Master Parent gives it to us. In their "sphere of influence" we give them real power, because *their lives belong to them.*

Just as God cannot stop being God—cannot stop his ownership, his foundational nature, his authority, so we cannot stop being parents. But we can stop our exclusive use of authority and our resistance to power-sharing. If God can share ownership with beings so much less perfect than himself, then we should be able to share ownership with beings just as imperfect as we are.

BEING IN AUTHORITY

If you're going to do anything worthwhile as a master parent, you'd better take charge of your children.

Our Master Parent is absolutely clear on his authority related to his children. "The earth is the Lord's, and everything in it, the world, and all who live in it." We simply and totally belong to the Lord. We can't escape it. "Where can I flee from your presence?" Nowhere. He'll find us, because we belong to him.

The Master Parent transfers this authority to us: "Obey your parents in everything, for this pleases the Lord." I'm sure you would agree that "everything" is pretty comprehensive. There's not much wiggle room there. We can expect our children to listen to and obey us whenever we choose to give direction. We can expect it because that's how the Master Parent set it up, both in our relationship with him and in our children's relationships with us.

When we obey our Master Parent, life goes pretty well. "If you are willing and obedient," he says to us, "you will eat the best from the land." This is good news! But "if you resist and rebel, you will be devoured by the sword." Not such good news. And there is no question: "For the mouth of the Lord has spoken."

Master parents take this same approach with their children. They say, "You determine what you get from me, soft or hard."

Master parents don't exercise their authority based on moods or whims or personality conflicts. If their children are "willing" (they do things with a positive spirit and sometimes even volunteer) and "obedient" (they actually listen and follow directions), master parents deliver the goods. And if their children "resist" (procrastinate, do it sloppily) and "rebel" (give an outright "no"), master parents also deliver the goods—*different* goods.

Master parents have grown up in their understanding of what obedience really means. Obedience doesn't mean "Do this because I'm more powerful than you, even if what I'm asking is dumb." Obedience means, "Do this because I'm sure that it will make you a better, more complete, more mature, more effective, more *power-ful* human being."

Master parents use their authority as representatives of their Master Parent. The command "Obey the Lord by doing what I tell you" implies that what parents tell their children should be what God would say if he were standing there instead. Master parents don't make up their own commands.

Because parents are representatives of God, a child's obedience is not optional. Neither is it random. Obedience is *expected*. This is so important that a person often can't even be a leader in the church if his children don't "obey him with proper respect." Many churches make exceptions here, although God never does.

Master parents are not like the priests who "rule by their own authority." They know that the only real authority they have comes from God and that it's divine authority. This means that they're careful not to make their authority into something it's not. What does this mean for master parents? If God says it, they say it. If God doesn't say it, they don't either. They try to parent just like God. They don't want to fall short, and they aren't presumptuous enough to try to do it better. They don't translate their own out-of-control lives into a desire to control their children. "He who would govern others," says Philip Massinger, "first should be the master of himself."

What about all of the problems we face as parents that the Bible doesn't seem to specifically address? Should my toddler use a pacifier? Should we choose public, private, or home school? Should we require daily Bible readings? Should my children be allowed to date? Is dating even a reasonable approach? *God doesn't say anything about these things,* you might think.

While he does leave a lot unsaid, God *does* say something about these things. Will we find a verse on pacifiers in the Bible, or on types of school, or on routine devotions, or on dating? No. But we will find all sorts of principles in the Bible that have a bearing on these points. For example, it's a good thing to bring peace into heart and home (use a pacifier), but it's not a good thing to substitute a tool for learning self-control (don't use a pacifier to stop a tantrum). We're free to select the form of schooling (the choice is open), but we're not free to expose our children to vulgar, arrogant, or incompetent training. We're told to teach our children spiritual disciplines (have a regular Bible reading) but not to make an unbreakable regulation about it (skip it sometimes or lose it for a while). We're told to protect our children from harm (restrict or redefine dating), and we should show them how to have healthy relationships (create safe but free environments where friendships can flourish).

If we're honest, we'll admit that we want the Bible to spell it all out for us. It does, but maybe not the way we'd like it to. It doesn't always tell us, "Do this exactly this way, don't do this specific thing." Rather, it gives us principles, often paradox principles that force us to think and bring to bear on our parenting two apparently contradictory principles.

Master parents take great care to make sure that their "commands are not burdensome." This means that we don't tell our children to do things that are beyond their ability to do (or to do well). We don't tell them to do too many things at one time. And we don't give them orders that are petty ("get down there and pick up every crumb") or repugnant ("I'm telling you this is great music, so sit down and listen").

Master parents know that they don't own their children. Paul said, "I am free and belong to no man." Authority is not a question of ownership, or even stewardship; it is, at its core, a question of *relationship*. Someone needs to steer the ship.

Master parents also avoid exasperating their children. The great command to children to "obey your parents in the Lord, for this is right" is followed closely by another great command: "Don't make your children angry by the way you treat them. Rather, bring them up with the discipline and instruction approved by the

Lord." Why make obedience hard or distasteful because of the *way* we demand it?

Master parents don't define "divine authority" like the monarchs did in the middle ages. Those people claimed the "divine right of kings," meaning they could do whatever they wanted to do and claim that God was behind them. Master parents reject autocracy and dictatorship. They don't claim an all-encompassing "divine right of parents." They know they have no right—no authority—to go beyond, or to be different from, God.

I have heard pastors complain about "rebels" in their churches who don't "obey" them and who have a "problem with authority." The truth is that these "rebels" often have a problem with how leaders are *exercising* their authority, not with the authority itself. God has never authorized any leaders to rule by their own authority. I have heard parents make this same bogus complaint about "rebellious" children. Everyone who struggles with authority is not a rebel, and everyone who disobeys is not a sinner. The badge of authority comes with no blank checks, and disobedience can be a wise and courageous act.

Master parents know and believe the truth that "no one can serve two masters. Either he will hate the one and love the other, or he will be devoted to the one and despise the other." Parental authority becomes a disaster when two parents or authority figures don't speak as one. What does this look like in practice?

The parent whom children seemingly "love" and are "devoted to" is usually the one who lets them do what they want more frequently, even if it isn't in their best interest. Often, the parent who tries to hold up some semblance of order or decency is in for a good measure of being "hated" or "despised." This is hard on the parenting and hard on the marriage.

It is very unhealthy for parents or authority figures to disagree in front of the children about decisions or directions that affect the children. These holes in authority can be big enough for crafty children to drive a truck through (even if they're not old enough to drive).

It is not, however, unhealthy for parents or authority figures to disagree in front of the children about, say, political opinions and perspectives, as long as they are agreed on basic values. This lets the children see that there can be both unity and diversity in a power relationship.

I recently read an article in which the author wrote about his relationship with his wife: "We try to remember that ultimately we both want the same thing." The problem is, sometimes two people (parents) *don't* ultimately want the same thing. One wants responsibility, the other wants fun; one wants open communication, the other wants no disagreements or confrontations. Sometimes we can't get past the differences. The important point is not to pretend they don't exist, nor to exhaust ourselves in an effort to find common ground, but rather to make sure that the lack of common ground doesn't create a "two-master" home. Parents must be united in the task of raising their children.

What do master parents do with their God-given authority?

MASTER PARENTS USE THEIR AUTHORITY TO BUILD BETTER CITIZENS

Our Master Parent says to us, "As obedient children, do not conform to the evil desires you had when you lived in ignorance." Master parents do the same, reminding their children that obedience is designed to keep them from conforming to the evil desires that *always* grow out of ignorance. Ignorance is a human specialty that's destined to produce evil desires, and obedience is the cure.

Master parents use their authority to make sure they're moving their children *away* from evil desires, rather than *toward* those desires by being nitpicky about unimportant details and thus breeding inevitable rebellion. For example, dialoguing about movies and agreeing about the movies that are strictly off-limits is a good use of authority to develop children with unperverted minds. Wide freedom with clearly defined restrictions or fences will connect well with most children. But making movies the enemy, waxing on about the corruption of Hollywood, and critiquing every minor thing with which we disagree in every movie that comes along is not only oppressive, it's also a surefire way to cause our kids to toss out all of our teaching on movies and to want to see them all.

Master parents know that authority used well can lead children to holiness, and authority used badly can lead them to sin. Master parents want to be effective in their use of authority. They give directives that eliminate ignorance ("Read this article about the effects of using drugs and we can talk about it later") and increase enlightenment ("Let's sign up for a conference on creationism, evolutionism, and intelligent-design theory").

MASTER PARENTS USE THEIR AUTHORITY TO ENCOURAGE AND REBUKE

"Encourage and rebuke with all authority," Paul encouraged his "true son in our common faith," Titus.

We discussed the "rebuke" part of this command in chapter 5. Here we see that we're to do it "with all authority." What does this mean? We have all the authority of heaven—all the authority we need. We don't need to feel sheepish, guilty, or ashamed about rebuking our children. In fact, if we don't do it when necessary, we're disobeying our own Master Parent.

How can we *encourage* with all authority? We encourage with all authority when we put our full weight behind the encouragement. We should be just as intense about encouraging as we are about rebuking. We draw on everything in the Bible, in our knowledge, and in our experience to come up with a specific, detailed, and powerful encouragement. We, like Paul, use our authority for building our children up. Master parents are relentless, unapologetic, and convincing encouragers.

Master parents use their authority to strongly encourage their children to do the right things and to strongly rebuke them when they don't.

MASTER PARENTS USE THEIR AUTHORITY TO PAVE THE WAY FOR WORSHIP

"To obey is better than sacrifice," we're told by the Master Parent. It does us no good to write a big check out to our church if we're telling God to buzz off.

Master parents don't let their children "make up" for disobedience in one area by doing something in another. Volunteering to vacuum doesn't make up for disobedience in another area. Disobedience must be erased with repentance, not sacrifice. The order is this: obedience first, sacrifice and worship second.

MASTER PARENTS USE THEIR AUTHORITY TO GAIN PROOF OF LOVE

The Master Parent makes obedience to his authority a proof of love: "If anyone loves me, he will obey my teaching. . . . He who does not love me will not obey my teaching."

Hard as it is to do, master parents do the same. They make obedience to their authority a proof of love. They've learned that talk is cheap; children can't disobey and then try to convince their parents that they love them. Master parents say with John, "Dear children, let us not love with words or tongue but with actions and in truth." To paraphrase, they say, "Don't butter me up with your lovey-dovey words; prove it by how you behave this weekend."

Master parents know there are some things that can't be delegated. We read earlier that "the highest heavens belong to the Lord." The Master Parent has given us the earth, but he hasn't given us the heavens. There are some things that parents must be responsible for and decide. This is part of being a parent, just like ownership of the highest heavens is part of being God. Some of these critical "highest heavens" areas for master parents include:

- **Their own spiritual lives.** As master parents, we don't allow our children to direct our relationship with God. If they don't like praying before meals, that's *their* problem, not ours. If they don't want to read the Christmas story before they open the Christmas presents, tough rocks.

- **Intimate relationship details.** Our Master Parent is actually a Trinity, a community of divine persons. Their relationship has characteristics and dimensions that we will never get to look into, now or later. Master parents don't generally expose the details of their relationships to their children (to find support or get advice, for example).

- **Career decisions.** We're not in a position to tell our Master Parent what to think about or what to do, and master parents don't put their own children in that position with themselves. We didn't have these children so they could tell us what to be when we grow up! They might say, "I hope you keep working where you work; all my friends think you're cool for working there." That's all well and good. But we can't let their stray comments and immature reasoning direct our paths. Our children are not the Holy Spirit, nor are they career counselors. They probably don't even know what *they* want to be when they grow up. You can listen to their input, especially as they become adults, but the call is yours.

- **Major financial or investment decisions.** While it's a good thing to involve our children in the financial life of the family and to give them some preparatory training, master parents realize that their children don't have the perspective to make major decisions, and they don't need the pressure of thinking about them. They simply need to know that provision is there. The Master Parent wants us to be free of too much thinking or concern here as well: "So do not worry. . . . For the pagans run after all these things, and your heavenly Father knows that you need them. . . . All these things will be given to you."

Many of us, when we decided to become parents, pictured decorating the nursery, playing with babies, and taking walks with the stroller. We knew that we would always laugh, always connect, and always like each other.

And at first, it seemed to work that way. We put them somewhere and when we came back, they were still there. They smiled when they saw us coming. They were happy just to play with our fingers.

They didn't throw temper tantrums in the middle of the grocery store because we wouldn't buy them a box of the new sugar-coated cereal. They didn't have one-word answers to every question when they came home from school. They didn't argue with us every time we asked them to do something, no matter how small. And they didn't give us "the look," the scowl that says, "I wish you would go away" (or "How did someone as dumb as you live as long as you have?").

Most of us probably didn't plan on this change. We didn't want these power struggles. But that's part of parenting. Master parents accept this, and purpose to do it well.

Master parents take Jesus' directive seriously that they teach their children "to obey everything I have commanded you." They take charge and are comfortable with their role as authority figures.

Being in authority can be a glorious thing, and it can be a positive thing, and it can be a tough thing, and it can be a terrible thing. But whichever it is, master parents take the lead.

SHARING POWER

If you're going to do anything worthwhile as a master parent, you'd better let your children take charge of as much as possible, as *soon* as possible.

You've probably heard it said, in one form or another, that good parents can't abdicate responsibility, but master parents reject this myth. In fact, master parents have learned the critical lesson that they *must* abdicate responsibility. They can't be in charge of everything, and they *shouldn't* be in charge of everything.

It's not their job to be omnipresent, omniscient, or omnipotent. That job is already taken by the Master Parent. And the startling truth is that *he* has already abdicated responsibility, giving it up so that we can share in running his kingdom.

He has shared fantastic power with us. "You are awesome, O God, in your sanctuary; the God of Israel gives power and strength to his people." He is awesome, having all authority and power and strength. And at the same time, he shares his power, giving it to his children. "He gives strength to the weary and increases the power of the weak."

He's given us even more. "I have given you authority to trample on snakes and scorpions and to overcome all the power of the enemy; nothing will harm you." We've been given such awesome authority, such magnificent power, that we can overcome all the power of the enemy and not be harmed in the process! "[He] gave them authority to cast out evil spirits," we are told. In fact, "he gave them power and authority to drive out all demons and to cure diseases."

"Ask whatever you wish," he tells us, "and it will be given you." If we're wise enough to ask for a wise and discerning heart, he is gracious and grants us other things that we haven't even requested, as he did with Solomon. If we just reach out to touch him, the power flows to us, as when a woman who had been bleeding for twelve years merely touched his cloak, "at once Jesus realized that power had gone out from him."

SO WHAT DOES "SHARING POWER" MEAN?

Consider the following verse and try to fill in the blank: "Jesus knew that the Father had put all things under his power, and that he had come from God and was returning to God, so he
_____."

At this point in time, Jesus was at the pinnacle of power. All things are under his power. *All* things.

What would most people do if all things were put under their power? Start giving orders? Whip the laggards into shape? Take charge of the government? Jesus didn't do any of those things. Not even close. What did he actually do? He "got up from the meal, took off his outer clothing, and wrapped a towel around his waist. After that, he poured water into a basin and began to wash his disciples' feet."

Jesus, at the pinnacle of all authority and power, at the very moment of coronation, washes dirty feet.

It's easy to begin thinking as a parent, *It's about time somebody else did some feet-washing around here!* Gulp. It always starts with us. Master parents know the truth, the upside-down biblical truth that authority is all about service, that being in charge means being a servant. They know that sharing power requires us to forego our own foot massage so we can wash those dirty feet.

Our Master Parent has all authority and power, which is why he can share it with us. And he does. Master parents know that their job is to model him and to take the authority that they have and share it with their children. And they do.

Our Master Parent is not into "big shot" authority, and master parents aren't either. "You know," instructed Jesus, "that the rulers of the Gentiles lord it over them, and their high officials exercise authority over them. Not so with you." Is it possible that Jesus was excluding parents from this? that there is a "parental exception," because kids are so little or immature or childish? Not likely. Compared to Jesus, you and I are *really* little and immature and dumb, and yet he practices this feet-washing, upside-down, servant brand of authority with us.

The biggest "big shot" authority was the devil, tempting Jesus by showing him "all the kingdoms of the world. And he said to him, 'I will give you all their authority and splendor, for it has been given to me, and I can give it to anyone I want to.'" Jesus didn't think much of the devil's power play. Big-shot parents don't stand a chance.

Great leaders have always known that authority isn't automatically good or right simply because it has power. This is where the great "authority" teaching of Romans 13 has been contorted. "Obey the government, for God is the one who put it there" seems to say that "might makes right." Many have taught us that we are to obey authority, regardless of what it says, simply because it has the position and the power.

But this is leaving out the rest of the teaching: "The authorities do not frighten people who are doing right, but they frighten those who do wrong. So do what they say, and you will get along well. The authorities are sent by God to help you." But what if the authorities frighten people who are doing right and *don't* frighten those who do wrong? What if you do what they say and you *don't* get along well? What if you need help and they *don't* help you? In other words, what if the so-called authorities don't do what Romans 13 says God-ordained authorities do or should do? Well, at some point we have to say that this authority is not from God, because it doesn't meet the definition. Hitler had position and power but no legitimate authority, and those who disobeyed him did well by rejecting his authoritarian absurdities. It's too bad more churches didn't disrespect his authority and disrespect his power.

We have to make sure that *our* authority meets the biblical definition. What if we're frightening children who are trying to do well? What if we're not frightening the mischief makers? What if our directions cause our children harm? What if we use them to serve us, rather than the other way around? At some point, parents can be so rotten that they lose their legal authority over their children. At an earlier point, many parents have already lost their *moral* authority over their children.

How do we lose moral authority? By being hypocrites, for example, and telling them not to lie, then lying to a friend to get out of a commitment. We can lose moral authority when we pound their souls into the ground through insults and degrading verbal abuse. We lose it when we approve activities and then change our minds at the last minute, or forbid things and then allow them to be done. We lose it when we treat our children like serfs or slaves, or even like employees. In the final analysis, real authority never comes from a position or title; it comes from character—a character that is set on enhancing the life of the follower.

Paul understood this when he said that God had given him authority that he did not intend to use harshly. Why not? Because the Lord gave him the authority "for building you up, not for tearing you down." Destructive authority is no authority at all.

So let's say that we're exercising parental authority in line with God's exercise of authority with us, in line with the full definition of Romans 13. We've got legitimate authority. Why should we share this with our children? Don't children need a strong hand? Don't we need to control our children? For all sorts of reasons, some reasonable and some dysfunctional, most of us cringe at the thought of sharing power.

Part of the problem with our resistance to power-sharing is in our definition of authority. Consider these incomplete or incorrect definitions:

- **Control.** In my experience, a huge percentage of parents think it's their responsibility to control their children. The first problem with this is that control is an illusion. Who among us could really, fully control just one teenager for a week? To ask the question is to know the answer. The second problem is that any attempt to control children pushes them to break free, which in practice may mean swinging to the other extreme. Third, attempts to control children damage your relationship and distort all of your communication. Master parents don't waste their time on an approach that their Master Parent never uses with them.

- **Management.** I've heard people talk about "managing" their households. As with control, management is an illusion. It's wonderful when applied to organizing kitchens and files or planning a project, but it's a terrible thing when applied to human beings. Peter Drucker, known as the "Father of Management," has even said he is not comfortable with the word *manager* anymore because it implies "subordinates" and control. Master parents know that children will be led but not managed. To paraphrase leadership expert Warren Bennis, most homes are overmanaged and under-led.

- **Empowerment.** This approach is a bit better than control or management, but its basic premise, in the home as well as in business, is wrong. It says, "I'm the king or queen and you're not; but I'm such a nice monarch I'll share a little of my power with you." Too often, this means that more responsibility and accountability are given, but not equivalent authority or power. The reins are kept in the hands of the monarch. This is a trickle-down approach, not a true sharing of power.

Why should we share power with our children? The main reason is that this is what our Master Parent does with us. But many other reasons flow from this principle:

1. There's no better way to train them in how to exercise authority than by actually allowing them to exercise authority.
2. The home is a safe laboratory where children can learn how to use power without blowing the world up.
3. Learning to exercise power under self-control is a great way to

develop effective power. We have to show them that the greater their self-control, the more power we can share with them and the more effective they can be. Chaining them with rules might look like self-control, but *our* control works against *self*-control and will actually disempower them. Self-control is a prerequisite to power-sharing and controls how much and how fast the power-sharing can be increased. If they see that self-control is the pathway to power, we've given them a fabulous incentive to manage themselves.

4. They can learn to use power rather than having power use them. "Power tends to corrupt," said Lord Acton, "and absolute power corrupts absolutely." But it's not the power itself that corrupts, it's the way the power is used. To say it another way, power doesn't corrupt the person as much as the person corrupts the power. Most positions aren't bad in and of themselves, but we can make them bad by *being* bad and abusing power. We can teach our children what is good, and what is corrupt, about power.

As master parents share power with their children, the first thing they do is define "sharing power" correctly. Power-sharing is more about responsibility and accountability than it is about privilege. This is where many parents go wrong. They think they are sharing power when they remove needed restraints, give their children lots of spending money, and indulge their desires. But what's the fruit of this approach? Self-centeredness, a focus on privilege, and a growing sense of entitlement.

Privilege can be a good thing, but only as a reward for being responsible and accountable. Power-sharing begins with responsibility and accountability and ends with privilege. The extent of the privilege equals the extent of the responsibility and accountability.

This is the way our Master Parent is with us. "Everyone who has will be given more, and he will have an abundance. Whoever does not have, even what he has will be taken from him." The context of this dramatic statement is the parable of the servants who were assigned responsibility for the master's property and were then required to give an accounting of how they handled this full-fledged power-sharing.

The servants who did well—those who didn't look at their power as a privilege to be exploited but rather as a responsibility that would end in accountability—were not only praised but were given greater responsibility "for many things." The servant who irresponsibly sat down on the job was called wicked and lazy and had all of his responsibility—all of his power—taken away and given to the most responsible servant.

Master parents model this behavior. They trust ten "talents" (units of money) to one child, five to another, and one to another. They parcel out the responsibility unequally, based on the child's readiness for power-sharing. When a child does well (allowing, of course, for honest mistakes), we praise him and trust him with more power. If he's struggling and wants to do well, we help him and train him and coach him.

You agree, for example, on some general principles of dress: You expect your child to dress modestly and appropriately for the situation. Your eleven-year-old gets it. You tell her you appreciate her and give her even more freedom to buy her own clothes and to decide what to wear. Your thirteen-year-old, on the other hand, doesn't quite get it. She isn't being deliberately over the edge, and her attitude isn't really bad, but she simply makes poor choices: short skirts to youth group, shorts to a fancy restaurant, beat-up jeans to the family reunion. You stick a little closer to her. You guide her selections and exercise a veto where appropriate. And you let her know that you'll back off as soon as she can see for herself how to stay inside the wide fences you've set up.

When children don't do well because of an attitude problem, we remove the power and reduce the responsibility because power-sharing is all about accountability. We want to see them doing something useful with the power we've entrusted to them. If they don't, we say to them what our Master Parent says to us: that what we have "will be taken away from [us] and given to a people who will produce its fruit."

Master parents know that power-sharing means giving room to their children to learn how to share power with each other. Our Master Parent doesn't intervene in every problematic interaction that we have with our peers, and master parents follow his example with their own children.

Sibling rivalry is often really a quest for authority and power among our children. "Sibling rivalry enables children to work out differences and explore emotions in a safe place. This helps them deal effectively with friends and classmates . . . and later, with other adults." But they don't learn the lesson if we jump in and take charge of every unpleasant situation. Children in this case don't learn how to share power; instead, they learn how to manipulate us.

The same is true with peer relationships. For example, if you see someone taking advantage of your son, the most normal thing in the world is to jump in, criticize the friend, and perhaps limit or eliminate further involvement. Unfortunately, you've just created a "parent vs. friend" scenario, forced your son to defend the peer, and eliminated a wonderful opportunity for him to learn how to get himself into an effective relationship—and out of an ineffective one.

In all cases of dealing with others, whether siblings or peers, master parents use their authority to structure or alter situations so their children can learn how to share power safely. That might mean that your daughter can only meet with a certain "tough" friend at your home, where the friend will be on better behavior and you can make sure nothing gets out of hand. Or it might mean that your son can baby-sit his siblings for the first time for a limited amount of time and with activities agreed upon in advance.

Every power-sharing situation involves the transferring of authority. There are simple guidelines for how much:

- The amount of authority is equal to the responsibility and accountability that we give. It isn't fair, for example, to tell the son who is baby-sitting that he can't correct his siblings. I've seen parents put their children in charge of their siblings, only to scold them if they exercise any authority. Not fair.

- The amount of authority is only what is needed to take care of the responsibility. The baby-sitting son needs to know the restrictions, or you might find his siblings cleaning up his room.

- The amount of authority is not more than they know how to use. This can be based on their maturity level or the previous handling of authority. We don't let the son baby-sit if he is too young or immature, and we might have to be more restrictive in the future if he misuses his authority.

The amount of authority is also based on how the child shares power with others. We use the child's power-sharing with others as a benchmark for how much power-sharing we can do with him. Our motto is one the Master Parent uses with us: "With the measure you use, it will be measured to you—and even more."

If your son never gives his sister a say in what they will play, he should expect less opportunity to help you decide what to eat or where to go. If he defers to his sister often, he can expect you to defer to him often. Master parents don't focus on how little or immature their children are. They focus on how big and mature they want their children to be. They realize the truth of the great tension described by General Lewis B. Hershey: "A boy becomes an adult three years before his parents think he does, and about two years after he thinks he does." Our children probably aren't ready for as much power as they think they are, but they're probably ready for a lot more than most of us feel ready to share.

How extensive is our Master Parent's power-sharing with us? "You put us in charge of everything you made, giving us authority over all things—the sheep and the cattle and all the wild animals, the birds in the sky, the fish in the sea, and everything that swims the ocean currents." (Now you know who should be given authority over all the pets!) The psalmist considers this grand sharing of power and then adds, "O Lord, our Lord, the majesty of your name fills the earth!"

So the question is, how much have you put your kids in charge of? Is it everything you own: home, car, money, vacation plans? How much have you given them authority over? Do they have a say in all things? Will they ever?

Like God with us, master parents don't ask, "How much power should I share with her?" The question they ask is, "How can I share it all with her?"

THE BLEND

Master parents recognize that power is a tool rather than a goal. It's not "I'm the parent, so I make the decision," or even "I'm the parent, but I'll let you decide this one," but rather "I'm the parent, so you get to decide."

Master parents use their power, but they use it to liberate their children rather than to dominate them. They're like their Master Parent, whose "divine power has given us everything we need for life and godliness." Are we using our power to give them what they need for "life and godliness," or to give them what *we* need?

One of the most amazing facts in a creation full of amazing facts is this: The main purpose of authority is not to limit, restrict, or kill freedom but to *give life* and *protect freedom.* "For [God] granted [Jesus] authority over all people that he might give eternal life to all those [God has] given him." The purpose? "It is for freedom that Christ has set us free." Master parents use their divinely delegated authority not to shackle their children but to break the shackles. "God seeks comrades and claims love," said Rabindranath Tagore. "The Devil seeks slaves and claims obedience."

"Those who exercise authority over them call themselves

Benefactors," Jesus taught, not without sarcasm. "But you are not to be like that. Instead, the greatest among you should be like the youngest, and the one who rules like the one who serves." Master parents don't push their kids around and say, "I'm only doing it for you" (the Benefactor approach). Instead they ask, "How can I be like the youngest?" Well, the youngest is needy and struggling and a long way from being glued together; we are all like that. "I will serve you," says the master parent, "because I am like you."

I've heard some parents say, with certainty and often with humor, "This isn't a democracy around here!" But the question is, "Why not?" What's wrong with democracy? Democracy doesn't mean that there isn't any authority or respect for authority. Democracy is all about the balance between authority and power-sharing. It means that those who are governed are given some say in how the thing is run.

This is just like the Master Parent does with us. He is on the throne, fully in charge, with unquestionable authority and unlimited power. And yet he consults with us, gets our input, lets us "vote" with our actions and inactions. He asks for, and makes room for, the great democratic principle of the "consent of the governed." King David, for example, asked the people if he should bring back the ark of God, and "the whole assembly agreed to do this, because it seemed right to all the people."

The irony is that parents end up granting this "consent" in any case, because reality intervenes. We can take the approach of "my way or the highway," but the fact is our children can choose the highway. They can choose it in the short run by ignoring our commands and sloughing off on their responsibilities, and they can choose it in the long run by actually leaving on the highway. Kids get to vote, first with their hearts and then with their feet.

We are still in charge when we share power. We are deciding not to act so our children will have room to act. Master parents use their authority to create room for their children to exercise their own authority, step up and make some real decisions, and share power with others.

Power-sharing involves trust. We have to trust our children with power, always slightly ahead of their real readiness to handle it well. But our trusting comes at a price, as the Master Parent's trusting of us has a price: "Now it is required that those who have been given a trust must prove faithful." It's our mission to trust and our children's mission to prove faithful. Some trust must be granted, while the balance must be earned.

We want to share power with our children so they will learn early how to be in authority and do it well. The wise use and sharing of power on their part is critical to themselves, the people they serve, and the kingdom of God, since "the kingdom of God is not a matter of talk but of power."

Power-sharing means using authority to structure situations where sharing power is a viable option. Some of those grand applications are:

1. **Making agreements in advance.** Master parents don't expect their children to do something that hasn't been agreed to in advance. They don't wait until after the activity to push or "nag" for responsibility. They say instead, "If you'll agree to put your clothes in the hamper and wash yourself when you come in, you can go play in the mud. Agree?" Or, "You can take the car if you run it through the car wash. Agree?" And they let their children know that a violation of the agreement won't bring a lecture. It will bring the loss of a next time in the mud or the car.

2. **Agreeing on consequences.** Master parents make it clear in advance when certain actions will get certain consequences. The agreement here is on *understanding* the consequences. "If you get anyone home late after the game and upset their parents, then you will have to apologize to them in person and miss the next game. Do we understand each other?"

3. **Expanding options.** Master parents start when their children are young to offer as many options as are appropriate. "The zippered or the buttoned coat?" "Green beans or carrots?" Then they expand the options, both in number and complexity, as the children show an ability to handle the maddening array of life's offerings. "You can go out in a foursome to dinner and the movies and be back here by midnight, or you can have two friends here and keep it going until 1:30, or you can go to your friend's house if an adult is there, or you can suggest some other plan." Life isn't simple. Sharing power early is good preparation.

Master parents use their authority to back up the authority of their children. If you've allowed your children to set up and run their own party, you don't pull the plug because the music is too loud. If you've given your daughter the car for the week without restrictions, you can't get upset with her if she uses it to haul around her sloppy friends. If our children use their authority poorly, we can correct and guide them later. But in the midst of the action, our role is to back it up.

Master parents share the most power with those who have the most respect for their authority—the ones who understand it. They should be able to use power properly.

Master parents don't share power with those who demand it. They don't yield their authority to those who despise it, because they know that in this case, they're dealing with "those who follow the corrupt desire of the sinful nature and despise authority."

We know that there is a difference between sharing power and spoiling. Sharing power means inviting our children to walk in the corridors of responsibility before we invite them to tour the corridors of power. They have to do their part or we cut back on the power-sharing—just like the Master Parent does with us: "From everyone who has been given much, much will be demanded; and from the one who has been entrusted with much, much more will be asked."

Spoiling is a totally different parental activity. Master parents know that spoiling produces eternal (and infernal) adolescents, while power-sharing produces giants.

Only when we're secure in our own authority are we really free to share power in an intelligent and constructive way with our children. Insecure parents swing to one of two extremes. Some become control freaks because any power-sharing seems like a threat to their shaky thrones. They are destined to be like King Nothing, who "points his finger, but no one's around." Others become anarchy freaks. They are uncomfortable in their authority, so there seems to be no alternative or balance to sharing power. The result is kids who run wild.

We need to be secure, because what we're really trying to create is—are you ready for this?—a positive, guided rebellion.

It's positive because the whole goal of this authority/power-sharing business is to create effective adults. It's guided because we're in charge and we're not going to abdicate. And it's rebellion because we want them to discard everything that doesn't fit with who they are or who God has designed them to become, including all bogus authority.

This is all part of obeying our Master Parent, who tells us to "submit to one another out of reverence for Christ." Master parents know that this applies to them as well as their children. They expect their children to respect authority, to yield on decisions and directions, and to find ways to utilize parental power for their own good. And they expect their children to develop their own authority, to determine their own decisions and directions, and to enhance their own power for their own good. Master parents know that there will be no conflict if they and their children are willing to "submit to one another."

At the end of the day, what master parents really do is use their authority to make their power-sharing effective. They allow their children to make decisions, to change directions, to impact people and situations, to question their parents' ideas and decisions. Master parents make it safe for their children to speak truth and ask questions—first, because the parents have the power, and second, because they are willing to share it.

In an irony of power, master parents *order* their children to share the power with them. We order them to be partners and joint owners. We order them to take charge of their own lives, to keep themselves under control, to exercise their own authority, to make a difference for the kingdom of God.

"Do it," we say. "This is your life. Do something good with it. Don't get outside of the boundaries we've agreed to, but instead, be an original person inside those boundaries. Shake things up. Let the heavens and the earth know that you were here. You have the power. Use it. And we'll back it up with ours."

"The spirit of liberty," wrote Judge Learned Hand, "is the spirit of Him who, near two thousand years ago, taught mankind that lesson it has never learned, but never quite forgotten: that there is a kingdom where the least shall be heard and considered side by side with the greatest." Master parents may be bigger, more educated, and more experienced, but they *have* learned the lesson. Without relinquishing their position, they hear their children as equals and walk with them side by side.

"Give him some of your authority," the Lord commanded Moses about Joshua. As a parent, you have that same authority and power. And as a master parent, you know what to do with it.

LAST THOUGHTS

If we exercise authority without sharing power, we create children who rebel against us and mindlessly follow their peers. If we share power without exercising authority, we arm children to do what they cannot or should not do.

"I don't like the wallpaper you picked for my room," a young girl said unhappily. Her mother looked at her face, the beautiful brown eyes glistening in the midst of a current surge of acne.

"I don't either," the mother said, turning back toward the sink.

"You don't?"

"No."

"Then why did you pick it?" the daughter asked.

"Because I thought it was beautiful and a perfect match for everything else in your room."

The daughter stopped eating her cheese cracker in midbite. "Then why don't you like it?" she asked, confused.

"Because you don't, and it's your room," her mother said, turning to face her. "I'm sorry I picked it up without talking to you. We'll return it later, and the choice is all yours, as long as you pick something within our price range and our ability to put it up."

"Oh," the daughter said thoughtfully as she finished eating her cracker. "Oh," she said again as she finished chewing. "Cool."

Master parents know that if they want to be the best parents possible, perhaps among the greatest parents ever, they have to use their power to serve their children and use their authority to increase their children's power. "Whoever wants to become great among you must be your servant," said Jesus, "and whoever wants to be first must be your slave—just as the Son of Man."

Parent as authoritative servant. Not a bad plan at all.

Seven

MASTER PARENTS
INSIST ON "THE WAY"
AND
INSIST ON FREEDOM

———— • ————

"I will show you the most excellent way"
~ But ~
"Where the Spirit of the Lord is, there is freedom."

We want our children to follow "the Way," to be on the right path, with all of our hearts. But we can't force them to do it, because that doesn't work and it isn't right.

Master parents show their children the Way, and master parents let their children find the Way themselves.

You want your kids to be on the right path? The Master Parent is tracking with you on that. That's his very plan for us. "I am the Lord your God, who teaches you what is best for you, who directs you in the way you should go." If we want to know "the Way"—the way to him, the way to live—he's right there, telling us all we ever could need or want to know. Even if we show the slightest interest, he's there.

In fact, even if we *don't* express a need or desire to know, even if we don't express the slightest interest, he is *still* there, telling us to know and be sure that there is only one Way.

And in an incredible exercise in self-restraint, the all-powerful Master Parent is totally committed to our freedom. He allows us to decide what we will do with the Way that he has been pressing us to accept. He insists on the Way, but he doesn't try to manipulate or force us into following it. If we want other "ways," he steps aside and lets us have them. He's even made us creative, so we can make hundreds of "ways" up in our heads if we want to.

Our Master Parent is, in fact, quite pushy about our freedom. So much so that we're told our freedom is the reason he came to save us: "It is for freedom that Christ has set us free." He didn't set us free so we would be mindless followers of the Way. He set us free for *freedom*, so that we could really choose to live as free people, free of the chains of sin and despair, free of the yokes of other people.

Many people talk about their "calling," but the calling of the Master Parent for all of us is freedom: "For you have been called to live in freedom," we are told. What great news! We haven't been called to live in religious chains, or dogmatic narrow-mindedness, or subservience to human rules and traditions. We've been called to live in *freedom*.

God's message to us is clear. There is only one Way—and let freedom ring.

INSISTING ON THE WAY

If you're going to do anything worthwhile as a master parent, you'd better insist that your children follow the Way.

"And now I will show you the most excellent way," Paul opens his magical thirteenth chapter of 1 Corinthians.

WHAT IS THE WAY?

The Way is first and foremost about the way to life. The Master Parent tells us to take the time to get it right. "Stand at the crossroads and look; ask for the ancient paths, ask where the good way is, and walk in it, and you will find rest for your souls."

Master parents give the same direction to their children: "Take time to see what life is all about. Ask me some good, probing questions. Ask me where the Way is, and I'll tell you. If you choose to see it and walk in it, the deepest sort of peace will be yours. I hope you do. I'm going to be pretty bold in telling you about it."

The way to life means, in part, the way to *eternal* life. Although the way to life culminates in eternal life, it's also a way of enjoying the journey and enjoying the life we've found here. Eternal life is about *quality* of life as much as it is about *length* of life. To say it another way, there are many who have found the destination—eternal life—without appreciating or enjoying the journey, or squeezing all of the power, meaning, pleasure, and satisfaction out of it.

So what is this "way to life"? The Bible is very clear about what this way is, or rather, *who* this way is. "Thomas said to him, 'Lord, we don't know where you are going, so how can we know the way?' Jesus answered, 'I am the way. . . . No one comes to the Father except through me.'"

This verse may sound uncompromising or "unfair" to people who don't want to believe it, but it's reality. Jesus doesn't claim to be *a* way but *the* Way. There may be some nice people who don't think Jesus is the Way. But he really is, and those nice people are on the road to nowhere.

There aren't a thousand ways, or a hundred, or even ten. There are only two: God's way, and all the others. All the others are just different variations on one bad plan. "This day I call heaven and earth as witnesses against you that I have set before you life and death, blessings and curses. Now choose life." "Anyone who chooses to be a friend of the world," wrote James, "becomes an enemy of God." God's way is the only game in town. "Salvation is found in no one else," said Peter, "for there is no other name under heaven given to men by which we must be saved." People may not like it, but God set up the rules. If we don't like it, we'll have to start our own universe.

Master parents teach their children the way to life. Master parents insist on Christianity as the way because it *is* the Way. They love their children too much to let them live in ignorance of the way to life.

They refuse to be trapped by the thinking of so many parents who take a hands-off approach to their children's futures in order to "let them figure it out for themselves." Master parents know that if there is a way to life (and there is), then it isn't something to mess around with. They say to their children, "You can take it or leave it, but I'm at least going to make sure you know about it."

At the same time, they refuse to let their family get caught up with, or stay caught up with, narrow religious viewpoints or petty religious rule making. They focus on the Way with a capital *W*. They teach their children that Christianity is a very big tent, with room for lots of diversity of thought and practice. They teach that the way is spacious: "And a highway will be there; it will be called the Way of Holiness."

Too many people in this life confuse the Way with their own ways—or to say it differently, they declare their own "way" to be *the* Way. They baptize their own little view of truth and rename it "the Way." We want our children to find and live the Way. Although we want them to listen respectfully to any respectable person or viewpoint, we don't want them to find and live every "way" that any person might cook up. They can listen without accepting all of those "ways."

Master parents explain that one of the great attractions of the Way is that it's the way of freedom. It's not the Way *or* freedom; it's the Way *and* freedom.

Master parents don't put up with any arrogance about the Way. They remind their children that the only difference between those on the Way and those not on the Way is a simple choice, a choice between life and death. We shouldn't look down on anyone because he or she hasn't yet made the choice, hasn't yet found the Way. If you and I made the choice for life, anyone can. And lost people will always act . . . lost.

But master parents insist on the way to life. They say to their children what the Master Parent says to them: "See, I am setting before you the way of life and the way of death." They press their children to choose life, not because they are dogmatic, but because they know there is a way to life and they want their children on it.

The Way is also about the way to live. The Master Parent tells us clearly that he will make the Way plain. "I will instruct you and teach you in the way you should go; I will counsel you and watch over you." He continues, warning us not to be stubborn about going our own way: "Do not be like the horse or the mule, which have no understanding but must be controlled by bit and bridle or they will not come to you."

Master parents make the way to live plain and make clear requests that it be followed: "My son, give me your heart and let your eyes keep to my ways." We ask for an all-out commitment to the Way. We know that we have to help, because all of us are lost and must be shown the Way. Our children must search for it; we must help them find it.

Master parents know the power of example in teaching the way to live. Jesus put his finger on it, in his own relationship with the Master Parent: "The Son can do nothing by himself; he can do only what he sees his Father doing, because whatever the Father does the Son also does." How will our children know which way to go if we don't show them? They will do what they see us doing. They will go where they see us going.

The Way is not just about the destination, the way to life. It is very much about the journey, the way to live. It is about the really important things we're supposed to be doing, and the way we are supposed to be doing them, while we're on the road to eternity.

There are far too many Christians with a "salvation and rapture" theology, whose only "way" is a way of escape. In the meantime (meaning the other eighty to one hundred years of life), their truncated, decrepit theology drags them and those who believe them into an abyss of negativism and pessimism, where the only "joy" they experience is a perverse joy in pointing fingers at the evils of this world. Their way to live is marked by misery and depression. They won't find any master parents on their path.

It's too easy for parents, even well-meaning ones, to have a siege mentality, where the enemy is at the gates and all could be lost in the next battle. It's a "Custer's last stand" approach to parenting that echoes the escapist theology of much of Christianity. Our goal becomes to protect our children, hide them, shield them, worry about them, fear for them. We just want to see them accept Christ and not get into anything too horrible. The Way becomes a panic room, a place to hide while evil controls the rest of the house.

Master parents don't fall for this. They know the Way is full of joy and goodness and peace and blessing. They know it's not "salvation and rapture" but *salvation and life.* Salvation is not one event that occurs to a seven-year-old, followed by a long empty space and a second event when she's eighty-seven. Salvation is an event that triggers an eighty-year, joyous journey on a way like no other, the Way of ways.

Master parents point the way. They heed the advice that Jethro gave to Moses: "Show them the way to live and the duties they are to perform." The way of journey and destination includes:

- **Vision.** What is the vision for your family? Master parents try to be like their Master Parent, "who went ahead of you on your journey, . . . to search out places for you to camp and to show you the way you should go." Vision is all about the "why" of life: Why are we here? What is our purpose? Where can we make a unique contribution? This can be written down if parents and children agree, but we have to be careful not to let words bind it up and put it in too small a box. It's more important to talk about it a lot, to develop it and add content and color to it, to end up with a picture of the future that is worth spending a life on. It's less about a formal statement and more about an idea of the direction in which we'd like to see our family move. Above all, vision always has an eternal perspective.

- **Mission.** Mission is all about the "what" of life: What will we do to achieve our vision? What major steps will we take on the journey to make sure we end up at our desired destination? In part, it means that we go ahead of our children on life's journey, always looking for the Way but finding the best places to stop—here with this church, there with that youth group, here with this school, there with that teacher. We want to be able to say to them, "Then you will know which way to go, since you have never been this way before."

- **Values.** Values are all about the "how" of life. How will we live while we are moving toward our vision? Master parents focus on planting and growing first-rate values like integrity, commitment, humility, and self-control. We teach what these values mean and what they don't mean. For example, integrity means that we're transparently honest and consistent in our words and actions. It doesn't mean that we can say rude, hurtful things under the banner of being honest, or that we can be arrogant with people who are floundering in inconsistency. We teach values all along the journey, since it takes a lot of tries to really understand them.

- **Responsibility.** The journey includes responsibility for each of us. Master parents teach their children about expected responsibilities and how they (and God) will measure the children. For example, what is our responsibility to people who are lying along the side of the road, broken by life and the school of hard knocks? Is it to avoid stepping on them? to pray for them? Or is it to help them resume the journey? We teach our children what it means to be a responsible pilgrim.

- **Trust.** What is the role of mutual trust in your family? Master parents know that trust is a fragile thing. We have to grant our children some trust so they can get started on the journey, even though they might do quite a bit of stumbling. And we have to expect our children to earn some trust as they walk in the Way with integrity. We know that nothing energizes a traveler on the Way like being trusted.

The question we face as parents is this: Are we going to build our teaching and family and unity around structure, rigid rules, and supervision, or around shared vision, values, and mutual trust? We can't build a home around both sets. Master parents choose a journey of clear vision, world-class values, and trust that isn't shattered by the first mistake.

Master parents know that the best plan for teaching the Way to their children is to walk it themselves. We let them see us focused on the destination, walking on the Way, picking up speed so we can "run in such a way as to get the prize." We teach our children to be disciples—followers of the Way—by being disciples ourselves.

Master parents also do more. They know that "the corrections of discipline are the way to life." When they themselves are undergoing discipline from the Master Parent, they let their children peer into the experience and watch the lessons learned. We can do this because we know that "he who heeds discipline shows the way to life." What a great work we can do, showing our children the way to life by simply learning from discipline in our own lives!

Master parents work hard to create an alignment between the passions and interests of their children and the way to live. They teach that the way to live includes service, but then they search their children's souls to find what service could look like for them: Is it being busy and running errands? working on a home for Habitat for Humanity? being on the youth worship team? collecting food for the poor? finding spontaneous ways to make others' lives easier? We show them that the things they want to do and the way to live are not in conflict—that they can serve people and enjoy it immensely at the same time.

Master parents know that there is a "big Way" and a "little

Way." The big Way is the one we must all find, the way to life and the way to live. The little Way belongs in a unique form to each person. "Who, then, is the man that fears the Lord? He will instruct him in the way chosen *for him.*" Master parents pay attention to see what way has been chosen for their children, and then they instruct their children in this way, this little Way. They work to "train up a child in the way he should go."

And on the other side, they don't try to "motivate" their children to do things that, for some reason or another, the children fundamentally do not want to do. We don't force all of them to work with us in the local food pantry. We don't push all of them to raise funds for charity. We don't insist that they all join us on a visit to the elderly. We listen for the melody of their souls, and then we show them where that fits in the grand chorus on the big Way.

How important is the Way? The Way—to life, to live—is *everything.* If we find it, we've found a priceless discovery. If we teach it to our children, we offer them a priceless gift.

The Way. It's worth teaching with resolve, with tenacity, with dogged persistence. Master parents insist on the Way.

Always.

INSISTING ON FREEDOM

If you're going to do anything worthwhile as a master parent, you'd better insist that your children find their own way.

And you'd better not shepherd your children with a firm hand, in spite of the centuries-long tradition that this is what good parenting is all about. The reality? The idea that parents should always guide their children with a firm hand is a myth. It's also a formula for producing rebellion in children and exhaustion in parents.

Freedom. God tells us that the way of the Lord is the way of freedom. He created us to be free, saved us to be free, intends for us to walk in freedom, warns us to be careful about keeping our freedom. "It is for freedom that Christ has set us free. Stand firm, then, and do not let yourselves be burdened again by a yoke of slavery."

Master parents act on the premise that "where the Spirit of the Lord is, there is freedom." This verse is chock-full of good stuff, but there's an important application to parenting that most parents miss. It's this: Whatever else we know about our home—its values, its structure, its activities—we know this: *If there is no freedom, the Spirit of the Lord isn't there.* How do we know this? Because if he were present, there would be *freedom.*

If we don't have freedom, we are blocking out the Spirit. In fact, the only way to really create an oppressive environment—in the home, the church, or anywhere else—is to block out the Spirit. Many parents do this, believing that parenting is all about order, control, rules, and getting kids to toe the line. Too many parents don't believe that parenting is all about freedom, which is why too many homes have a big hole where the Spirit ought to be.

"The greatest gift that God in His bounty made," wrote Dante in *The Divine Comedy,* "was the freedom of the will, with which the intelligent creatures were and are endowed."

Master parents know that if they move to the side, their children will be free to say, "I have chosen the way of truth." The Way is about the "ought to" of life, while freedom is about the "want to" of life. Even when children are clear on the "ought to," it will only be theirs if they can choose in freedom to *want* to do it.

Now, right up front, we have to face a fact: Freedom is a very dangerous thing. By creating a life rife with freedom, God took a chance—a very big risk. Freedom allows his children, the children of the Master Parent, to go their own way and miss the mark. It allows them to reject him and the way to life and the way to live.

Master parents take the same chance, the same risk, as their Master Parent. They know that freedom allows the offspring of a good parent to make wrong choices, and yet they create a life for their children that is rife with freedom. Like God, we allow our children to go their own way and miss the mark. Like God, we allow them to reject us, and the way to life, and the way to live. We know that no one was ever forced into the kingdom of God, and our children won't be the first.

We don't insist on freedom because we think we have good kids who won't ever fail but rather in spite of the fact that they *will* fail. They will make bad choices; they will misuse their freedom. We don't wait until they are totally mature and flawless before we grant them any freedom. That day will never come. We insist on freedom now. We want them to learn how to live free under our guidance now, when the choices are more easily reversible and the mistakes are generally far less costly.

Insisting on freedom means insisting on the freedom to fail. A free home is a mistake-friendly home. How do you react when you let your thirteen-year-old redecorate his room (and yes, you should give him that freedom) and the end product looks more like a scene from *Friday the 13*th than a cover story in *Good Housekeeping*? The colors clash, the wallpaper is crooked, the posters . . . oh, the posters. Master parents find something to praise: the creativity, the effort, certain details. Mediocre parents find something to criticize, and there's plenty there to criticize. Master-parenting is really concerned with the possibilities of life, while mediocre parenting is all too often concerned with the limitations of life.

The greatest leaders in any field are focused on possibilities rather than limitations, results rather than methods, outcomes rather than processes, freedom rather than control. In order to insist upon freedom, master parents know they must avoid these very typical tools:

- **Policies rather than vision.** When we define vision as where we want to be over the next five years, we're talking about possibilities. We get into trouble when we say, "Let's get this vision down into some family policies that will make sure we all work toward the vision." When we agree on where we want to go, we don't need a policy manual to get us there.

- **Rules rather than values.** When we talk about gratitude and modesty as important values for the journey, we are on the right track. We head for tension and possibly disaster when we overdefine either term. We move the Holy Spirit to the corner when "gratitude" becomes formal words of thanks and forced thank-you notes, and "modesty" becomes dictates about hair length and style, makeup, jewelry, and clothing length and style.

- **Supervision rather than responsibility.** If, as early as possible, we've emphasized personal responsibility and accountability, we're building free people who can make a difference. When we've structured our home life so things like homework only get done if we're cracking the whip, we've done a good job of turning a free society into a prison camp.

- **Reporting rather than trust.** We do well when we work on creating an open, free environment where our children are able to talk with us about problems, mistakes, concerns, and doubts. We go down in flames when we turn parenting into interrogating. We may be giving our children less freedom to make bad decisions, but we're also giving them less freedom to make *good* decisions.

Master parents know that although there is only one Way to God, there are a million ways to God. We know that the Way can be walked with great diversity. We know that our children's approaches may be better suited to them; they may, in fact, be better than our approaches. So we insist on freedom for diversity of thought.

We also know that a big part of insisting on freedom is insisting on the nonsense of rules and regulations. That's right. The *nonsense* of rules and regulations. This is what the Master Parent tells us through his Word:

> *See to it that no one takes you captive through hollow and deceptive philosophy, which depends on human tradition. . . . Do not let anyone judge you by what you eat or drink, or with regard to a religious festival, a New Moon celebration or a Sabbath day. . . . Why, as though you still belonged to [the world], do you submit to its rules: 'Do not handle! Do not taste! Do not touch!' . . . They are based on human commands and teachings. Such regulations indeed have an appearance of wisdom, with their self-imposed worship, their false humility and their harsh treatment of the body, but they lack any value in restraining sensual indulgence.*

There are more human traditions floating around than could ever be counted, much less followed. And there are people who will not only teach these things, but also will try to take us prisoner with this empty bag of tricks. We are commanded not to let ourselves be taken captive, not to let people judge us in the many areas where they want rules but God wants freedom. One of the great delights of finding the Way is that we no longer need to submit to anyone else's rules!

Other people will try to tell us that these rules aren't really as awful as they really are. They have an "appearance of wisdom" and can make us stop and say, "Gee, that sort of makes sense that I shouldn't drink this (or eat that, or go there, or do that)." These regulations seem to offer a quick path to worship ("All godly people spend at least thirty minutes a day in prayer"). They appear to be humble ("It's a sacrifice, but I don't go to movies anymore"). They can even play tough with the body ("I stayed on my knees in the cold for three hours!").

The R&R (Rule and Regulation) salespeople are those who "infiltrated our ranks to spy on the freedom we have in Christ Jesus and to make us slaves." We say to them, "If you need to do this—not drink certain drinks, eat certain foods, go to certain places, participate in certain activities—because this is an area of personal conviction (or more likely, an area of personal weakness), then go right ahead. But don't inflict it on me or my children."

Churches and youth groups are easy prey for this deadening truckload of religious concrete. It's all too easy to make an insidious appeal to the youthful idealism of our children with talk about "higher standards" and the penchant to reduce the meaning of being "all-out for God" to being "all-out for rules." Master parents smell this stuff from miles away and don't allow it into their children's souls.

And master parents don't put any of this in there themselves. They know that it's all right to have some family traditions and "house rules," but they also know that these things are merely tent pegs in time and will need to be pulled up and moved and changed as times change.

For example, when formal family devotions or regularly scheduled "quiet times" become distractions to the Way (and let's be honest, they *can* become distractions), it's time to jettison them. If those family devotions cause our children to hate things spiritual and we press on anyway, we've missed the whole point. We've reduced the Way down to "human commands and teachings."

And master parents know another ugly truth about these regulations that most parents don't: They don't work! They lack any value in restraining sensual indulgence. Master parents lose the human commands and teachings and regulations and restrictions because they know these things are *worthless.* They're great for taking up time and energy, and for taking our eyes off the Way, and for annoying our children (or worse, turning them into arrogant religious monsters because they follow "higher standards"), and for wrecking our relationship. The only thing they're not effective at accomplishing is making better children. "There is a way that seems right," we are told, "but in the end it leads to death."

Rules are also great for killing creativity. A "house rule" that forbade writing on the walls or floors would have prevented a little preschooler named Blaise Pascal from writing out his own self-intuited Euclidean geometry all over the floor of his nursery on the way to becoming one of the greatest mathematicians of the last millennium. Insisting on freedom might mean we show our children how to write on the walls well (beautifully but with washable markers) rather than forbidding it. "Don't do that" or "don't do it that way" are top suspects in the murder of a child's inborn creative fire.

Master parents know that true spirituality is about freedom because God is about freedom. Religious systems that emphasize rigid rules for living, enforced from the top, might make room for methodical behavior but little or no room for freedom of thought. "Dogma does not mean the absence of thought," said G. K. Chesterton, "but the end of thought."

Insisting on freedom is different from insisting on independence. Independence is a bad plan. One authority said that the goal of parenting is separation, planned obsolescence, and getting them ready to leave. Is this really what our hearts want? Not likely. This is not only discouraging, it's unbiblical.

The Master Parent certainly doesn't have this goal for us. His goal is connection (not separation), renewal of relationship as we mature (not planned obsolescence), and interdependence, in which we each have our part in the ongoing relationship (not getting us ready to leave).

As the Master Parent says to them, master parents say to their older children, "I no longer call you servants, but friends." People who push independence almost seem to be saying that if we want ongoing friendship with our children and no clear break, we're somehow deficient. They treat mutually developing, interdependent relationships and friendships with our adult children as dysfunctional. If so, then God is dysfunctional, and master parents are happy to join him.

Master parents know that they've been given freedom, and they follow Jesus' command: "Freely you have received, freely give." They freely give gifts to their children, including the gift of freedom. They "proclaim liberty throughout the land to all its inhabitants," even—perhaps especially—to their own children.

Freedom is what we find at the end of history. We can easily think of the "end times" as times of warfare and judgment and punishment. But the Master Parent has a far better end to the story than that. "All creation anticipates the day when it will join God's children in glorious freedom from death and decay." The end of God's story is freedom from death, not death itself. And that is glorious freedom indeed.

Heaven itself, the Master Parent's home, is a place of freedom. "The Jerusalem that is above is free." And the rest of the verse brings it right into our relationship with the Master Parent: "The Jerusalem that is above is free, and she is our mother."

Master parents insist on freedom, because we come from a free place, and that free place is our home.

THE BLEND

God knows we won't really commit our souls to the Way unless we choose it for ourselves. None of us walks very quickly on unchosen paths. The Master Parent is totally committed to insisting that we find and walk in his way, and he is totally committed to insisting that we have complete freedom as to whether or not we do it.

Master parents take the same approach with their own children. They are not so committed to freedom that they take a hands-off approach and avoid being insistent about the Way. They aren't crippled by the malady of thinking that they have no "right" to try to direct their children into certain paths. They have big enough minds that they don't confuse speaking about life-critical truths with "brainwashing."

Because they are so committed to the Way, they know better than to push it down their children's throats. They are equally insistent about freedom, because they know that "it is for freedom" that Christ has made us all free. They also know that freely made, fully informed decisions are the only ones worth making, the only ones that "stick."

Master parents know that the Way is critically important, and they want their children to know it and follow it. But they say to their children, "Follow the Way because of what it is, not because I say so. Choose it because it's the best. Choose it because *you're* the best. But no matter what, I accept and honor your right to choose." We are free to choose, to accept or reject the Way, because the Master Parent has built freedom into the Way's design. Master parents insist on the whole Way, including the part that allows freedom to reject it.

They can do this with some confidence because of the intimate connection between the Way and freedom. One of the great points about the Way is that it is the only way to be free, the only path to freedom. "Then you will know the truth," Jesus said, "and the truth will set you free."

The Way is all about truth, and truth is all about freedom. If we teach our children the Way, we will automatically teach them the way to be free. One reason is that they can't run with confidence if they don't know where they are going. "I will walk about in freedom, for I have sought out your precepts."

Master parents know the difference between their way and *the* Way. They know that an insistence on their way—preferences, rules, convictions—is wrong and wrongheaded. It's wrong because we have no right as parents to convert our personal approach to the Way into the *only* approach to the Way.

And it's wrongheaded because these transient preferences and details add nothing to children's approach to the Way. At the worst, these things are a distraction to our children, and perhaps even an arrow through their hearts. Master parents avoid the approach of mediocre parents, who in effect say to their children, "When we want your opinion, we'll give it to you."

"Too often," wrote Dr. Richard and Jerilyn Fowler, "we force our children to abide by our opinions, tastes, desires, and demands, as though obedience were the primary goal of parenting. . . .

Children who are given the blessing of choice within a solid core of absolutes are children whose hearts easily, willingly, freely turn toward their creator."

Master parents know that there is only one Way to God, and yet there are a million ways to walk that Way. There's one destination but many paths. Because we know there is one Way, we insist on it; because we know there are many ways to walk it, we insist on freedom.

We define the Way for our children, but we are careful not to create too narrow a path. This is often the tendency of leaders—to keep people on the "straight and narrow." Jesus did say that the way to eternal life was narrow, but he didn't say *how* narrow. If we're not careful, we can make it into a tightrope.

Master parents insist on the Way in terms of goals but insist on freedom in terms of methods. Great leaders in any area focus on goals rather than methods. The Way might include a goal of nothing less than a B on core courses, with a cutback in other activities if the goal isn't met. But, insisting on freedom, master parents let their children decide when and how to study to meet that goal. A strict regimen of supervised homework can arguably help achieve the goal, but it will be at great cost—the loss of freedom and a little less of the Spirit in the home.

Our Master Parent sets boundary lines for us, but "the boundary lines have fallen for me in pleasant places." Master parents are careful to mark out the Way—to set boundary lines—but to make sure that those boundary lines fall in pleasant places. What exactly is a "pleasant place"?

- **A boundary line that our children realize will keep them from disaster.** If our children can't see how this boundary line will protect them, they'll surely call it unpleasant.

- **A boundary line that our children realize will keep them from wasting their time or energy.** It could be you saying, "There's no reason for you to explore this or that, because everyone I've ever known who has tried that has flopped big-time." Or it could be you saying, "You can do it if you meet certain conditions." For example, suppose your children want to organize an event to raise money for the poor. It's not a bad goal, but you know how hard it is to get people involved, how easily youthful vision can melt away, and how discouraging it is to move ahead with an idea like this and have no one show up. So you tell them, "If you get ten people to commit in writing that they will help you, and fifty people to commit in writing that they will come to the event, you can take it to the next step and I'll help you. Otherwise, we end it there." Our children have to see that it's a waste preventer before they can call it a pleasant boundary.

- **A boundary line that our children realize will keep them focused on their own goals.** To say, "That new activity you want to do will take ten hours a week, so the music lessons and acting in the school play will have to go," is a healthy reminder that the good is the enemy of the best. Even if they're disappointed, they're likely to think of the boundary as pleasant, at least eventually.

- **A boundary line that our children see getting moved out farther** as the children are clearly and freely making good choices of their own. "I originally intended to move your curfew from 11:00 to 12:00, but you're so on target that I'm going to make it 1:00."

Master parents are careful not to confuse boundary lines with rules. "Clear limits tend to reduce power struggles," suggested one article, "because children don't need to constantly test you to discover where the boundaries lie." This is true if the limits are truly boundary lines—wide fences with lots of free space inside. But if these limits we set are rules, then the tighter they are and the more inflexible we make them, the more we will tend to *increase* power struggles. Why? Because the kids are always bouncing up against the rules. Master parents think about wide boundaries, few and far between, and ask about every power struggle, "Is this really a boundary line rather than a rule? And is it really worth fighting over?" Rules say, "Don't do this, period," or "Do it this way." Boundaries say, "You can do everything *but* this," or "Do it any way you want, with these few exceptions."

A very practical application of this is in the way that master parents assign work to their children. Let's say you're going to have your fourteen-year-old clean up and reorganize a section of the basement. Mediocre parents tell their children to do it, often without a clear picture of what the end result is supposed to be, and then tell them how to do it: "First, pull this stuff out, then sweep, then put this part of it over there," etc. Then they keep dropping in with little "suggestions." They think the Way is a focus on the "how" rather than the "why" and the "what." The result is not what these parents want, so they end up nitpicking and complaining, even though they themselves are the real cause of the problem.

Master parents are thinking, in every assignment or other serious interaction, about the balance of the Way and freedom. They want to focus on the desired result and leave many of the details up to their children. So as a master parent, you might approach the job of cleaning the basement like this: First, talk about the "why" of the mission, so your son can see the Way. "Honey, we want to get out as many things as we can that we're not using and give them to the needy. We also need to clear that area out because I think we might have a leak, and we need to take a look. And here's the other reason why we're doing this: I'm thinking about putting in a Ping-Pong table if we can make room."

Second, be very clear about the end result, so your child will know in advance what victory looks like. "Everything that we keep needs to be able to fit on the shelves along the wall. All of the paper items can be thrown out. Everything that we're not using and can be given away should be put together so we can look at it. You can separate out anything you want to keep or that you're not sure of. Questions?"

Third, be very clear about any restrictions, any limits, any boundary lines. "This has to be done by the end of next weekend, by bedtime on Sunday night. You can get your brother to help you but not your sister. She's too little and likely to annoy you or get herself hurt. Clear?" And here's the key: Anything not specified here can't be brought up after the fact. You give him freedom on the "how," the methods he uses to get the job done. You can't come in at the end and say, "You shouldn't have used that broom!" or "Why did you put those heavy things way up there?"

Fourth, tell your son what resources he has to get the job done and ask him what additional resources he might need. "Here are dust masks for you to wear. I've bought you a box of trash bags. If you get into this project and see that you need anything else, like shelves or whatever, let me know."

Finally, open the way for his input to improve the end result. "If you get into this and see a way to make the results better, let me know. If you see a way to get the job done more easily, just do it."

To summarize this "delegation plan":

1. Tell them what the mission is and why they need to do it.
2. Tell them what you're expecting the end product to look like.
3. Tell them what they can't do, and give them freedom on everything else.
4. Ask them what tools or resources they need to get the job done.
5. Ask them to offer suggestions or make improvements as they get into it.

"Never tell people how to do things," said legendary U.S. General George S. Patton. "Tell them what to do and they will surprise you with their ingenuity."

On the subject of the Way and freedom, the Master Parent gives us a stunning declaration: "Everything is permissible." Whoa! *Everything* is permissible? You don't hear that verse preached about very often! But there it is, right there in the Bible, repeated four times. It is one of the clearest, boldest statements of freedom you can find in any religious text. If you say you want to teach your children the Bible, then you have to teach them that "everything is permissible."

But, of course, it doesn't end there. This part of the passage captures totally our need to insist on freedom. But the rest of the passage captures our need to insist on the Way:

> *"Everything is permissible for me"—but not everything is beneficial. "Everything is permissible for me"—but I will not be mastered by anything.*
>
> *"Everything is permissible"—but not everything is beneficial. "Everything is permissible"—but not everything is constructive.*

We're free to choose the Way (or not), free to walk on the Way in freedom (or not), and free to do anything on the Way *as long as it doesn't violate the Way.* This means that what we do in freedom, what we do with God's full support, must be:

1. **Beneficial.** Whatever we do must produce good, not bad; benefit, not loss. Master parents teach their children to get rid of the things that they are free to choose if those things don't produce benefit for themselves, benefit for others, or benefit for the Way. This qualifier is repeated in both verses. "Who will benefit from this and how?" is a great master-parent question.

2. **Constructive.** To construct is to build. Master parents teach their kids to use their freedom to build something new for

themselves and others. They remind their children of God's warning: "Be careful, however, that the exercise of your freedom does not become a stumbling block to the weak." We say to our child, "If you can handle that movie, and your friend can't, you would be abusing your freedom to take him to it."

3. **Not enslaving.** We're free to do many things in moderation that become disastrous in addictive form. Master parents show their children that this is one of the great ironies: In choosing things that are permissible, we can lose our freedom and become slaves. "There's nothing wrong with that video game in itself. It makes a great source of entertainment, but it will make a terrible slavemaster."

Insisting on the Way means that we teach our children all that we know, including our sense of judgment, with all of the authority that we have. But we do this so they can freely apply it for themselves, and perhaps go on to new and different heights.

As master parents, we even teach our children to disagree with us, in a way that honors our authority and wisdom, because we want them to be wise and we want them to be original. If we call all disagreements rebellion, we've made ourselves out to be infallible—popes of the home.

"The apprentice," wrote Richard Rhodes about the system of masters and apprentices, "learned high standards of judgment from his master. At the same time he learned to trust his own judgment: he learned the possibility and the necessity of dissent. Books and lectures might teach rules; masters taught controlled rebellion. . . . Original work is inherently rebellious."

Master parents know that insisting on freedom is the best approach to insisting on the Way, because then our children will make it their own. Who knows, we might even learn something new from them! They might even make the way better for us, if we have the wisdom to listen and to learn what they have learned about the Way in their own free pursuit of it.

What do we do if we have children who are resistant to the Way, perhaps older children who seem to be throwing the Way out the window? Do we keep insisting that they go to church, participate in family devotions, read the Bible, and attend youth group? At some point, led by the Spirit, we know that we must insist on freedom, perhaps the most fundamental freedom of all—freedom of conscience.

But we still insist on the Way as the best and only path. We never back off from that insistence but only from the insistence that focuses on the way our children act. We do this because we treasure freedom, love freedom, and want to protect the freedom of our children.

Master parents know that insisting on the Way without insisting on freedom is tyranny. They work hard to find the balance between strictness and flexibility, demanding and accepting, unity and diversity, the Way and freedom.

"What you have inherited from your father," said the great German philosopher Goethe, "earn over again for yourselves, or it will not be yours." The Way is the "inherited" part. The "earn over again for yourselves" is the freedom part. Both parts are necessary to master-parenting.

Master parents say to their children, as the Master Parent says to them, "Choose for yourselves this day whom you will serve. . . . But as for me and my household, we will serve the Lord." We declare ourselves followers of the Way and put the free choice clearly before our beloved ones.

Master parents want their children to serve the Lord. But they also want their children to be able to say, "I have chosen the way of truth."

LAST THOUGHTS

If we insist on the Way without insisting on freedom, we cause our children to hate the Way and seek freedom *from* it rather than *within* it. If we insist on freedom without insisting on the Way, we lead our children toward unfettered license and crippling narcissism.

"To lead the people," said Chinese philosopher Lao-Tze, "walk behind them."

Master parents walk behind their children and let them freely choose their own steps. But always, like their Master Parent, they say to their children, "Whether you turn to the right or to the left, your ears will hear a voice behind you, saying, 'This is the way; walk in it.' "

And, if you do it wisely and well, "what you have whispered in the ear in the inner rooms will be proclaimed from the roofs."

No parent could ask for more than that.

Eight

MASTER PARENTS PROTECT THEIR KIDS' INNOCENCE AND EXPOSE THEIR KIDS TO REALITY

———— • ————

"I want you to be . . . innocent about what is evil"

~ But ~

"I am sending you out like sheep among wolves."

We now enter one of the greatest ongoing, seemingly contradictory challenges of parenthood.

We want our children to keep their innocence, to get to be "little," to know that life can have happy endings. At the same time, we want them to be savvy, to be street-smart, and not to be easy marks for those who would gladly victimize them.

Master parents relentlessly protect their children from harm, while at the same time they relentlessly expose their children to danger.

Do you cringe at the thought of your babies losing their innocence? Join God's team. "In regard to evil be infants," we're told. How much does a baby think about evil? Not much. In fact, not at all. Now, this might sound as if God is out of touch with real-world events. Evil is all around and the world is a tough place. How on earth can he expect us to look at it like an infant would?

But that's what he says. "In regard to evil be infants." He also offers us a great reason to remain innocent: his promise of protection. "The Lord protects the simplehearted." Innocence does not lead to destruction but instead invites God's protection.

The Master Parent is so totally committed to protecting his children that they are able to say, "He protected us on our entire journey and among all the nations through which we traveled."

On the other hand, it's a hard world out there, full of deception and dangers. Because of that, you know your babies need all of the experience they can get—and fast! The Master Parent shares your concern. And he takes action. "I am sending you out like sheep among wolves," he says. No hesitation. He's not asking us or permitting us to go out; he's sending us.

Why would he do that knowing how many wolves are out there and how big their teeth are? He does it because he knows that's where we will spend our lives. That's where we can make a difference. That's where we can have an impact.

He exposes us to reality so that we'll be able to live in truth and have no illusions about the world, its people, or ourselves. He lets life hold up a mirror, because we need a clear picture of what our lives look like.

And he expects master parents to do the same. He expects us to expose our children to reality, while at the same time protecting their innocence every step of the way.

PROTECTING INNOCENCE

If you're going to do anything worthwhile as a master parent, you'd better protect the innocence of your children with dogged vigilance.

What is innocence? It's sometimes defined as "freedom from sin or moral wrong." Oops. That can't be it, since "all have sinned and fall short of the glory of God." How about "freedom from legal or specific wrong; guiltlessness." Nope. Same problem. Then how about "simplicity; absence of guile or cunning; lack of knowledge or understanding"? Now we're on to something.

Innocence doesn't mean that we have a frontal lobotomy or go under heavy sedation so we'll be incapable of doing anything wrong. It means that we're "simple"—not a mixed bag, not hypocritical, not protesting evil while enjoying it. We have an "absence of guile or cunning"; we don't claim that we're being shrewd when we're really being deceitful or treacherous. And we have a "lack of knowledge or understanding"; we deliberately turn away from, and fight to ignore, the wrongdoer's guidebook.

We need to emphasize that ignorance of evil is not the same as innocence. And it's not the source of innocence. Instead, innocence is refusal to comply with evil in any of its forms. Choosing to ignore evil can be a positive thing up to a certain point; it can help us preserve our innocence. But it's only a component of true innocence.

Innocence is critical to faith. "[Jesus] called a little child and had him stand among them. And he said, 'I tell you the truth, unless you change and become like little children, you will never enter the kingdom of heaven.' " Why? Because God has given us a massive challenge: to believe in something that we can't see. Who are the only people on the planet who easily believe in something that they can't see? You got it. Little children.

This tells us that we have to do more than protect our children's innocence; we have to go back and find our own. Only little children have the faith—the imagination—to be "sure of what we hope for and certain of what we do not see." "Great naïveté is needed to perform great deeds," wrote René Crevel in "L'esprit contre la raison."

We don't need to worry about getting little children into the kingdom of God. They're already there. We just don't want them to grow out of it, and when they do (as children do when they reach the age of moral responsibility), we want them to head right back in. The really amazing thing about this passage is that it tells us that we, too, need to go back to being innocent in order to enter the kingdom.

People often attack the idea of wearing "rose-colored glasses." But what's really wrong with rose-colored glasses? What's wrong with seeing the world a little better than it is—seeing the potential in a rough situation? Isn't that the basis for optimism and hope? The Master Parent expects us to live in hope, to "do everything without complaining or arguing," and to really believe in redemption. Master parents do the same. We want our children to believe that ugly doesn't have to stay ugly—that if we look at it differently, we can make it be different.

In order to give our children this perspective, we have to be careful how we talk about problems and challenges. Protecting innocence means avoiding talking in sarcastic, cynical, nasty tones. We don't take a position of despair: "I don't think we'll ever be out of debt." We don't put people down, even when we think they deserve our remarks. We don't even restate the obvious: "As I've said before, she's just a greedy, selfish person, so give up trying to expect anything out of her." Life can be ugly. We try not to make it uglier than it already is.

Protecting innocence means we really protect the innocence of our children. For example:

- **We work to eliminate our kids' interactions with rotten people.** "In the shelter of your presence you hide them from the intrigues of men," the Bible says about our Master Parent. "In your dwelling you keep them safe from accusing tongues." This doesn't mean that God stops rotten people from planning or talking. It means he hides us from them and keeps us safe. Master parents say to their Master Parent, "You will keep us safe and protect us from such people forever," and "Protect me from men of violence." We say to our children, "I will be a refuge for you when people come after you, and this home will never be even slightly open to anyone who abuses you (or others) in any way. And all of this will still be true, even when you're seventy and I'm one hundred."

- **We guard against family members who live far from the Master Parent's values.** The Bible tells us clearly, "Your enemies will be right in your own household!" Master parents stay away from these people and protect their children from them. We don't nitpick them, but we do *pick* them. We pick the people we spend time with and how much time we spend with them and at what kinds of events or situations we interact with them.

- **We don't let our kids "run the neighborhood" or assume they're okay because they're at church or school or youth group.** Peers can teach our children a lot, including a lot that they should never have to learn. Again, we don't nitpick their friends, but we do *pick* them. We literally pick them when our kids are small, and we help them pick friends when they're older.

- **We don't flip television channels and hope to find something good,** or plan to use fast-forward to skip fifteen unsavory scenes in a rented movie. This is like looking for a ham sandwich in a garbage can. We don't become hermits, and we remember that our Master Parent "richly provides us with everything for our enjoyment," but we don't deliberately wipe out the innocence of our children. We know the difference between exposing to reality and exposing to slime.

- **We don't talk about cults and their strange beliefs,** a popular staple on Christian radio and television and in bookstores. Our Master Parent commends those who "have not learned Satan's so-called deep secrets." What's the point of listening to talk about untruth? Or talking about it? This won't make cults any better, but it can make our children a whole lot worse.

- **We don't welcome fanatics or members of bogus religious groups into our lives or homes** to try to "convert" them, or to let our children see us "defend" the faith. Why not? Because the Master Parent forbids it: "If anyone comes to you and does not bring this teaching [about Christ], do not take him into your house or welcome him. Anyone who welcomes him shares in his wicked work."

Our Master Parent wants us to be "wise about what is good, and innocent about what is evil." He wants us to spend a lot of time thinking about good and very little time thinking about evil. Master parents focus their children in the same direction. Unlike the nightly news, we focus on "whatever is true, whatever is noble, whatever is right, whatever is pure, whatever is lovely, whatever is admirable," and we teach our children to "think about such things."

Master parents pray for the protection of their children, as Jesus prayed for them: "Holy Father, protect them by the power of your name." We pray that our Father will guard their lives, watch over them, deliver them from harm, and otherwise surround them with about 2.6 million angels. And we know God listens because he's our Parent, and he understands.

Master parents are able to say to their Master Parent, "You are my hiding place; you will protect me from trouble and surround me with songs of deliverance." We want to be and to do the same for our children. We want to be a hiding place for them, because life is tough and it's nice to have a shelter from its many storms. We do want to protect them from trouble, because it's the right thing to do and will protect their innocence. And we want to surround them with songs of deliverance—because we've protected them and delivered them, let there be music and dancing.

Master parents pray, as the Master Parent does for them, for the protection of their children from the evil one. "The Lord is faithful, and he will strengthen and protect you from the evil one."

Because it's a tough world out there, the Master Parent taught us to pray a very interesting (if not downright peculiar) prayer: "And lead us not into temptation." What's that all about? Why do we need to pray that? Surely God wouldn't lead us into temptation, would he? But there it is, a prayer taught by Jesus: "Lead us not into temptation."

We know that our Master Parent does not ever tempt us: "For God cannot be tempted by evil, nor does he tempt anyone." And yet, "Jesus was led by the Spirit into the desert to be tempted by the devil." It seems that God doesn't tempt us, but he might let us be led into situations where we could be tempted. This may be exactly where the prayer "Lead us not into temptation" comes into play.

Jesus confirms this when he says to his disciples, "Watch and pray so that you will not fall into temptation." Later, frustrated with them for falling asleep right before he was arrested, he said, "Get up and pray so that you will not fall into temptation." There is a war going on all the time, a war designed to annihilate human souls.

Master parents pray this prayer for their children: "Lead them not into temptation." And they teach and encourage their children to pray this prayer—a lot. They warn them to "watch and pray so that you will not fall into temptation." When they see their children drifting off to worldly sleep, they say, "Get up and pray so that you will not fall into temptation." Better to be innocent than battle scarred.

Are our kids innocent because they haven't sinned? Hardly. In a remarkable statement, Jesus says, "If you had known what these words mean, 'I desire mercy, not sacrifice,' you would not have condemned the innocent." He says that we wouldn't condemn the innocent if we were merciful. *But why would we need to be merciful unless they had sinned?*

One of the greatest examples of mercy claimed by a sinner was Paul. Here was a man who zealously attacked the young church and hauled Christians off to their deaths, just as zealots are doing with Christians today in Africa, the Middle East, and other parts of the world. Paul, then called Saul, was an all-out murderer. And yet he was able to say, "Christ Jesus came into the world to save sinners—of whom I am the worst. But for that very reason I was shown mercy." How? How could he get mercy after killing Christians *because* they were Christians? For the simple reason that his Master Parent desires "mercy, not sacrifice."

Master parents don't condemn the innocent. In practice, this means we don't express disapproval of the innocent; we don't attribute wrong or evil motives to them just because they make a mistake. If they don't clean their rooms, we don't immediately call it rebellion. If they try to make funny comments that come out as insults, we don't automatically assume it's disrespect. If they drop dishes, we don't conclude they must have been fooling around. We rely on the tested principle "Innocent until proven guilty," a great rule of law that traces its roots all the way back to the Master Parent.

We avoid those kinds of reactions because we are merciful. And we don't attack our children even if they do miss the mark as badly as Paul did. We are eager to show mercy so our children can once again, like Paul, declare themselves to be receptacles of God's mercy.

How do we know when they're losing their innocence? "The conduct of the innocent is upright," we are told by the Master Parent. Master parents know that bad behavior is not a phase or a stage and that it shouldn't be explained away by tiredness, sickness, birth order, or anything else. Bad behavior is bad behavior; it is *not* upright, and it is a powerful sign that innocence is disappearing. The verse tells us that if people *were* innocent, they would be upright.

But even at these times, we protect the innocence of our children. Can we find a way to protect their innocence, even as we see that it's disappearing? Love will find a way, if we'll let it. Let's say we find that they've been sneaking off to watch tough R-rated and PG-13-rated movies. They've seen things that you couldn't see in *any* movies a generation ago, and the simple truth is that you can't erase those images from their minds. But you can *replace* them.

Over their groans, you can go on a steady diet of PG- and G-rated movies, with a lot of caution on the PGs. You can help them find their way back to being entertained by something dramatic or funny that's also *innocent*. You can shove the garbage out the back door as you fill the front room with stuff that will refresh their souls. They have developed a taste for junk food of the mind, but they can rediscover their taste for nutritious mental meals, with a little help from a protective master parent.

The Master Parent protects us, and we should protect our children at all times because of love. Love "always protects." So do master parents.

The value of innocence and of being free from grime and sin is beyond measure. Daniel, as an older man, was able to say about his delivery from the lion's den, "They have not hurt me, because I was found innocent in [God's] sight." He had kept himself out of the garbage of life, and the lions couldn't hurt him because of that.

May your children be ever safe from lions because they, too, are found innocent in God's sight.

EXPOSING TO REALITY

If you're going to do anything worthwhile as a master parent, you'd better expose your children to reality with relentless vigilance.

And the first thing you ought to do is be better aware of what is going on in the world around you.

Master parents know that the first thing they have to do is expose themselves to reality. Every one of us has a "theory of reality," some sort of idea about what reality is like. We have theories about why children behave as they do—why they yield to peer pressure, why siblings fight, why they dodge responsibility—theories about everything that parents have to face. These theories are based on our perceptions.

But the old saying "Perception is reality" is a lie. Perception is *not* reality. *Reality* is reality. If we perceive our son's friend to be a nice boy, and he's really a diplomatic monster, our perception isn't reality and won't change the reality. That "nice boy" will still devour our baby.

We can be very resistant to actual reality and to hearing that our "theory of reality" is out of whack. Every human being is, to one degree or another, learning impaired. Even more important, every human being is *reality impaired*. We don't always want help, and we can be very upset with people who try to offer it. "If you speak the truth," says the old Turkish proverb, "have a foot in the stirrup."

A fact that shows how resistant we can be to reality is that the word *disillusioned* is in the dictionary, but the word *illusioned* is not. How can we be disillusioned unless we were first illusioned? We find out that our child is into something awful, and we are shocked. But if we were paying attention and trying to see the reality that is there, how could we be shocked? The signs were there; it was only the vision that was blurred. We were "illusioned."

Master parents open their eyes to reality. How do they do it?

- **They resist easy answers.** It's too easy to conclude that a child is motivated by one thing when the truth is that his motivation comes from someplace else completely. We think his behavior reflects apathy when really he's lonely. We think he's rebellious when really he's struggling with depression. We blame peers for our children's poor behavior when really we should be blaming ourselves. Master parents resist the answers that allow them to avoid thought, relational work, or personal responsibility.

- **They listen to observers.** Master parents listen to the observations of others regarding their children. They don't brush aside criticism from their parents and in-laws and people at church. Instead, they comb through it to see if there is a shred of truth in it.

- **They ask good questions.** Master parents talk to their kids and ask good questions: "How are we doing? Where are we missing something important?" If they have more than one child, they might ask, "What's going on in your sibling's heart that I might be blind to?"

- **They analyze strong responses.** Master parents pay close attention to strong responses, both their own and those of their children. They ask, "Why are we reacting so strongly to one another's words? Are there problems that we'd really rather ignore?"

- **They watch for differences.** Sometimes it's the thing that's "different" that offers a clue into reality. Master parents watch for these differences: a good student suddenly gets a bad grade in only one course, a quiet child gets angry when she's around a certain person, a decent kid gets on the Internet after everyone has gone to bed. Master parents pay close attention to these differences and won't let them go until they find the truth.

- **They allow healthy disagreement.** Master parents allow their children to share contrary views, because they know that buried ideas and resentment are not healthy. Most parents worry about how to manage conflict so it doesn't get out of hand. Master parents focus on how to manage consensus so it doesn't get out of hand.

- **They give permission to speak.** Master parents authorize their children to speak up whenever they see Mom or Dad taking a trip to la-la land. They create a safe forum for illusion-busting— a regular "permission to speak freely" session, for example.

We need to make sure that we're communicating with our children to find out what they're already being exposed to. The junk will fall into a couple of categories. The first is the stuff that's true but horrible: two middle-school classmates who are having sex, a group of friends who are experimenting with drugs, kids who are stealing from the local store. Our role here is to clarify what really happened and then put these things into perspective: What will the results be? How will this affect people's lives?

The second category of junk is the stuff that's untrue but horrible: the young boy advising his friends on "safe sex," or the young girl sharing unfounded gossip about a friend's family. Our role here is to correct the error and then help our kids rethink the time they are spending with certain people who perpetuate these false ideas.

In dealing with all of this junk, we need a reality check if we're going to be effective. We've got to know where our kids are coming *from* before we can know where we need to take them *to.*

Master parents can then move to the next step: exposing their children to reality. We don't let them hide behind bogus perceptions that will only bring them harm. We teach them how to bring their perceptions in line with reality.

Our Master Parent gives us "tips" to help us discern reality. The book of Proverbs is full of them. Master parents follow God's example and load their children up with tips and clues.

For example, humorist Dave Barry has said that if you're out to dinner with someone and she treats you well but treats the waiter badly, whatever else you know about this person, you know she is not a nice person. This would apply directly to your kid's friend who treats her well but treats others badly. "Watch out," you say. "It's only a matter of time until she points her tongue at you."

We need to teach our children the ABCs of street smarts—how to stay safe while remaining confident, not fearful. "There's a fine line between teaching kids to be cautious and making them afraid." We want them to know what's going on, but not in such a way that it makes them afraid (steals their innocence). So what are the ABCs of street smarts?

- **Acknowledge the dangers.** Admit that there are real and serious dangers in this life. The Master Parent does this with us, through countless, colorful teachings and examples in the Bible. Master parents do the same. We give our children the "scoop." We clue them in about evil people who kidnap the unwary, seductive people who will butter people up to steal from them or hurt them or take advantage of them sexually, parasitic people who attach themselves to others and drain the life out of them. "A good scare is worth more to a man than good advice," wrote Edgar Watson Howe in *Country Town Sayings.* We need to teach our children about dangers and give them lots of examples. *Everything* becomes a parable for a master parent.

- **Bury the illusions.** The Master Parent does this with us. You think you can be safe at last in a "church home"? Think again. God warns us about wolves in sheep's clothing, shepherds who only feed themselves, teachers who spread "gangrene," and a time "when those who kill you will think they are doing God a service." Master parents banish "Pollyannaish" nonsense in their homes. We don't let our children be illusioned, because we don't want them to end up disillusioned.

- **Create effective strategies.** Develop tools to deal with reality. The Master Parent arms us with hundreds of these. Master parents gladly take on the role of family spiritual weapons manufacturers. If we don't teach our children how to handle the wolves, who will?

We teach our children Mike Murdock's great principle "Go where you are celebrated, not tolerated." We teach them superinvestor Warren Buffet's great principle "Never work with anybody who makes your stomach churn." We teach them to avoid the bad guys, to be cautious with the good guys ("A righteous man is cautious in friendship") and to be fully trusting of few. We teach them George Washington's great principle "Be courteous to all and intimate with few."

As another example, we can arm our children to think clearly about how to spend their lives. We can show them how the best decisions about work and career come at the meeting point of three great questions that require clear and honest answers:

1. What am I passionate about?
2. What can I be really good at?
3. What can I earn sufficient money and resources by doing?

We can help them answer each of these questions and then help them find the one or two or three things that might be on all three lists. For now, at least, these are the realistic areas to pursue. If our children are passionate about dancing, for example, but have little talent or ability to earn a living at it, it's just not an effective choice—at least for now. If they've got some talent and can possibly even earn some money at it, but they just don't care about it, it's almost certainly not a good choice. They won't have the inner care and drive to make it go for a lifetime. Too many people have taken this numbing path.

Master parents expose their children to reality early and often. Some practical ways to do this are by:

1. *Not* interfering when our children are struggling with siblings or friends. We let them see, in ways that hurt, that selfishness and nastiness don't work in human relationships.
2. *Not* making excuses for our children when they fail to do their homework or live up to a commitment. We simply say, "I bet that hurts."
3. *Not* telling them the old lie that "there aren't any monsters." We tell them, in general but effective ways, that there are indeed monsters.

4. *Not* telling them that the Christian life will be easy. We let them know that if they do anything for God, anything worthwhile at all, they'll likely become a target of the evil one, of nasty people, or of their own doubts.
5. *Not* acting as though the church is a safe place. We, like Paul, are "in danger from false brothers," and we let our children know that they are too. We tell them that many of the most dangerous people will be *in* the church, not outside it. Wolves hang out in two places: wolf dens and sheep pens. "There were also false prophets among the people," wrote Peter, "just as there will be false teachers among you."
6. *Not* telling them to give "equal time" to all Christians. We tell them that there are people in the church who are negative—who will criticize and nitpick and make other Christians' lives miserable if allowed to do so. This judgmentalism has no logic or reality. We warn our children to flee, for example, from the person who slanders other people under the guise of "praying" for them.
7. *Not* viewing their peers as only a problem. Peers are an opportunity for our children to learn about the reality of relationships. "Children need your help to learn how to connect with others, to stand up for themselves, to be comfortable taking risks and failing, and to learn new skills. If they do those things in their early friendships, they will be able to do them throughout their lives." Peers can be an effective sociology lab.
8. *Not* paying for their college education. The reality is that college-age people are adults, or ought to be, and they need to assume adult responsibilities. This includes paying their own way at college, or at least a majority of it. This is a bigger gift to them, in many ways, than the money would be. Among other things, this prevents them from cruising through a program they might not really care about because it doesn't cost them anything.

Like all master parents through the ages, we need to teach our children about the evils of our own time and not just about the many evils of history. It's easy—now—to talk about slavery, but it wasn't so easy in most parts of the United States in the early 1800s.

In fact, it's always easy to talk about the problems of other people, problems that are already solved. But what about the evils that haunt us today? If we condemn those who didn't speak out against slavery while we don't speak out against modern evils, aren't we hypocrites? Master parents take a stand on the "slavery" issues of our own age. Consider some of these evils at this moment in time:

- **Assaults on the innocent unborn.** How can we claim to be a civilized society when we allow mothers to collaborate with doctors in the murder of their own children? Master parents teach their children what the Master Parent teaches them—to "speak up for those who cannot speak for themselves." We teach our children about the need for twenty-first-century abolition.

- **Assaults on the disabled and elderly.** How can we stand quietly by while authorities debate whether disabled and elderly people have enough "quality of life" to allow them to live? Master parents teach their children that life is not less worthwhile because it has problems. We don't fall for the lie that dragged the German medical profession into the Nazi muck, that there is such a thing as a life not worthy of being lived.

- **Sexual wastelands.** How can we allow entire generations of young people to stain their souls in a cesspool of sexual sickness? Somewhere well beyond individual choice and freedom of the press lie depravity, disease, and destruction. Master parents teach their children that sexual perversity in all its forms is a trip into a black hole. We tell them what our Master Parent tells us: "Flee from sexual immorality." We warn them about the soul-draining effect of sex outside of marriage and the disempowering addictiveness of pornography in all its forms, including the explosion of private, accessible, seductive corruption on the Internet.

Master parents teach their children to fight these evils. They also teach them that this fight might not always make them popular and might even get them some grief. We expose them to this reality and to the reality that there are some things worth taking a beating over. "You don't hold your own in the world by standing on guard," said George Bernard Shaw, "but by attacking and getting well hammered yourself."

Our Master Parent has little patience with persistent immaturity and never confuses this with "innocence." The author of Hebrews said, "You are slow to learn. In fact, though by this time you ought to be teachers, you need someone to teach you the elementary truths of God's word all over again. You need milk, not solid food! Anyone who lives on milk, being still an infant, is not acquainted with the teaching about righteousness." God expects all of his children to grow up and know the score. Adolescence, largely a modern invention, has allowed young people to be *childish* a lot more than it has allowed them to be *childlike*.

Master parents expect their children to grow up and know the score. They train their children to know that "solid food is for the mature, who by constant use have trained themselves to distinguish good from evil." Exposing our children to reality means putting them into a rigorous training program in which they are taught to distinguish good from evil. The only way to do that is to push them into the world and expose them to reality.

This push will probably make them feel insecure. It will probably make us feel like we're stripping them of their innocence. "Growth demands a temporary surrender of security," says Gail Sheehy. Our children grow by being exposed to reality and by surviving the temporary surrender of their security. But they can rest in the certainty that they will be exposed to reality, not disaster.

Why? Because their master parent is only a heartbeat away.

THE BLEND
Master parents know that they have quite a challenge here.

On the one hand, they know they need to fight to protect their children's innocence. When children lose that, they lose something irreplaceable.

On the other hand, they know they need to push their children out into the real world so they don't get slaughtered in their ignorance. They refuse to believe the myth that it is their responsibility to shield their children from all bad influences.

Many parents make the mistake of thinking that protecting innocence is the same thing as shielding from reality. In the short run, it looks like they are protecting the innocence of their children, but in the long run, they're really exposing their children to disaster. Children who've been shielded from reality have had no preparation, no advance warning, no opportunity to grow strong in the face of ugly situations or dreadful people.

Master parents make no such mistake. They define innocence in part as careful exposure to reality. We actually protect the innocence of our children by exposing them to reality. This is what the Master Parent does with us. "I am sending you out like sheep among wolves," he says, no argument expected. "Therefore be as shrewd as snakes and as innocent as doves." What does this mean?

SHREWD AS SNAKES
The Master Parent expects us to know the score. He tells us to "be on your guard against men." He prepares us so we won't need to learn everything the hard way. Master parents expect their children to know the score, to be on guard, to learn so they won't fall into disaster. We define *shrewd* as being smarter and wiser, not tougher and more experienced. We're the ones talking about issues with our children, and we're doing it first. We have no taboo subjects.

Jesus told a story of a crooked manager who lost his job because he mismanaged a rich man's possessions. The manager, instead of simply giving a final account of his work, seems to take his crookedness to another level as he gives the rich man's debtors big credits so they'll think well of the manager. The crowd that heard Jesus tell this story was probably waiting for the punch line, where the rich man gave the crook what he deserved.

It is a seemingly simple story, but the punch line Jesus actually used was complex and shocking: "The master commended the dishonest manager because he had acted shrewdly." Whoa! The master praised this guy after firing him for dishonesty, because he went on to give discounts at the master's expense? Yep. And Jesus tells us why: "For the people of this world are more shrewd in dealing with their own kind than are the people of the light." So, in effect, Jesus praises the crooked but shrewd manager, and he praises the master who values shrewdness.

But Jesus isn't done with the shock. He goes on to give the moral of the story: "I tell you, use worldly wealth to gain friends for yourselves, so that when it is gone, you will be welcomed into eternal dwellings." Double whoa! Use the wealth that actually all belongs to God to "gain friends for yourselves"? Yes. Use money to buy friends. That's another idea you won't hear preached very often, if ever.

But master parents preach it. They preach this whole story. They commend their children for acting shrewdly. They praise them for being more shrewd than their peers: "Wow, Kiddo, that was really well said! I'll bet he didn't know what hit him." We teach them to be shrewd with both the "people of this world" and "the people of the light." And we teach them the real value of money— that it can be used "to gain friends for yourselves." Shrewd people give money away because it will make a better life for them here than holding on to it for themselves will. It will get them a rousing reception in glory, where they "will be welcomed into eternal dwellings" by the people they helped.

The point of shrewdness isn't to make others look bad.

Shrewdness teaches our children to live well, to choose with wisdom and savvy, and not to be taken advantage of because of willful ignorance.

But shrewdness is not just about protecting ourselves and what we have. On the contrary, biblical shrewdness includes generously and strategically giving away what we have. We teach our children to work hard to keep what they have in order that they can work hard to give it away.

How do master parents teach shrewdness? Using money and possessions is a powerful place to start. These resources hit every one of us where we live and plan—and worry. When most people talk about being "shrewd about money," they mean being skilled at getting more money for oneself. At first, God seems to teach the opposite: We should be skilled at getting more money in order to give it away. So generosity is certainly a part of it.

But why is this shrewd? This is the question that master parents grapple with and try to get across to their children. It's shrewd because it really does pay big dividends now. We can have an impact, we can help people enjoy life and be successful, we can show people how to be generous, and we can experience people (at least most people) showing appreciation and even returning kindness. And we're using only what the Master Parent gives us, because there isn't anything that he hasn't given us.

But that's only part of the shrewdness. We teach our children that it's also shrewd to accumulate and distribute money because it has long-term growth potential. It will pay off in heaven with "well dones," rewards, more responsibility, appreciation, and a celebration of their investment. Shrewdness to gain money returns zero on our investments in heaven. Shrewdness to invest in others returns more than we can even imagine.

So we show our children how to be shrewd about money. We teach our little children to share their toys and treats, and we teach them to sometimes give part or all of them away. Then, just like the Master Parent does with us, we give them even more, because they've shown themselves to be trustworthy, to be shrewd. We don't feel like our children are being taken advantage of when they give things away; instead, we commend their shrewdness. It's an upside-down principle, just like most kingdom principles are. Master parents get it, and love it, and teach it.

Shrewdness always has this interesting blend of "You can't put one over on me, but I can put one over on the world." People will still try to take advantage of our children, but they won't be able to pull it off. And then our children will turn right around and freely share or give away what people were trying to take by force or deception: money, possessions, time, energy, love, affection. Many people will think our children are smart when they protect themselves and stupid when they give themselves away. But both actions in God's world are driven by the same thing: shrewdness.

The Master Parent values shrewdness highly, and so do master parents.

INNOCENT AS DOVES

Our Master Parent expects us to steer clear of the details of evil. He expects us to walk with our eyes straight ahead, veering neither to the right or the to left. Master parents also expect their children to steer clear of the details of evil and walk the same straight path.

So we talk about purity and abstinence, and we emphasize virginity of the mind. We teach our children that being pure is not simply about avoiding direct actions; it's also about avoiding the direct thoughts that lead to the direct actions. We teach them that anything they can say yes to, they also have the grace and power to say no to.

We also talk with our children about recovering lost innocence. If they slip, all is not lost. They can rally by flying far away from the dirt that sullied them. "Oh, that I had the wings of a dove! I would fly away and be at rest. . . . I would hurry to my place of shelter, far from the tempest and storm." They can fly to God, and they can fly to us. We will protect them from the tempest of guilt and the storm of shame.

Shrewdness and innocence, protection and exposure, have application to our interface with evil. In a striking biblical passage, our Master Parent tells us to "live as children of light. . . . Have nothing to do with the fruitless deeds of darkness, but rather expose them. For it is shameful even to mention what the disobedient do in secret. But everything exposed by the light becomes visible."

The key question is, "How can we expose the deeds of darkness if it is shameful to talk about them?" We see that:

- God expects us to have "nothing to do" with evil, but he does expect us to "expose" the "deeds of darkness." The shrewd part starts with not participating in these deeds, but it goes beyond that. We're supposed to expose the deeds—get them out in the open, out in the light, where people can see them for what they really are, the sin that deceives and destroys but cannot satisfy. Master parents do the same with their children. We encourage them not to participate in evil (like being cliquish and exclusive with people at school), but we get these things out in the open and put the light on them, where our children can see all the warts and scars (e.g., the effects of arrogance and meanness on them or other people they know). Exposing our children to reality means exposing the deeds of darkness.

- He expects us not to talk about—not even to *mention*—what sinful people do in the hidden, evil corners of their lives. The "innocent" part starts with avoidance of the details that devour. We don't wallow around in the stories and gory or sensual details that fill up a huge percentage of daily newspapers and newscasts. Master parents avoid this garbage with their children. We don't talk about these details, and we don't join conversations with others who do. We know there is an attraction to these particulars, but we say no to them and teach and show our children to do the same.

Let's say you have opened up communication with your thirteen-year-old daughter. You've talked in general terms about sexual issues, including areas that are sinful and areas that are just not beneficial. You keep the lines open and revisit this topic on a regular basis. This is being shrewd and exposing the potential disasters with the light. Then one day your daughter comes home and tells you that she overheard a boy asking a girl for sex "in a certain way," and that the girl agreed.

At this point, you are at a crossroads. If you do the easy and natural thing and ask, "What did he *say?*" or "What did she agree to do?" you've gone beyond being shrewd and entered into "shameful" conversation that will destroy your daughter's innocence. But if you do the harder and supernatural thing, you'll instead ask questions like "Why would a girl even listen to a request like that?" or "What do you think the long-term effects on those two young people will be?"

Now you're bringing the light to bear. You've exposed the barren nothingness of the situation without talking about what those young people might have been planning to do. You've exposed your daughter to reality while protecting her innocence. Master parents work hard to develop their skills in talking about the substance of important issues without talking about the titillating details.

On the matter of protection and exposure, our Master Parent tells us that he will protect us if we do things for him and the kingdom. He "protects the way of his faithful ones." At the same time, he tells us that he will let us be exposed to danger and suffering if we do things for him and the kingdom. "Dear friends, do not be surprised at the painful trial you are suffering, as though something strange were happening to you. But rejoice that you participate in the sufferings of Christ."

It's not that sometimes God is protecting us and sometimes he isn't. He's always protecting us. There is never a time when we're floating around out there on our own. But he does allow some things into our lives to challenge us, to allow us to "participate in the sufferings of Christ."

Master parents take the same approach with their children. We protect them, and we let them be exposed to danger and suffering. We show them how to avoid evil and to respond well and quickly to punishment, how to persevere and grow under discipline, and how to rejoice when they suffer for doing good. And we let them see that there are three ways to suffer: first, for doing wrong—a poor option; second, for discipline—a growth option; and third, for doing good—a blessed option.

Master parents push their children out into the world even as they fight to protect them from the world, just as the Master Parent does with us. "My prayer is not that you take them out of the world," said Jesus, "but that you protect them from the evil one. . . . As you sent me into the world, I have sent them into the world." He prays for effective exposure and effective protection, and we should do the same for our children.

As we go out into the world, Jesus warns us, and we should warn our children, "Be on your guard against men." To be effective, to give them a really useful tool, we tell them to do what our Master Parent tells us to do: "Watch out for false prophets. They come to you in sheep's clothing, but inwardly they are ferocious wolves. By their fruit you will recognize them."

Master parents know that the key is to get their children to look at the "fruit" people produce, rather than listening to their philosophies or scrutinizing their behavior. Are they helping people, displaying generosity, and teaching truth with humility? Then they're probably not wolves. Are they brutalizing people, making demands on people, and teaching (even truth) with arrogance? Then they're probably wolves.

We don't need to study people's private lives or dissect what they say. If we get into those things, we're probably going to lose our innocence. We need to look at the fruit, just like Jesus said: "Do people pick grapes from thornbushes, or figs from thistles? Likewise every good tree bears good fruit, but a bad tree bears bad fruit. A good tree cannot bear bad fruit, and a bad tree cannot bear good fruit. . . . Thus, by their fruit you will recognize them."

Master parents spend a lot of time with their children looking at the fruit of people's lives and drawing lessons for their own lives from this review. We teach our children that talk is cheap. We show them that people can make mistakes, but this doesn't automatically mean they're producing "bad fruit." And we show them that the Master Parent is talking about the *quality* of the fruit, not the *quantity*. Size of ministry is no measure of the quality of the fruit, although size is used as a benchmark—erroneously—all the time. The question is a quality question: Is the fruit good, or is it bad?

The challenge master parents have in both protecting innocence and exposing to reality is highlighted in the very tension between being told, "In regard to evil be infants," and being told, "Then we will no longer be infants, tossed back and forth by the waves, and blown here and there by every wind of teaching and by the cunning and craftiness of men in their deceitful scheming."

What does "in regard to evil be infants" mean to master parents who are trying to raise innocent children? It means we:

- **Shield our children from the details of evil.** We teach our children to say with the psalmist, "I will walk in my house with blameless heart. I will set before my eyes no vile thing." We don't need to stick our head in a sewer to know that it stinks.

- **Fill them with the many good things of life.** Why focus on the crud when there are so many wonderful facets of life to enjoy? We don't have time to spend on miserable corruption. We teach our children to focus on the glory road and the flowers crowding the path.

- **Walk away from corrupting conversations.** We teach our children that it isn't rude to walk away from filth. We teach them that it *is* rude to stay put—rude to God. Our children learn that Christian graciousness isn't defined as "trapped by trash."

What does "Then we will no longer be infants" mean to master parents who are trying to raise children who understand reality? It means we:

- **Show our children that life comes in "waves"**—good days and bad days, times of success and times of failure, friends who go the extra mile and friends who betray our souls. We train our children to be aware of this and to take it in stride.

- **Teach our children that there are a hundred interpretations of every possible issue**—that ninety of them are completely bogus, only seven or eight have even a bit of truth, and only two or three have strong validity. We explain that these interpretations will blow in like the wind, coming out of nowhere, swirling around and creating storms, and probably be carried on the wind—in the form of radio and television programs. In other words, we teach them to be very skeptical of what they hear. We say with Jesus, "Consider carefully how you listen."

- **Tell our children about the schemes that people can come up with to deceive them,** and the great "cunning and craftiness" these people have at their disposal. Master parents don't just talk about the schemes that are "out there" in the "world"; they spend even more time on the schemes that are "in here" in the church. "Where do the wolves go?" they ask their children. "To where the sheep are, of course."

To win any of life's important battles, our children have to have enough innocence to maintain their idealism and enough reality to fight the devil. We need to show them how to do this and let them know that it requires hard work. "Doubting everything or believing everything are two equally convenient solutions," wrote Henri Poincaré in *La Science et l'hypothèse,* "both of which save us from thinking." We have to teach our children how not to doubt everything (to be innocent) and how not to believe everything (to be shrewd) at the same time.

A model for the blend of these two great initiatives is the greenhouse. When a plant is small and tender, we keep it inside, away from the elements. As it matures and grows stronger, we can put it outside during the day, whenever the weather is not too extreme. When, after a healthy combination of greenhouse protection and exposure to the elements, the plant becomes hardy, we can trust leaving it outdoors through the night and into the more extreme weather. In fact, it is actually the exposure to the elements that makes the plant strong and ready to spend the night outside on its own without being damaged or destroyed.

Let your little ones stay inside, but put them out when the day is gentle and full of promise. And let your older ones stay outside, but pull them back in when the day is rough and full of storms.

Your Master Parent is also the Master Gardener, and he'll show you the Way.

LAST THOUGHTS

If we protect our children's innocence without exposing them to reality, we prepare them to be slaughtered by big monsters because they've never had to battle the little ones. If we expose them to reality without protecting their innocence, we replace the great childlike virtues of faith, hope, trust, and creativity with early onset-cynicism.

All of us, no matter how battered, long for the days of innocence and simplicity. We don't want innocence at the expense of being street-smart, or because of the loss of hard-won experience. We want both sides: protection and exposure, simplicity and street

Nine

MASTER PARENTS KEEP THEIR DISTANCE AND CONNECT AT THE SOUL

He asks, "Should you not tremble in my presence?"
~ But ~
"In him we live and move and have our being."

One of the great balancing acts in all relationships is between separation and togetherness, and parenting is no exception.

We want our children to respect us and give us space. At the same time, we want them to be right there with us, enjoying the wild ride at our side.

Master parents continually keep their children at arm's length, and master parents continually draw their children as close as the beating of their own hearts.

So you, along with Aretha Franklin, want a little R-E-S-P-E-C-T? You're disturbed that your children won't "look up" to you, even though they're only three feet tall? The Master Parent will add his "amen" to that. "Should you not tremble in my presence?" he asks of people who are obviously not predisposed to tremble in his presence. "As the heavens are higher than the earth, so are my ways

181

higher than your ways and my thoughts than your thoughts." Now that's distance!

Attempts on our part to break down the distance, perhaps all the way to zero, fall on hard times. "You thought I was altogether like you," God says angrily. He isn't altogether like us, just as we are not altogether like our children. We are like God, but we are not God. Our children are like us, but they are not us.

On the other hand, you want your children to like you and love you and want to be with you. Our Master Parent has cried over this one. "O Jerusalem, Jerusalem," Jesus cried out. "How often I have longed to gather your children together, as a hen gathers her chicks under her wings, but you were not willing."

Any parents who have tried to get close to their children, to talk with them or hug them, but in return have been brushed off or rejected, understand this cry. Our Master Parent sets his heart on getting close to us. "I will bring him near and he will come close to me. . . . Who is he who will devote himself to be close to me?" You can hear the longing and feel the pain. What parents *don't* want their children to devote themselves to closeness?

So the Master Parent has quite a balancing act. What a complex and interesting Parent he is! "Stay outside the Holy of Holies," he warns. "Come inside the veil," he woos. He wants both. He can have both. If we are willing, so can we. And as master parents—if we are willing—we can have both with our own offspring.

KEEPING YOUR DISTANCE

If you're going to do anything worthwhile as a master parent, you'd better keep some distance between you and your children.

Our Master Parent wants us to respect who he is, his place in the scheme of things, and his unmatchable power.

Master parents want the same things. We want our children to respect our person, our position, and our power. What does this mean?

- **Person.** Disrespecting or cursing our Master Parent is a very bad plan. Master parents know that this plan doesn't get any better if our children disrespect or curse us. "If a man curses his father or mother, his lamp will be snuffed out in pitch darkness," we are warned. "The eye that mocks a father, that scorns obedience to a mother, will be pecked out by the ravens of the valley, will be eaten by the vultures." Eye pecking, vulture eating, and death, simply for mistreating a parent? Not simply. In this, there is no "simply." The Master Parent demands respect for himself and for us. There is no viable alternative.

- **Position.** Our Master Parent says, "Do not come any closer. . . . The place where you are standing is holy ground." Although they're most certainly not God, master parents know that their position requires some distance. There is something holy about the role, and we know that there should be some measure of respect, even awe, for the position. This is why children are told to "honor your father and mother." There are no qualifiers, like "Honor them if they are honorable." Just honor them, period. This is so important to God that he makes it "the first commandment with a promise—'that it may go well with you and that you may enjoy long life on the earth.' "

- **Power.** The Master Parent is a force that can't be reckoned with. No one can successfully challenge him. "Great is our Lord and mighty in power." In the same way, master parents should be a force that can't be reckoned with. We intend to use everything at our disposal—our prayers, our wisdom, our knowledge, our passions, our convictions, our resources—to have maximum impact on our children. We will share power (see chapter 6), but we won't abdicate our responsibility or yield to rebels.

We make it easier for our children, of course, if we actually *are* people worthy of respect, if we actually fulfill our responsibilities as parents, and if we use our power in a way that builds our children and families up. But even if we're stumbling around, even if we miss the mark, we still want and need our children to respect who we are, what we do, and how we do it.

The good news is that our children want and need this as well. "Parents are the pride of their children," we are told matter-of-factly. We aren't told that we are the pride of our children if we're perfect, or very good, or even just okay. All of us have known people who have really awful parents, and these people are still trying to honor them, still trying to make something of the relationship, still fighting a no-win situation, because "parents are the pride of their children."

You might be one of these people, still wanting your parents to be better, more honorable, more respectable than they actually are. At some point, you have to face the truth and admit that they aren't these things. You have to move on. But know that your desires are completely appropriate and entirely understandable. "The voice of parents is the voice of gods," said William Shakespeare, "for to their children they are heaven's lieutenants." The Master Parent has built the need to honor parents into our souls.

So master parents work hard to make this honoring business as easy as possible. We rise up and act like the parents we have chosen to be. We refuse to let our natural desire to be close to our children keep us from being honorable parents. We resist the devilish deception that if we broach a certain subject with our children, or correct them on this, or punish them on that, then all will be lost in our relationship. We may not have understood all this when we decided to have children, but we understand it now.

We want our children to love us, but not at the expense of our responsibility as parents. We know we're going to have to give an account of how we handled our stewardship of these human beings and we're not going to get a bad evaluation because we wanted to be liked. This means we have to be willing to stare down some oft-used and well-worn weapons:

1. **Rejection.** We can't be surprised by our children's rejection of us, just as the Master Parent isn't surprised by ours: "When I have brought them into the land flowing with milk and honey . . . and when they eat their fill and thrive, they will turn to other gods . . . rejecting me and breaking my covenant. . . . I know what they are disposed to do." We have to be willing to accept our children's rejection. No great leadership has ever occurred where the leader wasn't willing to take it on the chin. If Moses got rejected after leading God's children out of slavery, we shouldn't be too amazed if we get rejected for leading ours out of adolescence.

2. **Emotional blackmail.** The Master Parent accepts no "bargains" offered as blackmail: "Indeed, God does not listen to their empty plea; the Almighty pays no attention to it." Master parents don't listen to empty pleas either. What is an empty plea? It's a phony appeal to relationship made to get something. "If you loved me, you'd let me go!" "I hate you!" "You're a bad mommy." Ouch! It does hurt to hear our beloved children committing such relational felonies. But there's only one thing worse than hearing them: *giving in to them.*

3. **Anger.** Our Master Parent is no friend of temper tantrums. "If you remain hostile toward me and refuse to listen to me," he warns, "I will multiply your afflictions seven times over, as your sins deserve." Master parents take this to heart. We never, under any circumstances, yield in the face of hostility. That's why we have parental power. Many parents make the mistake of catering to tantrums and bribing children away from anger. Master parents say, "Keep it up, and I will multiply your afflictions seven times over, as your sins deserve."

4. **Misuse of our care.** The Master Parent expects his children "to be content whatever the circumstances." Master parents expect this of their children as well. In the midst of all-too-common youthful narcissism, our kids can transform our care for

them into a tool of their own selfish desires. "Mom, I really would like to have that new bedroom furniture. I know you want me to have nice things. I know you don't want me to be embarrassed by this little-girl stuff." We know that allowing and feeding this self-centered angling destroys any hope of our children being satisfied with their lives, or of us being satisfied with them.

The Master Parent doesn't allow us to use these "tools," and we won't allow our children to use them either. He uses distance as a solution, and master parents do the same. If our children act like this, we move away.

There are a number of ways we can keep our distance. Keeping our distance can mean that we allow our children freedom from the unforgiving microscope of parental scrutiny. Our Master Parent is the same way. He's not constantly focusing on every deficiency of our lives. He doesn't keep score. "If you, O Lord, kept a record of sins, O Lord, who could stand?" The answer is "no one." He's able to keep us in existence, in spite of our many failings, because he doesn't keep records.

In the same way, master parents know that their children also need a measure of "benign neglect." We need a sort of blissful unawareness of much that they are doing. Otherwise, some of those things will drive us crazy, and then we'll drive our kids crazy. We'll end up focusing on and obsessing about some problem until we create a Frankenstein out of our own bits and pieces of concern. What was a normal problem can be turned into a monumental one by parental overfocus.

Master parents provide the distance that lets some of the warts disappear on their own. We always remember to add a bit of overlooking to our oversight.

But what if our children march over into real wickedness? Well, what does our Master Parent do? He is "too pure to look on evil." Even though he is aware of all the evil that we do, he chooses not to dwell on it. In fact, he can't stand to look at it. He puts a lot of distance between himself and people who are way off the mark. "The Lord is far from the wicked," we are told.

This is why he said, when thinking about the sin at Sodom and Gomorrah, "I will go down and see if what they have done is as bad as the outcry that has reached me." Why would he need to go down and see, if he is God? Because his eyes are "too pure to look on evil." He knows that it's there, and he'll deal with it at the appropriate time, but under no circumstances is he going to fill up his mind with this corruption.

Master parents follow his example. We are aware of what's going on with our children. If they get out of hand, we'll "go down and see" what they are doing. But even if they're way off base, we don't allow ourselves to get into the details of their sins. It won't do us or them any good.

We ask our Master Parent to help us not to dwell on the details, not to "look on evil." We put distance between ourselves and the wrongdoers. This is a time for distance, so that we can be fair judges. And the distance itself might help bring our children to their senses, as it did with the Prodigal Son. Most Christians have come to understand this great principle through experiencing one of the greatest negatives of sin: separation from God.

Let's look at an example. Say you have two children, and you overhear the older one involving the younger one in a game of "let's do this and lie about it if Mom asks" in the basement. So, like the Master Parent, you "go down and see" and break the situation up, reprimanding the older child for his role in the situation. This would be a good time to isolate the older child from the younger for a while, of course, but also a good time to put some space between the older child and you. Leave this child out of some family dinners and events, do some reading and projects with the younger one alone, leave the older one out of participating in some family decisions. Let the distance work for you by letting him see that his behavior has a cost.

For some reason, our Master Parent thought it was important to let us know that "Jesus often withdrew to lonely places and prayed." He was only on earth a short time, and yet he often went off by himself. Why? Because he was lonely? No, it was the *places* that were lonely, not Jesus. He needed space. Time to think and pray. Time to be alone.

In the course of normal life, we need space as well. Master parents know that space holds great advantages for families. First, we give each other the opportunity to think about how we're doing in our relationships, including the ones we have with each other. Second, we avoid the buildup of friction, the little ongoing annoyances and frictions that can destroy great relationships. Third, we allow each other the room to grow in different and interesting ways. And fourth, we lessen the chance that family members will think negatively of one another.

We need and want our children to give us space. This means we want them to know we're not their maids, janitors, gofers, or chauffeurs. We have lives of our own, things important to us that don't include them, and we intend to make some space—lots of space—for these things to occur.

Master-parenting means making keeping our distance an important part of the relationship. We don't spend 100 percent of our time with our children. No friendship could survive that unending contact, and no parent-child relationship can either. We don't let our homes revolve around our children, because God is the center of the universe, not them. We want to produce closeness, not selfishness. We have to find a way to do the authority thing, do the friendship thing, and still have a life.

Often people in Christian circles will refer to the goal of being a "Proverbs 31 woman." Without actually reading the passage, we can be led to believe that Proverbs 31 talks about someone who is a "full-time mother"—someone who has few, if any, serious interests outside mothering. But it simply isn't so.

This woman is a full-time dynamo. She "works vigorously,"

selecting wool and flax, shopping "from afar," planning the day before anyone else is awake, evaluating and buying real estate, using her earnings to expand her business into vineyards. She trades and multitasks to carry on a fine garment business as well. She makes time to care for the poor. And she takes care of herself, dressing "in fine linen and purple" (no frumpiness here).

Only three out of twenty-two verses even refer to children, and two of those (verses 15 and 21) are indirect. The other verse says simply, "Her children stand and bless her." Why do they do this? Perhaps they respond so differently than most children do to their mothers because they have a mother who is their model, not their master (or their slave). She's showing them what it means to live a full life by living one, right before their eyes.

This amazing woman is too busy having a wide impact (which most certainly includes her children) to take a narrow view of "full-time mothering." She is a mother full-time—she always has her children in her mind and heart—but she doesn't "mother" full-time. This is why her children appreciate her rather than resenting her (if she is acting as master) or taking her for granted (if she is acting as slave).

This Bible-time master parent somehow learned that every child needs a woman who is his mother full-time, but no child needs a full-time mother.

The wonderful side benefit of giving ourselves space is that we give our children space at the same time. Life is not "Dad" or "Mom"; life is life—a wild and adventurous ride, with Dad and Mom at the wheel (for a while).

There are a number of roles that our Master Parent never asks us to play as his children. Master parents avoid putting their children into these roles. We don't ask them to be:

- **Counselors.** The Master Parent says, "Who is this that darkens my counsel with words without knowledge?" He doesn't expect us to give him counsel, and we should follow his lead. Our parental position makes any "child-as-parental-counselor" action very problematic. It can become more difficult to avoid this as our children become older, seem to know more, and are willing to express their opinion about everything (including us). If you're a single or divorced parent and doing it alone, you can also be more tempted to find help from the nearest available source: your kids. If we allow our children to become our therapists, they end up trying to recreate us in their image. With all our other problems, we don't need to be remade into an adolescent.

- **Sounding boards.** Good advice is hard to find, and these children are our own flesh and blood. It's easy to start bouncing ideas off them when they are simply not ready to react with wisdom and balance. For example, you might be thinking about moving to another home. Perhaps you begin talking with your daughter about it. Rather than giving you useful input and advice, your daughter could end up feeling great amounts of anxiety over the issue. Or she might get her heart set on the new house, and if it doesn't happen, she might end up disappointed and disillusioned. It's good to share ideas with our children when those ideas have a measure of form, but doing so too early in the game can create lots of personal and relational problems.

- **Shoulders to cry on.** Life is tough. After we've had a hard day, it's nice to have someone to "let down" with. Master parents don't let that someone be their kids. It's fine to fill them in on issues and challenges in our lives so they can learn about life and follow our example, but it's not okay to make them our outlet for anger, grief, or other emotional pain.

In an article about turning children into peers and buddies, one expert expressed great concern over parents: "The power [has] shifted to children. Parents said, 'I have to focus on making my child happy,' as opposed to 'I have to parent most appropriately.'"

The director of the Center for the Family at Pepperdine University has added, "Problems also arise [when parents make] an effort to avoid 'harming' the relationship, rather than teaching children moderation and the limits of life." When we're afraid to keep our distance, we become afraid to be the parents that our children need.

It's clear that there is a place for distance in our relationship with our kids. There are times of failure, when they should tremble in our presence. There are times of manipulation, when we should walk away. There are times of personal need or wounding, when we should go to our Master Parent instead of them. There are times of great and useful work, when we should do things other than parenting so that we can parent with excellence. And there are times when we just make space for the sake of space.

Master parents use all these strategies.

CONNECTING AT THE SOUL

If you're going to do anything worthwhile as a master parent, you'd better connect with your children intimately at the soul.

Master parents don't fall for the old myth that you can't be in charge if you try to be their friend.

Our Master Parent created us for *relationship*, not so he would have something to do. Master parents created their children for relationship as well, not so we would have something to do. Nursing and caring for children's needs and training them and educating them are not the "stuff" of parenting, not the core. As it is with our Master Parent and us, it's all about connection. E. M. Forster, the English novelist who wrote *Passage to India*, once summed up life by saying, "Connection is everything." When work and jobs and vacations and activities are distant memories, the only important things that remain are the connections we have with other human beings. And surely our children are at or near the top of the connection list.

The Master Parent is ardent in his desire to see us as close to him as possible. How close? "In him we live and move and have our being," taught Paul. "As some of your own poets have said, 'We are his offspring.' " Our very existence is *in* him. That's where we live—in him. That's where we move—in him. And that's where our very being resides—*in him.*

Master parents want an "inside" relationship like that with their children. They make sure that their children are living and moving inside them—inside their prayers, their spirits, their thoughts, their hearts, their *beings.* Our children are our offspring, as we are God's. In a very real sense, they are part of us.

And master parents take the time to crawl inside their children's hearts. We know that entering a human heart is a time-consuming, difficult, and at times frustrating activity, but we persist because no matter what else happens, we are going to connect at the soul. Hearts are like intricate caves, and we become relational spelunkers who dedicate ourselves to exploring and finding the holes. We know our children have a parent-sized hole in their hearts, and with the help of heaven, we are going to fill it.

Our Master Parent "sets the lonely in families." As Christians, we are in his family, the family of God. As parents, we have created a family and our Master Parent has set some new people in it. The lonely.

Who are the lonely? We are. Our children are. "It is not good . . . to be alone," God says in one of the simplest and most powerful statements about togetherness. Indeed, it isn't good to be alone. If we're honest we'll admit that at least one of the main reasons we had a family was so that we would never have to be alone again.

Once we are in a family, however, we can choose to "love" in a way that doesn't end loneliness. We can translate "love" into caretaking and teaching and punishing and entertaining, and we can totally miss the mark on ending loneliness. The simple truth is that we can "love" in a way that doesn't connect souls. When all the schoolwork and chores and discussions and disagreements and shared experiences are done, the crucial question for our hearts is "Is she my friend?"

Why do we often feel so disconnected from our children? Probably because we *are* disconnected from our children. If we feel this way, it's probably reality. Master parents face it, acknowledge it, and set their hearts on redemption.

How can you know if you are disconnected? There are clues. Are your children coming to you and talking about real things? Are they talking about mistakes and problems? Do you have healthy discussions and disagreements? Any real relationship has give and take, change and growth. Do your children like hanging out with you, because you're as "cool" as their friends (because you've learned that "cool" means you're interested in them, not that you dress like them or act like them)? Connection doesn't dry up because it's older. It dries up because it's not watered.

What is connection? Connection certainly includes hanging out together and being buddies, but it goes well beyond those spending-time activities. It is too easy to think we're connecting when we're really just occupying the same moment in time.

"Connecting at the soul" means going for the deepest variety of connection. We are vulnerable with each other; we share our thoughts and feelings and questions and doubts and observations. We trust each other—not because we're related but because we're *trustworthy*. We make time for each other; we're a high priority, not a no priority. As I was writing the book *1001 Ways to Connect with Your Kids,* I was struck over and over again by the many ways there are to turn ordinary days into extraordinary relationships.

And master parents never confuse nearness with closeness. We can have the illusion that we're connected because we're in the same room as our children. This is not connection. We can't expect connection to happen just because we're living in the same place. It won't. We can think that conversation will bring us together, but it will push us apart if we use talk that's disconnected from our children's world or that sounds like we're checking up on them.

Master parents use unexpected questions to open up real dialogue. They ask questions designed to get more than one-word answers. Instead of asking, "Did you have a good time at the party?" they ask, "What were the three most interesting (or surprising) things that happened at the party?" They ask themselves, *Does she care about what I'm asking?* and *Will my questions really grab his interest?* We ask questions about the home, like "What would you do differently if you were the parent?" and "What one thing would you change about our family if you could?" No subject is off-limits: "What three things in the Bible bother you most?" and "Why do you think our culture is so obsessed with sex?"

"What other nation is so great as to have their gods near them the way the Lord our God is near us whenever we pray to him?" the author of Deuteronomy asks with obvious awe about the closeness of the Master Parent to his children. He wants us to talk with him, to ask him for what we need, to have dialogue. When we do, he's as close to us as our own being. Whatever other god is being prayed to, there won't be any connection, because no one is at home.

Master parents respond like the Master Parent when their children talk to them or ask for what they need or have dialogue. We get near them. We *really* get near them. We stop putting away the dishes or cleaning the garage, and we focus on this wondrous being who is before us. We ignore the distractions, refuse to even answer the phone, forget for a moment the "to do" list in our heads. We're not omnipresent like our Master Parent, but for one or two blessed moments we can be totally devoted to being connected.

The psalmist says, "Yet I am always with you; you hold me by my right hand. . . . As for me, it is good to be near God." God touches us. Jesus "took the children in his arms." He couldn't keep his hands off his Creation, off his children. He touches us every day, every time we let him. No one else in our lives will ever get to that level.

Master parents know that it is okay to be all-out, crazy-nuts connected with their children. There are times when *no* distance is the best—when we want them in our laps or in our arms, even when they are ten, or fifteen, or thirty. We are like our Master Parent, who "gathers the lambs in his arms and carries them close to his heart." We know that no one has ever been loved too much, and we're determined to give as much love as possible to our children.

In times of trouble, we can say to our Master Parent, "O Lord, do not forsake me; be not far from me, O my God. Come quickly to help me." We don't want a distant God; we want a Velcro-close God: "My soul clings to you; your right hand upholds me." It's too scary out here; we want to be *in there:* "Your life is now hidden with Christ in God." That's what we want—to be hidden in him.

Master parents won't forsake their children. We are close to them, quick to help, and willing to hold them up no matter the cost. "Here we are," we say. "You can hide your life in here." We know that times of grief and heartbreak are perfect opportunities to draw close to our children. Our Master Parent is "close to the brokenhearted and saves those who are crushed in spirit," and we can do the same.

Master parents watch their children with their hearts and notice the start of little sicknesses of the soul. We tell our kids that life is scary, that it's normal to be afraid. And we illustrate this by talking about how we've dealt with our own fears and worries. We can share our losses and wash them with two sets of tears. Times of sickness—ours and theirs—are also wonderful opportunities for building closeness. In the upside-down world of master-parenting, we know that some of the best opportunities for building closeness occur during times of weakness. Similarly, some of the best relationship building takes place after our children have been punished or have spent some time in the school of hard knocks.

One of the delicious aspects of connecting at the soul is that through it we show our children how to connect with our Master Parent, who is also *their* God. Perhaps the best way to develop the spiritual life of our children is to let them experience real relationship with us. To paraphrase John, "Anyone who does not love his [parent], whom he has seen, cannot love God, whom he has not seen."

Think about how you can say, "I love you" like you never have before. In new and different and more effective ways, let your kids know that you love them. Ask them what topics they would like to discuss, things that lie deep in their minds and hearts. Holidays and traditions are a great time to share your love. Keep working through traditions until you find two or three that do more than fill time and discharge your duty. Catch them being good. When your kids do something really outstanding, find as many ways as you can to show them how proud you are of them and how much you understand them. Pull their friends into your heart and create a "triple-braided cord [which] is not easily broken."

One authority said, "You may have moments with your teenagers when you actually do feel like friends. . . . Just don't forget, those moments are illusory. You aren't friends, not really." What a sad teaching. What a depressing picture of family life. Don't believe it for a minute. Deep friendship with your children is no illusion; it can be as real as the longings for it in your heart.

It's never too late for us to connect with our children, not as long as both of us are still on the planet, not as long as we're both still breathing. God is the God of second chances. We can make a comeback and reconnect at any age. Someday you will both want connection again. And the magic of relational redemption can help erase a lifetime of lonely distance.

In one of the great and humbling ironies of life, we care for our children when they are young and helpless, and they care for us when we are old and helpless. The loop closes. The circle is completed. When all the battles have been fought and all the problems have been faced, the only thing still standing is connection.

At the soul.

THE BLEND
We have been given the challenge of having our children tied to us, flesh and blood, but needing to move them to some safe relational distance.

"Am I only a God nearby," declares the Lord, "and not a God far away?" The answer is that he is a God both nearby *and* far away.

The birth experience gives us a picture of this. The baby is inside the mother, intimately connected to her through a cord. Birth brings a distance that was never there before. The cord is no longer useful and must be cut—but then the baby is immediately put into the mother's arms. There is closeness, and there is space.

This is the rhythm of distance and connection.

The Master Parent's answer to distance is closeness. After his resurrection, Jesus could have condemned Thomas for his doubting (although later, at the Ascension, some of the disciples who had *seen* him were doubting!). Instead, he visits Thomas and tells him to put his hand in Jesus' side. "Touch me," he says. "Get as close as you can and be sure."

If we feel our Master Parent is too distant, we can cry out to him, "Why, O Lord, do you stand far off?" It's okay to challenge the distance. It's okay to say, "Where are you?" And we can pray, "Do not be far from me." We know that we can't get too far away from him or we're done for: "Those who are far from you will perish."

Master parents follow God's example. When our children say—with words or tone or body language—"Why are you so far away?" we respond by getting closer. "Are you coming to the concert, Dad?" "Will you be there at the play, Mom?" "When will you be home?" We hear their words and see their faces, and we are there.

When they are small, it's easier to figure out. They actually say, "Get closer!" They come in without asking and crawl into bed with us. They get scared, and they say with trembling, "Don't move!" It gets trickier when they're older. They might not actually say the words or act on their impulses or let us see them tremble. But they're still saying that they need us. Master parents have very sensitive ears, and they can hear this.

The Master Parent's answer to closeness is distance. He uses distance to see if we will cross it to find him. "He determined the times set for them and the exact places where they should live . . . so that men would seek him and perhaps reach out for him and find him, though he is not far from each one of us." He puts us "out there," but not very far out there. And then he watches to see what we will do. Just a fluttering of an arm in his direction, and we find him. The distance wasn't as far as we first thought.

Master parents follow God's example. We structure our home and family routines so there is some distance, some separation, in part to see if our children will seek relationship. We want to find out if they will reach out for us. We want them to know that if they do they will find us, because we are right there, very close, not far from each one of them. To make it real relationship, we've got to create some distance and give them the opportunity to cross it first, to take the first step.

Master parents know that there is good distance and bad distance. Let's take a look at each of these.

GOOD DISTANCE

This is the distance talked about earlier in the chapter, the distance that keeps our roles and relationships clear. It keeps us from cluttering up our relationships with discussions and activities that muddle and damage connection. Good distance is actually the distance that keeps us close.

Good distance never means disconnection. God "perceive[s] my thoughts from afar." "Where can I go from your Spirit?" David asks. "Where can I flee from your presence?" Nowhere. Nowhere is too far for God.

We need good distance, but so do our children—more so as they get older. "I need to be alone," wrote a teen in an article I read recently. "When I'm alone, I can think, and believe me, I've got a lot to think about. . . . When I go to my room and close the door, it doesn't automatically mean I'm mad." Distance for thinking is a very good distance.

Good distance also includes the distance caused by shame, as when after Jesus was arrested, "Peter followed him at a distance."

JAMES R. LUCAS

When our children have really let us down, there is a place for distance until they can see what they've done and, like Peter, break down weeping. To use the distance effectively, to use it to rebuild our relationship, we've got to let them follow at a distance for a while.

And there is good distance when they've sinned. Jesus said, about a broken man, that "the tax collector stood at a distance. He would not even look up to heaven." If our children can sin and this puts no distance between us, we're not taking sin seriously enough. The break in the relationship gives them a second reason (along with any punishment) to stop sinning.

BAD DISTANCE

Bad distance can simply be the distance of disinterest. We can focus on the television or a computer program or our newspapers and never connect with those around us. Someone has wisely said that every technical advancement in communication has brought those far away closer and has pushed those close farther away.

Bad distance can enter our homes through relational misconnection or disconnection. If we don't solve it, if we don't close the gap, the result can be horrendous. "They detest me and keep their distance," said Job. "They do not hesitate to spit in my face." Too many parents have children who detest them and keep their distance, and some even spit in their parents' faces. Master parents have radar for this type of distance, this really bad distance, and they work to close it up by connecting at the soul.

They set everything aside until they can determine the cause of this detesting and spitting. They don't explain it away ("It's just an adolescent thing") or blame it on others ("It's those terrible friends of his"). They pray and ask God for guidance and read and pour their guts out to supportive friends and cry and work and ask questions until they get to the bottom of the ugliness. Their goal is not to assign blame. Their goal is to fix the relationship.

Bad distance can also be created when we've been oppressive, unfair, or simply petty. When we've beaten our children down with things big and small, we can't realistically expect them to want to be close to us. There is no trust, no warmth, no sense of unity. This sort of bad distance has demolished countless relationships. Master parents know that if we stop doing the things that create the bad distance, it will close from miles to yards, and from yards to inches, and will finally disappear completely. Parent-child relationships are seldom cast in concrete.

MORE ON THE BLEND

When people draw in close to try to "butter up" God even though they're completely disconnected from him, his response is a mixture of anger and sadness: "These people come near to me with their mouth and honor me with their lips, but their hearts are far from me." People can try to substitute physical nearness for true closeness, but God isn't buying it.

Master parents aren't buying it either. There are periods when the only time our kids will initiate contact is when they want something. They come near, say, "Hi, how's your day going?" and maybe even thank us for something. But their heart isn't in it. They don't mean it, and in our souls we know they don't. That's when we let them know that nearness and words are poor substitutes for closeness and truth. This is when we need to create a little physical distance to match the actual distance that is between us. The goal is not to create a problem but to recognize a problem that is already there. We're not trying to create distance; we're trying to close the gap.

In part, the closeness we have to our Master Parent is related to the distance we have to evil people. "I hate all crooked dealings; I will have nothing to do with them. I will reject perverse ideas and stay away from every evil." God makes it clear that we can't be close to both him and corruption: "Don't you know that friendship with the world is hatred toward God?"

Master parents expect their children to hate the deeds of faithless people and keep that slime off themselves. We let them know that if they draw in close to people of perverse heart, people who think evil is great fun, they're automatically putting distance in our relationship. Friendship with the world—with those who hate our God—is a wedge that must separate us from those who choose it.

In great measure, our children's attitudes determine how distant or connected we should be. Though our Master Parent "is on high, he looks upon the lowly, but the proud he knows from afar." He condemns those "who say, 'Keep away; don't come near me, for I am too sacred for you!' " When we act like we're everything and he is nothing, the distance grows to infinity.

Master parents must take the same approach. Arrogance, especially arrogance of the self-righteous or religious variety, is something we must condemn. If we have prideful children, we have to know them from afar. We cannot allow them to put their religious judgmentalism all over us, saying by their actions, "I am too sacred for you!"

They have put distance between us, from the high place they think they inhabit to the low place they think we inhabit. We can't "climb up there" to connect with them, and even trying would cause our Master Parent to condemn us. We can only connect with our children if they come down off their pedestals and act like what they are: flawed people, just like us. People in need of connection, just like us. We can only wait—and hope that they will see their nakedness.

The Master Parent has made the way to close the gap between us: "Now in Christ Jesus you who once were far away have been brought near through the blood of Christ. . . . He came and preached peace to you who were far away and peace to those who were near."

Master parents know that they, too, were once far away, but they have been brought near. We've heard the preaching of peace.

We see those rebels, flesh of our flesh, so far away from us, and suddenly we see the truth: They are far away, but they can be brought near.

And we preach peace.

LAST THOUGHTS

If we keep our distance without connecting at the soul, we leave a huge, parent-sized hole in our children's hearts that they will fill with something else—probably something awful. If we connect at the soul without keeping our distance, we lose our credibility and any ability to help our children steer their lives.

I am writing this just after the twentieth anniversary of my father's death. We had a lot of distance between us, most of it bad distance. But parents really are the pride of their children, and I wanted to close that gap. As it turned out—as it usually turns out—so did he.

Neither one of us knew what we were doing, but we stumbled around in the room of life together, reaching out and finally reconnecting. To paraphrase our conversation, I said to him, "Do not be far from me," and as it turned out, he was not far at all. We had six good years together, with the distance shrinking a little more each year.

Our Master Parent calls us from our distant places: "I took you from the ends of the earth, from its farthest corners I called you. . . . I have chosen you and have not rejected you. So do not fear, for I am with you. . . . For I am the Lord, your God, who takes hold of your right hand." Master parents never buy into the lie that a parent's goal should be planned obsolescence, separation, and the breaking of one family into two.

In the rhythm of distance and connection, the distance is always a target of connection for the Master Parent. He is always calling us. The warmth and comfort we feel flow from his fingers, slipping into ours.

Master parents get it. We keep our distance, but always with our voices calling out to our children.

And always with our fingers outstretched, slipping into theirs.

Ten

MASTER PARENTS KNOW THAT LOVE IS CONDITIONAL AND LOVE IS UNFAILING

He admonishes us, "Keep yourselves in God's love"
~ But ~
he tells us, "Never will I forsake you."

One of the greatest challenges of parenting comes down to a definition: What is love? If we get it right, love means everything. If we get it wrong, love is a sentimental charade.

Master parents display conditional love to their children, and at the same time, master parents display unfailing love to their children.

So you think that there should be some mutuality to this relationship? that your children shouldn't treat you like dirt? The Master Parent thinks you're on the right track. "O Lord," prayed Daniel, "the great and awesome God, who keeps his covenant of love with all who love him and obey his commands."

God only keeps his covenant of love, his unfailing love, with a certain group of people: those who love him in return and who show it by obeying him. The implication is clear: If we don't love him and obey his commands, there is no more covenant of love. We've broken it. God won't honor what we don't want.

Should we follow God's example? You're probably thinking that these are your children and you somehow need to love them, right? Stinky or no, they are your children forever, right? Yes, says the Master Parent. You're right on track. "I trust in God's unfailing love for ever and ever," rejoiced the psalmist.

His love won't ever go away. It's unfailing. It goes on and on, an unstoppable river of love, waiting for us to drink from it, waiting for us to jump in.

The Master Parent is clear. His love is unfailing, but only for those who access it, only for those who meet his conditions.

Master parents see this and learn how to live it in their parenting.

KNOWING LOVE MUST BE CONDITIONAL
If you're going to do anything worthwhile as a master parent, you'd better know that love must be conditional.

Wait a minute! We've always been taught that our love, like God's love, is supposed to be *un*conditional. Well, believe it or not, this "unconditional love" concept that's been flying around for years is only a phantom. The Bible knows no such commodity, for the simple reason that God knows no such commodity. You can try to find it in the Bible, but no matter how hard you search, you'll never find the term—or the concept—in the Word of God.

So where did this notion come from? And why is unconditional love such a popular idea? It probably came from the same people who tell us that we should forgive everyone even if they don't repent (which is a very different approach than God himself uses). It's an easy sell, which is why so many parents buy into it.

The idea of unconditional love has gained such popularity because it makes us feel good. To think that God will love us no matter what is a great comfort. It's particularly comforting if we don't want to change anything about ourselves but still want to be loved "as is." (This is another nice-sounding lie—that God loves us "just as we are"; the truth is that for most of us, he loves us in *spite* of what we are.)

We all want unconditional love from others. We don't want it to matter if we're fools or jerks or uncaring slobs. We just want to be loved unconditionally. If others don't love us, even if we're manipulating, using, or oppressing them, then we get to point the finger and say *they* have a problem. Don't they know that God teaches unconditional love?

Offering unconditional love to other people, including our children, sounds like such a noble thing to do. "I'm not expecting anything," we say, keeping a stiff upper lip. "I'm just going to keep loving them with God's love."

The only problem with all of this is that the Master Parent knows and practices no such thing. His love is conditional at its very beginning. If we reject him as Savior and Lord, nothing in heaven or on earth—including hoping for unconditional love—will save us from condemnation.

He is *not* the Father of everyone, but only of those who accept him as Father, as Master Parent. Everyone else has a different father. "You belong to your father, the devil," Jesus said without a trace of unconditional love. Ouch! "How can you get in on love," he's asking, "if you pick the wrong father?"

For master parents, the crucial lesson is that true love—yes, unfailing love—is conditional. And the conditions are absolutely essential if we want to develop a beautiful and mutual relationship. We want to make sure of course, that we set the right conditions; do it wrong and we've sterilized love. But if we set the right conditions, if our love is based on something that is both real-world and real-heaven, we can create the love of a lifetime with our children.

In a remarkable passage, the Master Parent tells us that he is anything but unconditional. He says:

Do not judge, and you will not be judged. Do not condemn, and you will not be condemned. Forgive, and you will be forgiven. Give, and it will be given to you. A good measure, pressed down, shaken together and running over, will be poured into your lap. For with the measure you use, it will be measured to you.

This passage is loaded with conditions. It is also loaded with a key biblical concept: *Don't expect to receive anything if you aren't willing to do it or give it.* All of the actions listed in this verse are related to our relationships with other people. They are related to our relationships with our children. And the implication of every one is "If you *don't* listen, if you *don't* do these things, you'll end up with an empty sack."

Let's look at each one in turn.

DO NOT JUDGE, AND YOU WILL NOT BE JUDGED

The condition for not being judged by the people in our lives is that we not judge them. "My conscience is clear," wrote Paul, "but that does not make me innocent. It is the Lord who judges me." We're supposed to leave the judging to our Master Parent, who actually has the wisdom to do it right.

The lesson is clear for master parents. Our children can't expect to judge us ("This church you picked is totally stupid!") and expect unconditional love ("That's okay, honey, I'm sorry I haven't found something you like").

Instead, we will weigh them in the scales and find them lacking: "That was pretty good, judging me and the church in the same sentence! You know, they really think you're a nice person at that church. I wonder if they have the whole picture."

DO NOT CONDEMN, AND YOU WILL NOT BE CONDEMNED

Our children can't expect to condemn us and not face condemnation in return. "All my friends' moms are nicer than you! You never let me do anything I want to do. You're a rotten mother!" The voice of "unconditional love" might respond like this: "I'm sorry I'm not more plugged in, sweetheart. Tell me what you want to do, and we'll see if we can make it happen."

But "You know what?" is the question asked by conditional love. "There are no trade-ins on mothers. I'm the only one you've got, and you just went down ten points. And if those mothers are as nice as you say—and I'm not so sure you're a good judge of 'nice'—I'm pretty sure they wouldn't want to have a daughter with your attitude anyway. Maybe if you finish one or two of your chores around here, and stop making ridiculous requests like staying out until 3:00 A.M., you might get to do a few more things."

FORGIVE, AND YOU WILL BE FORGIVEN

Jesus makes forgiveness, a key element of love, utterly conditional. If we forgive, we'll be forgiven. If we don't forgive, we won't be forgiven. "Forgive us our debts, as we also have forgiven our debtors," he taught us to pray to our Master Parent.

He elaborates in another passage and directly brings our Master Parent into it: "If you forgive those who sin against you, your heavenly Father will forgive you. But if you refuse to forgive others, your Father will not forgive your sins." Here is God himself not practicing "unconditional love."

Master parents practice this "conditional forgiveness" principle with their children. If they don't forgive us or their siblings, they get no forgiveness from us. "If you don't forgive your brother his sins," we say, "your master parent will not forgive your sins. And by the way, neither will God."

If we don't take this approach, we run the risk of creating a house full of unmerciful servants, people who want to be forgiven a mountain while they beat their sister over a molehill.

GIVE, AND IT WILL BE GIVEN TO YOU

Unconditional love keeps on giving, regardless of the return. But the Master Parent disagrees with that approach. He gives more than we do—a good measure running over—but always in return for something. That "something" is *our* giving.

Master parents give to their children the same way the Master Parent gives to us. We will give more to our children than they give to us (a difference in degree). But we will not suffer a difference in kind, with them giving zero and us giving everything.

And the Master Parent is concerned with how we give. "Be careful not to do your 'acts of righteousness' before men. . . . If you do, you will have no reward from your Father in heaven. . . . Do not let your left hand know what your right hand is doing, so that your giving may be in secret. Then your Father, who sees what is done in secret, will reward you." If we give for the wrong reason, we get nothing from God.

Master parents treat their children's "acts of righteousness" the same way. If they do a "good deed" to get praised or to get something, we give them nothing—no return, no reward, no recognition. Only if they do their giving out of love and care do we give them anything in return out of love and care. Only if they give in "secret" do we respond ("secret" here refers to the purpose, not to whether anyone might happen to see the gift).

Our giving is always puny next to God's. Our children's giving will probably be puny next to ours. Puny is okay. But it has to be there at some level, and it has to be genuine.

FOR WITH THE MEASURE YOU USE, IT WILL BE MEASURED TO YOU

This is Jesus' summary statement of conditions in our relationships. If we forgive a lot, we'll be forgiven a lot; if we forgive a little, we'll be forgiven a little. If we give a lot, we'll get a lot; if we give a little, we'll get a little. Whatever we measure out gets measured right back to us. If our children break something and we blast away, we can't expect sympathy when we break something.

The Master Parent set up this principle of life, and master parents purpose to follow it with their children. We say to them:

"Don't expect to treat your sister that way and have me treat you any better."

"Don't think you can treat me like dirt and have me treat you like gold."

"If you think you can hold a grudge against me after I asked you to forgive me, I'm pretty sure you're going to have problems being forgiven by others the next time *you* blow it."

"You want me to share my paints with you when you refuse to share your toys with your brother? Nope."

There are other conditions for love to be meaningful, for love to work. If we don't have conditions, love becomes a twisted, contorted mockery of itself. We pour ourselves out for nothing in return—not even, in some cases, bare-bones respect—and end up feeling resentful, angry, and very used. So conditions are there to enhance and elevate love, not to cheapen or commercialize it.

Some of the conditions necessary for real love are:

- **Light and truth.** "If we claim to have fellowship with [God] yet walk in the darkness, we lie and do not live by the truth." The Master Parent has no fellowship with people who live a lifestyle of sin and then lie about it. Master parents follow the same guidelines. They don't try to manufacture a relationship out of darkness and lies. There can be no love where there is no decency or reality. A child who often lies about what she's been doing—saying she hasn't watched television when you know she has, telling you that a friend didn't come by while you were gone when you can see the evidence to the contrary—might still pretend to love you, but that's all it is, a pretense. Master parents don't go along with the pretense so their children will "like" them; instead, they let their children know they've created a gap that won't easily go away. "What upsets me," Nietzsche once said, "is not that you lied to me, but that from now on I can no longer believe in you."

- **Knowledge.** "Continue your love to those who know you," the psalmist prays. The Master Parent is more than willing to "continue" his love—never stopping—to anyone, to *everyone* who knows him. If we take the time and make the commitment to know him, the love never ends. Master parents know that there can be no real love for someone who doesn't care about who we are. When they commit to know us, we commit to love. If our kids don't care to get to know us, will it really affect them if our love is conditional? Yes, just as it affects us when we don't have time for our Master Parent and he pulls away. The distance between us might not always be in the front of our minds, but the nagging thoughts will keep chipping away at our souls. The universe is designed by the Master Parent to aggravate us when we're disconnected from him, even if we think that's what we want. So it will be with master parents and their children. We will always be in the back of their minds, and the nagging disconnection will chip away at their souls.

- **Seeking good.** In speaking of the things we need to have in order to live, basic things like clothing and food, the Master Parent tells us not to worry about them: "He will give you all you need from day to day if you live for him and make the Kingdom of God your primary concern." He expects us to care as much about the kingdom as he does. Master parents apply this to their families. "I will give you all you need from day to day—including my love and attention—if you make this family a primary concern." If we are committed totally to the family, and they don't care about it at all, whatever else we've got, it isn't love.

- **Obedience.** "But if anyone obeys his word, God's love is truly made complete in him." Our Master Parent will bring his enduring love fully into our hearts, but only if we obey him. With disobedience comes the restriction of love. And continued obedience is mandatory if we want to continue in his love: "If you obey my commands, you will remain in my love." Master parents see and understand this. We tell our children that if they want to fully and continually experience our love, they have to do their part and obey (or at least, for older children, honor). We make it clear that love has not ceased but that they have exited that love.

The alternative to conditional love is unsatisfying and even abusive relationships. If there's no big problem when our children treat us like dirt, if they continue to "get" from us even if they only give us grief in return, what does that teach them? It will show them that they can treat people badly and still expect love in return. They'll think it's okay to treat a future spouse badly, friends badly, employees badly—and still be able to demand "unconditional love." It will also teach them that their parent is a sap.

Conditional love teaches a simple and very different lesson. "Keep yourselves in God's love," we're advised. His love is always there for us, on the condition that we keep ourselves in it.

KNOWING LOVE MUST BE UNFAILING
If you're going to do anything worthwhile as a master parent, you'd better know that love must be unfailing.

"What a man desires is unfailing love," we are told. And yet one of the great challenges of life is to find this unfailing love in a world full of impostors: "Many a man claims to have unfailing love, but a faithful man who can find?" We have to pay attention, because there will be many people who will claim to be giving us unfailing love. But not all of them will truly follow through.

"Though the mountains be shaken and the hills be removed," says our Master Parent, "yet my unfailing love for you will not be shaken nor my covenant of peace be removed." When everything else gives way, when the creation itself crumbles, there will still be one thing standing: his unfailing love.

This is so important to him that he puts it into family terms: "Can a mother forget the baby at her breast and have no compassion on the child she has borne?" he asks, expecting our answer of "No!" Mothers don't forget their children. They can't.

But even if a mother could forget, God won't: "Though she may forget, I will not forget you!" His unfailing love survives everything, even the death or absence of a mother's love. Some of you reading this may have been abandoned or abused by your mother. She forgot you. But the Master Parent never did and never will.

Unfailing love from our Master Parent means that there is no "performance test," no spiffing up that we need to do before he loves us. He just chooses to love us, warts and all, and then he loves us persistently and obstinately. We don't have to jump through any hoops for him to love us.

Master parents are careful to follow God's lead. We have no "performance test" for our children, asking them to do this or accomplish that in order to earn our affection or approval. They don't have to jump through any hoops, because there *aren't* any hoops.

The alternative is to replace relationship with barter. "I'll give you the love and affection you need if you will live up to this expectation and make no mistakes." This is no way for children to live. They'll walk on eggshells, work hard to please us, and fret about living on the edge of a relational abyss. But sooner or later they will come to resent us, and then finally to hate us, for using their built-in need for parental love as a tool of manipulation and control.

And our children will fail. They will make mistakes. Will we focus on those mistakes? Unfailing love says we must catch our children doing good. It's a no-brainer to catch them doing bad or wrong. The trick is to catch them doing good. Master parents catch their children doing good at least ten times for every time they catch them doing bad.

Like our Master Parent, we offer unfailing love to our children.

We are consistent and persistent in our love. We focus our spirits, our minds, and our hearts on loving our children like no one has ever been loved. We know that our love will pass any test. "To be capable of steady friendship or lasting love, are the two greatest proofs, not only of goodness of heart, but of strength of mind," said William Hazlitt.

Unfailing love is a grand thing, and as master parents we can and must pass it along. Our Master Parent tells us this about unfailing love:

- **It's everywhere.** "The earth is full of his unfailing love." Master parents have experienced this love and intend to let it overflow onto their children every day of their lives.

- **We can ask God to let us see it.** "Show us your unfailing love, O Lord." As master parents we let our children ask us to show our unfailing love, and we show it to them.

- **It's worth thinking about.** "We meditate on your unfailing love." "How priceless is your unfailing love!" As master parents we want our children thinking about, and being secure in, our unfailing love. We want them to know our love is so good that it's priceless.

- **It leads God to save us.** "Save me because of your unfailing love." "Have mercy on me, O God, according to your unfailing love." Master parents will spend themselves to help their children, and still have enough love left over to ignite an endless supply of mercy.

- **We can trust it.** "But I trust in your unfailing love; my heart rejoices in your salvation." Master parents never do anything to make their children doubt their love. They may not like our actions, but our motives are always above question.

- **Sin won't cancel it out.** "I will punish their sin with the rod, their iniquity with flogging; but I will not take my love from him." Rejecting Jesus as Savior and Lord will cancel his love out, but sin and failure will not. Master parents punish their children, but never in anger or hatred. No sin will make us pull our love away from our heart of hearts.

- **It keeps us from falling apart.** "Through the unfailing love of the Most High he will not be shaken." As master parents we know that tough things may happen to our children. When they do, our unfailing love will provide an immovable foundation for their lives. Our children will be able to say, as we are able to say to our Master Parent, "May your unfailing love be my comfort."

- **It makes us sing.** "Satisfy us in the morning with your unfailing love, that we may sing for joy and be glad all our days." Nothing kills singing and gladness faster than feeling unloved. Master parents love so hard that their children can't avoid singing for joy and being glad all their days. Even after we are gone, the memory of our unfailing love will *still* make them sing—and they'll never forget the words.

When we have problems in our relationship with our Master Parent, he's always willing to take the first step. "God demonstrates his own love for us in this: While we were still sinners, Christ died for us." He doesn't wait. When we are quite unlovable—in fact, when we are on the bottom—he loves us. He doesn't wait for us to make the first move. He demonstrated his unfailing love by loving us, while we don't even know what love is.

Master parents understand that a big part of unfailing love is *going first.* Whenever there are problems in our relationship with our children, we take action first. What if your child offends you? "You go and show him his fault, just between the two of you." You don't wait for him to initiate the reconnection. You search for him until you find him. Then you make it better.

What if you're the one who offended your child? You must clear it up, even if it means leaving a church meeting to do so. You should "leave your gift there in front of the altar. First go and be reconciled." You shouldn't stew about it and try to rationalize it or act like what you did wasn't so bad. You must acknowledge your error, first to your Master Parent and then to yourself, then to your child. Look for her until you find her. Then make it better.

So whether the problem is our children's fault or our own, the Master Parent says, "You go first." The sun will never come up on a day where a master parent doesn't fight with unfailing love to close any relationship holes between herself and her children.

We will, at times, face difficult situations with our children, times when they don't deserve our love and respect. But for the sake of unfailing love we always give these things to them. "Part of kindness is loving people more than they deserve," said Joseph Joubert. Master parents love their children more than they deserve.

Our Master Parent has given us a promise of unfailing love: "God has said, 'Never will I leave you; never will I forsake you.'" Master parents make the same promise to their children: I won't leave you, I won't forsake you. Wherever you are, whatever you're doing, whenever you turn around, I'll be there.

In a request made long ago by Jonathan to David, the cry of every child's heart is echoed: "Show me unfailing kindness like that of the Lord as long as I live."

Master parents hear the cry and they show it—forever.

THE BLEND

Our Master Parent hints at the connection between conditional love and unfailing love when he says, "Sow for yourselves righteousness, reap the fruit of unfailing love." We have a responsibility to sow for ourselves righteousness. We have to take steps to be right with God. Only then do we reap the fruit of unfailing love.

The unfailing love has been there all along, waiting to be "activated" by our sowing of righteousness. The unfailing love is always there. But we only access it and get its "fruit" by meeting the condition: sowing for ourselves righteousness.

Master parents take the same approach. We tell our children, "My unfailing love for you is always there. It won't go away. And believe me, there are a lot of advantages to accessing it. But you have to be right with me before that can happen." Master parents reject the myth that they must always offer unconditional love.

When we miss the mark, our Master Parent might have to make it tough for us. But "though he brings grief, he will show compassion, so great is his unfailing love. For he does not willingly bring affliction or grief to the children of men." He does what he has to do to get our attention. He has conditions that must be met to receive his unfailing love. But he's always just a fraction of an inch away from compassion.

A master parent's attitude is the same. If our children miss the mark, we may have to bring them affliction or grief. We may have to correct them, discipline them, punish them. We will do it, but we don't do it willingly. It's not our first choice. We'd rather just pour the good stuff out on them. We do these hard things because our Master Parent does them with us. We hold tight to our conditions.

But our unfailing love is always there, waiting to go into action, waiting to release compassion. As soon as our children change, as soon as they repent, as soon as they say they're sorry and ask forgiveness, we throw open the floodgates of unfailing love and a high tide of compassion overflows them. Master parents are always only a tiny fraction of an inch away from compassion.

So the connection is this: There is unfailing love, but it comes with conditions. And conditional love always opens a door into unfailing love.

The psalms are full of details about the conditions of the unfailing love our Master Parent has for us. They tell us that:

- **We have to trust him to receive it.** "Unfailing love surrounds those who trust the Lord." The condition is that we have to trust him for the unfailing love to surround us. "Let the morning bring me word of your unfailing love, for I have put my trust in you." As master parents we tell our children that the unfailing love we have for them can only surround them—make them secure—if they trust us. That means they have to listen to us, take our advice seriously, and believe we have something that they can't find anywhere else.

- **We have to fear him to receive it.** "But the eyes of the Lord are on those who fear him, on those whose hope is in his unfailing love." The condition is that we have to fear God before our hopes for unfailing love will be effective. When we show how much we respect and honor and fear him, we cause a joyous release of love: "The Lord delights in those who fear him, who put their hope in his unfailing love." Master parents make no promises to children who don't respect and honor and fear them.

- **We have to serve him to receive it.** "In your unfailing love, silence my enemies; destroy all my foes, for I am your servant." We can ask for unfailing help with our enemies, both physical and spiritual, because we have set our hearts on service for God. As master parents we will stand up and fight for our children unfailingly—if they have a servant's heart, if they are willing to help us, our family, and others around us to build a better life.

- **We have to hope for it to receive it.** "May your unfailing love rest upon us, O Lord, even as we put our hope in you." This verse says we shouldn't expect to rest in God's unfailing love if we can't or won't put our hope in him. Master parents tell their children, "If you have confidence in me, with God's help I will never let you feel unloved."

- **We have to hate evil to receive it.** "Let those who love the Lord hate evil, for he guards the lives of his faithful ones and delivers them from the hand of the wicked." He doesn't promise to guard the lives of people who love evil or who are unfaithful to him. Master parents remind their children that no claims of love will be believed if the children also claim to love evil. We can't protect them if they go outside our sphere of influence, outside the protection of unfailing love.

- **We have to love him to receive it.** "Turn to me and have mercy on me, as you always do to those who love your name." We can claim God's unfailing love and mercy because we love him; we even love his very name. As master parents we tell our children that unfailing love and mercy are there for them, as they show even the slightest care for us and our family name.

The Master Parent's unfailing love exceeds all imagination—if we release it: "For as high as the heavens are above the earth, so great is his love for those who fear him."

We want his love for us to go that high, right through the Milky Way and into forever.

And our love for our children will be trailing right behind.

LAST THOUGHTS

If we make love conditional without making it unfailing, we produce a performance-based relationship that is really no relationship at all. If we make love unfailing without making it conditional, we produce a twisted view of relationship that does not allow us to ask for or expect anything.

"All you need is love," goes an old song, hitting very near the truth. We all need love, and it's almost true that *all* we need is love.

But we need the right kind of love.

We need a love that's worth something—something other than money, because we don't have enough to buy it, and it isn't for sale anyway. Its worth comes from our wanting it, from our having to put ourselves into it, from our having to meet the conditions that all great treasures require. We need conditional love.

And we need a love that just won't quit, a love that is relentless and insistent and ridiculous in its tenacity. We need unfailing love.

Master parents need this kind of love, and they know that their children need it desperately as well.

They offer their children unfailing love that is worth the commitment of their very lives.

And they offer their children conditional love that just won't quit.

Eleven

PARENTING
YOUR CHILD LIKE GOD
PARENTS YOU

In 1793, Philadelphia was a bustling city.

It was the capital and largest city of the new United States of America. It was alive with the rumblings of new government and the presence of luminaries such as President George Washington, Vice President John Adams, Secretary of State Thomas Jefferson, and Secretary of the Treasury Alexander Hamilton.

But in 1793, at the pinnacle of national glory and focus, Philadelphia was hit by the worst epidemic ever to strike an American city—a vicious outbreak of yellow fever. "The Philadelphia yellow-fever epidemic of 1793 had been as savage as an attack of bubonic plague and doomed the supremacy of Philadelphia among the cities of North America."

During the epidemic, thousands died. There were many heroic efforts, none greater than those of Dr. Benjamin Rush, whose later work earned him credit as the "father of American psychiatry." Dr. Rush worked incredible hours, spent himself on behalf of the sick and dying, and exposed himself to the disease again and again. His very presence gave people hope.

But there was a small problem. Dr. Rush had two basic "cures" for yellow fever, both popular treatments of the day. The first was to "bleed" the patient, to drain blood from him in hopes of reducing the fever. In addition to this being a very bad idea, Dr. Rush thought the human body contained more blood than it actually did. He would drain patients of up to eighty ounces of blood.

The second cure was no less destructive. It was a "mercury purge," which required that the patient be given a vial of liquid mercury to drink. It didn't do anything for the yellow fever, but it certainly shortened the suffering—by hastening death. At a different time and place, American hero Patrick Henry had been finished off by a mercury purge.

What can we learn from Dr. Rush's story? Is there a lesson for parents in this?

The answer is a resounding "yes!" To do well at anything, we have to have good intentions and strength of will, both clear attributes of Dr. Benjamin Rush. But we also have to have good thinking and good strategy, which Dr. Rush (like most physicians of his day) was sorely lacking. He cared about his patients and tirelessly and selflessly devoted himself to their welfare. But his heroic care and devotion succeeded in adding to the death toll, while curing no one.

Parents surely need good intentions and strength of will to succeed in this most challenging assignment. But if we don't add good thinking and strategy to our heroic efforts, our very care and devotion will wreak destruction on our children and our homes.

After nearly thirty years of working with families, parents, and young people, my conclusion is that most parents have good intentions, and the majority have the strength of will to succeed. We really do love our children, and we will do whatever it takes to raise them well. The desire and will to parent well, even heroically, is present in great quantities.

But there is an enormous absence of good thinking and strategy. Most of us got our "basic training" watching other people (like our own parents) parent with an absence of good thinking and strategy. No one enrolled us in a crash course in parenting before we brought those little bundles of joy home.

Even if we had taken a course or read a book, we might still be deficient or worse. In 1793, medical courses and books elaborated on the medicinal value of bleeding patients and giving them mercury purges. Some of today's courses and books on parenting are no less toxic to children. If we follow them, we'll drain the life out of our children or give them "cures" that will eat them up from the inside.

Many of these books and theories offer tools we can supposedly use to parent well. Unfortunately, many of them are wrong in their core idea. There is no "one size fits all" approach. "Just understand their personalities, understand their birth order, understand their temperaments, understand their adolescent identity (whatever that is)," we are told. The old saying is true: If your only tool is a hammer, every problem looks like a nail.

Master parents know that they have many tools, all of which derive from a wonderful premise: We can parent our children like God parents us. We don't have to make it up as we go along. We don't have to stay on top of all the new psychological "buzz" in order to be good parents. We can lose the idea that our problems are unique.

There are many thoughts and strategies out there on parenting. Many of them contain ideas that are true and useful. Many of the examples can illustrate truth. But there is only one overriding vision, one grand strategy, that works to put us in a small but growing group of truly effective parents: Parenting your children like God parents you.

You can be a master parent. All you have to do is commit to the grand parenting vision and strategy. All you have to do is commit to parenting your children like God parents you.

MASTER-PARENTING

In this chapter, we're going to get very specific with this magnificent approach that we have called master-parenting. We'll take a look at ten common challenges for parents today, and we'll see how to put the principles of master-parenting to use.

First, let's review what master-parenting is all about:

We begin by watching God very closely in his role as our Father, the Master Parent. If we see him doing something with us, we will do it with our children. If we see him avoiding something with us, we will avoid it with our children. We will study his work in the Bible and in our own experience with him, and we'll apply what we've learned as his "representative parents" to our children.

We've studied eight great paradoxes of master-parenting, elements that each contain two seemingly contradictory ideas. In the following examples, you'll see how to make these ideas work together as you begin to parent your children like God parents you. Before we jump into our ten key situations, let's review the eight great paradoxes:

1. Master parents have high expectations and have high tolerance.
2. Master parents dispense justice and dispense mercy.
3. Master parents teach through values and teach through results.
4. Master parents exercise authority and share power.
5. Master parents insist on "the Way" and insist on freedom.
6. Master parents protect their kids' innocence and expose their kids to reality.
7. Master parents keep their distance and connect at the soul.
8. Master parents know that love is conditional and love is unfailing.

Armed with these principles, you can take on your parenting assignment with a high confidence of success. So let's pull this together and look at how master parents use the principles, the eight great elements, to handle some specific situations.

ARGUMENTS AND DISAGREEMENTS

Arguments and disagreements are natural characteristics of any relationship, especially that of parent and child—people who are living out a complex relationship in very close quarters. Let's say you find yourself in an argument with your daughter because she feels her midnight curfew is unreasonable.

As you discuss the situation, require that your daughter speak to you in a respectful tone *(being in authority)*, but make it clear that you're willing to listen to her arguments, and allow her to participate in the conversation on equal footing *(sharing power)*. Do your best to explain your reasons for a midnight curfew *(teaching values)*, and because her purity is related to the "big issues" of life, be very intense and passionate about what you say *(insisting on "the Way")*. Explain, in some detail, the dangers of staying out too late with her boyfriend *(exposing to reality)*, but don't let yourself go too far and say things that destroy her optimism or idealism *(protecting innocence)*.

Don't allow yourself to become overly involved in the issue's minor details, like whether the curfew should be 12:00 or 12:15 *(keeping your distance)*. Look her in the eye and tell her how much you care about her in order to keep the conversation on a relational level *(connecting at the soul)*. After that, allow her to work out her own thoughts and convictions on the matter, and be content not to agree on everything *(insisting on freedom)*, in part because you know that the school of hard knocks will modify any unworkable ideas *(teaching through results)*.

YIELDING TO PEER PRESSURE

When your kids face the inevitable problem of peer pressure, you have to be careful not to be the "outside voice" that tells them everything they should do *(sharing power)* because you know they will transfer that outside voice to their peers and you sure don't want that! Don't get involved in the details of all of their relationships *(keeping your distance).* Go ahead and veto the worst of their friends *(protecting innocence)* but cut your kids a lot of slack on the peers who seem much less than true peers *(having high tolerance).*

Talk to your kids and explain the best way to carry on a friendship *(insisting on "the Way")* and the dimensions of friendship *(teaching values).* At the same time, allow them great room to explore many friendships *(insisting on freedom),* even the "rough" ones *(exposing to reality),* in part to let them learn about the ups and downs of peers in the school of hard knocks *(teaching through results).*

If they align with their peers against you, you'll need to adjust your approach to the relationship *(love must be conditional).* Even as you see these peers leading your children in the wrong direction, ready yourself to be there when the inevitable crash comes *(love must be unfailing).*

SIBLING RIVALRY

Since you are a master parent, really believe that your children can get along with each other and even learn to love, protect, and develop one another *(having high expectations).* Know better than to leave this to chance, however, so go ahead and show them what great families do *(teaching values)* and be very firm in your expectations that they learn to live this way *(insisting on "the Way").*

Work very hard not to create sibling rivalry through your own sloppy or unfair decisions *(dispensing justice).* And make room for a lot of negotiation and noise, because you know that enforced "harmony" is a lousy teaching tool *(having high tolerance).* Don't add to the problem by becoming overly involved in their squabbles *(keeping your distance).*

Allow your children to learn how to live with other people by learning in this "small school" with their siblings *(teaching through results).* Let them work out their own solutions *(sharing power),* as long as those solutions don't harm one of the children *(protecting innocence)* or challenge your right to set the standards *(being in authority).*

POOR PERFORMANCE OR LOW
INTEREST IN SCHOOL

When it comes to education, refuse to lower your expectations to match a child's poor performance *(having high expectations),* but also avoid focusing on the performance instead of the person *(connecting at the soul).* When your son fails because he doesn't care, get pushy *(insisting on "the Way"),* but when he fails because he's struggling and just doesn't get it, be more understanding *(dispensing mercy).*

Recognize and accept that a low level of interest might come from the fact that he simply isn't interested in the topic *(having high tolerance)* and that he would do better if he spent more time on the things he's most passionate about *(insisting on freedom).* When he does this, allow him to learn how far to press it by the results he gets *(teaching through results).*

Teach him that school is a good minipicture of life, which is full of boring and uninteresting things *(exposing to reality).* If he doesn't work with you to improve his performance or interest level, you know it's time to take action *(dispensing justice).* But don't actively intervene at school unless the problem is caused by abusive teachers or classmates *(keeping your distance).*

DISAGREEING WITH YOUR BELIEFS

It's a common problem for many Christian families: A teenager refuses to go to church, claiming she no longer believes "any of that stuff." When this occurs in your family, don't apologize for what you know to be critical *(insisting on "the Way"),* but do allow a lot of room for questioning, doubting, and disagreeing *(insisting on freedom).* Cut your daughter a little slack over things that seem to be challenging to you or disrespectful to the Master Parent *(having high tolerance)*.

Don't let her unilaterally change your church plans *(being in authority)*, but do allow her to help you revise these plans *(sharing power)* and look at other churches or youth groups *(exposing to reality)*. As she grows older, allow her to change *her* church plans *(insisting on freedom)*.

Tell her that some decisions, like openly rejecting Christ, will negatively impact your relationship *(love must be conditional)*, but that most disagreements are nothing compared with your love for each other *(connecting at the soul)* or your love for them *(love must be unfailing)*.

REALLY BAD TASTE IN MUSIC, MOVIES, AND TELEVISION PROGRAMS

What parent hasn't faced this issue? In dealing with your child's bad entertainment choices, start by telling him that there is value in diversity of taste *(having high tolerance)*. You can also involve him in setting some mutually acceptable boundaries *(sharing power)*. Let him know that within those boundaries he's completely free to make his own choices *(insisting on freedom)*.

Tell him that as long as he's living under your "watch," you'll always have some boundaries that cannot be crossed *(being in authority)*. If there are younger, "weaker" children in the home, don't allow them to be led astray by things they aren't able to process *(protecting innocence)*.

Talk with your son about what's good and what's bad from a perspective of principles rather than personal preferences *(teaching values)*. Try to elevate the conversation by talking about things that raise your souls *(having high expectations)*. You might even agree to "trade," crawling inside each other's world and listening to the other person's music and watching their programs *(exposing to reality)*. No matter what, refuse to let these areas damage your relationship *(connecting at the soul)*.

ABSENCE OF GRATITUDE OR APPRECIATION

It's tough to teach a person to be grateful, especially in a day and age when kids seem to be overwhelmed with "stuff" and it's hard to tell the difference between wants and needs. Begin by explaining to your children what gratitude and appreciation look like *(teaching values)* and how important they are to any successful life, including a successful family life *(having high expectations)*. Talk to them about having an attitude of gratitude and not just mouthing the words *(insisting on "the Way")*.

Make it a point not to respond to your children's requests *(keeping your distance)* if their desire is not accompanied by a history of prior gratitude *(love must be conditional)*. You can ask family and friends to stop giving them presents until there is evidence of gratitude *(teaching through results)*. You should also refuse to give to them if they are not freely giving to others *(dispensing justice)*.

Be sure to recognize even small attempts at gratitude *(having high tolerance)* and quickly forgive any genuine repentance over prior acts of rudeness *(dispensing mercy)*.

LAZINESS

If it seems you're constantly nagging your children to do their chores or help out around the house, don't worry. There is a solution. Start by setting family standards for contributing labor *(having high expectations)* and insist that the only acceptable way to live involves adding something of value to others *(insisting on "the Way")*. Teach them about the meaning of work *(teaching values)*, including the fact that they won't get anything *(teaching through results)* if they don't work *(dispensing justice)*.

Be careful that you don't turn your home into an organized boot camp *(insisting on freedom)*, and don't expect children, especially young children, to do things as well as you would *(having high tolerance)*. Talk with them about "job restructuring" *(sharing power)* and try hard not to let this daily grind become a source of bitterness *(protecting innocence)*. Some days, just because life can be hard, cancel all chores *(dispensing mercy)*.

Show them that what they put in is very related to what they will get out *(love must be conditional)* and that your greatest response will be related to what they *volunteer* to do *(insisting on freedom)*. Through it all, emphasize over and over that they don't have to do anything to earn your affection *(love must be unfailing)*.

SELFISHNESS

To be a kid is, in part, to be selfish and self-centered. As you tackle this problem, begin by remembering how hard it is to be a kid *(having high tolerance)* and keep reminding yourself that kids can't love themselves enough to void the need for your love *(love must be unfailing)*.

Let the school of hard knocks lead the way on instructing them *(teaching through results)*. Refuse to be moved when they don't get what they want *(keeping your distance)*. On a selective basis, leave them out of activities or events to show them that the world will go on without them *(exposing to reality)*. Don't let them take advantage of their siblings *(protecting innocence)*.

Tell them they are free to act like this *(insisting on freedom)*, but remind them that it's the opposite of everything you believe *(insisting on "the Way")*. Ensure that the more they push for their way, the less they will get it *(love must be conditional)*.

SEXUAL CONCERNS

The topic of sex is a land mine in many households. If it is not handled properly, the ramifications can be very costly—even deadly.

As soon as your children are capable of understanding, tell them that you expect purity *(having high expectations)* and show them it is the only way your family will live *(insisting on "the Way")*. Discuss with them how valuable sex is and how wonderful it can be in the context of marriage *(teaching values)*.

Let them know that they can always—gulp—get everything

they need to know from someone who actually knows: *you (protecting innocence)*. Spend time thinking of ways to love them more *(love must be unfailing)*, and make sure to give them tons of good affection and touch so they don't need to look elsewhere *(connecting at the soul)*.

Show them the destructiveness of errors in this area by giving them truth *(teaching values)* and by sharing your own observations and challenges *(exposing to reality)*. Let them know in no uncertain terms that taking advantage of siblings or friends will create unpleasantness *(dispensing justice)*. Assure them that you will never approve of unhealthy pursuits *(being in authority)*, but you'll always be ready to understand *(having high tolerance)* and forgive failure *(dispensing mercy)*.

REALLY PARENTING YOUR CHILDREN LIKE GOD PARENTS YOU

It's amazing how often we think we can do it different from God and still win. Or worse, that we can somehow do it *better* than God!

When you're faced with challenging attitudes or situations in the future, you don't have to fall back on the "trial and (mostly) error" method, or do it the way (or the opposite of the way) your parents did, or try to find a role model at church. Instead, you can fall back on God, your Master Parent.

Find a quiet fifteen minutes—lock yourself in the bathroom and turn on the water if you have to—and review the challenge in the light of what the Master Parent has taught you. Open this book to the table of contents, and ask yourself, "How does each of these elements relate to my current situation?"

Until the principles of master-parenting are really inside your head and heart, go back and read about any of the principles that seem fuzzy. You can start by reading the summaries at the beginning of this chapter. If you need more, go back and read the chapter itself or whatever portion needs clarification.

Remember: You didn't have kids so your parenting of them

would be an unsatisfying effort at best, or a disaster at worst. You had them so you could help them be the greatest human beings ever, so that you could have the grandest ride human beings—*related* human beings—could ever have together.

You don't need to make it up as you go. You have the model: your heavenly Father, the Master Parent. And he's given you incredible detail about how to parent your kids. You simply need to look at how he does it with you.

You can, with his help, parent your children like God parents you.

I know you can. And I hope you will.

Epilogue

Here we are, two parents, nearing the end of a grand journey together.

I didn't write this book to answer every possible parenting question, or to give you a range of techniques you an use to train your children (kids aren't much like dogs anyway, except for the messy and noisy parts). No such book could ever be written.

What I've really been doing is trying to give you a different way to think about parenting—about parenting in general and about your own parenting role. Is it a job? No. A profession? Certainly not. As I've said, parenting is, above all, about relationship.

And if parenting is about relationship, then we have to go well beyond tools and techniques to turn it into world-class relationship. A relationship is much more difficult to sustain, but also much more soul-satisfying, than anything else you can try to build with your children. It requires an understanding of the complexities of human life and the knowledge that complex human beings will not be reduced to a formula.

We need a guide, a craftsman, someone who can show us how to build a special relationship with our own offspring, someone who can show us how to balance the seemingly conflicting needs in that relationship—like expectations and tolerance, justice and mercy.

If that's so, we've always had the answer at our fingertips. We need only to look at our own relationship with our heavenly Parent, the Master Parent, God.

You can't get any better than God.

Issues are bound to come up—and problems, and questions that I haven't directly addressed in this book. But once you realize what it means to be a master parent, you'll know how to find the answers. Just go to your Bible and to your own experience with God, and ask, "How does my Master Parent deal with me on this?"

You're his representative. He'll give you the answer.

Someday, after you've followed this model in your parenting, you will wake up in eternity to find that your own children did it, and so did their children. They all followed you and became master parents themselves. "Children are the living messages we send to a time we will not see," says Neil Postman. Think of it: a world transformed, a world full of master parents. They will be your message.

And so, master parent, I bid you a rich farewell, wishing you many blessings on the rest of your journey into deep relationship.

As you begin to really parent your children like God parents you, stop and listen.

You'll hear the heavens resounding with joy.

OTHER BOOKS BY JAMES R. LUCAS

Family and Other Relationships
Am I the One? Clues to Becoming & Finding a Person Worth Marrying
1001 Ways to Connect with your Kids
Proactive Parenting: The Open Approach That Really Works
The Parenting of Champions

Leadership and Organizational Development
The Passionate Organization: Igniting the Fire of Employee Commitment
Balance of Power: Fueling Employee Power without Relinquishing Your Own
Fatal Illusions: Shredding a Dozen Unrealities That Can Keep Your Organization from Success

Personal Life and Growth
Walking through the Fire: Finding the Purpose of Pain in the Christian Life

Fiction
A Perfect Persecution
Noah: Voyage to a New Earth
Weeping in Ramah

Sources

Chapter 1: Master-Parenting and the Paradox Principle
2: "To have a fool": Proverbs 17:21

4: "You are my friends": John 15:14

4: "I no longer": John 15:15

5: "They'll know": While we're saying that as God is with us, so we should be with our children, we are *not* saying that parents are somehow mediators between God and their children. We're told clearly that there is only one mediator, and that is Jesus. We are no replacement or substitute for him. We should expect our children to relate directly to God. He is *their* Master Parent just as he is ours. But this book is not directly about showing children how to relate to God as their Father, as their Master Parent, or how to develop their relationship with him. Parenting your children like God parents you will, however, give them indirect teaching on these things, as they learn how to relate to us as human parents and to develop their relationship with us. In other words, we teach indirectly about relationship with God by modeling relationship with God.

5: "Be imitators": Ephesians 5:1

5: "In everything": Titus 2:7

6: "It is for freedom": Galatians 5:1

7: "It is possible": For more on this, see my book *Proactive Parenting: The Only Approach That Really Works* (you can order it from the Relationship Development Center, toll free at 1-888-248-1733).

8: "put on the new": Ephesians 4:24

10: "Great blunders": As quoted in *The Most Brilliant Thoughts of All Time*, edited by John M. Shanahan (New York: HarperCollins, 1999), 54.

Chapter 2: Inadequate Alternatives to Master-Parenting
14: "You are worried": Luke 10:41-42

Chapter 3: Master Parents Have High Expectations and Have High Tolerance
21: "For you made": Psalm 8:5 NLT

21: "be like God": Ephesians 4:24

22: "The Lord is": Psalm 103:8-9, 13

22: "For all have": Romans 3:23

22: "There is no one": Romans 3:12

26: "he who sows": Proverbs 11:18

26: "run in such": 1 Corinthians 9:24

26: "in a race": 1 Corinthians 9:24

27: "anything is possible": Mark 9:23, 10:27 NLT
28: "be completely": Ephesians 4:2
28: "gentleness be": Philippians 4:5
28: "be holy in all": 1 Peter 1:15-16
29: "A foolish": As quoted in *Word Lover's Book of Unfamiliar Quotations,* by
  Wesley D. Camp (Upper Saddle River, N.J.: Prentice Hall Press, 1990).
31: "treasure in": 2 Corinthians 4:7
32: "The Lord helps": Psalm 145:14 NLT
32: "Nobody should": 1 Corinthians 10:24
32: "Love . . . is": 1 Corinthians 13:4-5
32: "do nothing": Philippians 2:3
32: "made himself": Philippians 2:7
32: "patience is": Ecclesiastes 7:8
33: "Frequently": As quoted in *Word Lover's Book of Unfamiliar Quotations,* by
  Wesley D. Camp (Upper Saddle River, N.J.: Prentice Hall Press, 1990).
33: "He knows how": Psalm 103:14
35: "There is only": As quoted in *The Great Quotations,* compiled by George
  Seldes (New York: Kangaroo Books, 1977).
39: "As a father": Psalm 103:13
40: "Minds are": As quoted in *Word Lover's Book of Unfamiliar Quotations,* by
  Wesley D. Camp (Upper Saddle River, N.J.: Prentice Hall Press, 1990).
41: "You could": As quoted in "Fast Track to the Future," by Harriet Rubin,
  Fast Company (May 2001): 168.

Chapter 4: Master Parents Dispense Justics and Dispense Mercy
44: "For the Lord": Isaiah 30:18
44: "Follow justice": Deuteronomy 16:20
44: "If you *fully*": Deuteronomy 28:1, 15 NLT (emphasis mine)
44: "the Father": 2 Corinthians 1:3
44: "he does not": Psalm 103:10
44: "For I will": Jeremiah 31:34
44: "God has even": Job 11:6
44: "They will celebrate": Psalm 145:7 (emphasis mine)
45: "You take no": Psalm 5:4 NLT
45: "Administer justice": Jeremiah 21:12
46: "Do not be": Galatians 6:7
47: "loves justice": Psalm 11:7
47: "When a child": Jennifer Mangan, "Army Secrets of Good Discipline,"
  Christian Parenting Today (May/June 2001): 36.
48: "Whoever has": John 14:21, 23 (emphasis mine)
49: "Better is open": Proverbs 27:5
51: "For the Lord": Hebrews 12:6 NLT
51: "We will talk": For an extensive treatment of this important topic of

discipline and punishment, see my book *Walking through the Fire: Finding the Purpose of Pain in the Christian Life* (Nashville, Tenn.: Broadman & Holman Publishers, 1996). Chapter 17, "Applying the Principles in Families," gives some very specific and helpful advice to parents.

52: "They make the": See Jeremiah 21:14.

53: "discernment in": 1 Kings 3:11

53: "Cursed is": Deuteronomy 27:19

53: "judge . . . your": Psalm 72:2

53: "We look for": Isaiah 59:11

54: "And we don't": See 1 Samuel 8:3

54: "Does God": Job 8:3

54: "My justice": Isaiah 51:4

54: "Correct me": Jeremiah 10:24

54: "I will make": Isaiah 28:17

54: "Let justice": Amos 5:24

54: "The Lord is": Psalm 9:16

54: "Blessed are": Psalm 106:3

54: "When I was": James R. Lucas, *1001 Ways to Connect with Your Kids.* (Kansas City, Mo.: Quintessential Books, 2002). This book has 1001 ways for you to establish a one-of-a-kind connection with your children. The ideas are organized into twenty-five topical chapters so you can find exactly what you need fast.

55: "There is no": As quoted in *The Most Brilliant Thoughts of All Time,* edited by John M. Shanahan (New York: HarperCollins, 1999), 127.

55: "The line separating": Aleksandr Solzhenitsyn, *The Gulag Archipelago* (New York: Harper Perennial, 2002).

55: "Those who are": François Fénelon, *Talking with God* (Brewster, Mass.: Paraclete Press, 1997), 22.

56: "If anyone": Matthew 18:6

56: "Now if I do": Romans 7:20

57: "searches every": 1 Chronicles 28:9

57: "God does not": Galatians 2:6

58: "He has helped": Luke 1:54

58: "If you, O Lord": Psalm 130:3

58: "Blessed are": Matthew 5:7

59: "Shouldn't you": Matthew 18:33

59: "I will spare": Malachi 3:17

60: "Go and learn": Matthew 9:13

60: "If you had known": Matthew 12:7

60: "I was shown": 1 Timothy 1:13

60: "In your great": Nehemiah 9:31

60: "I tell you": Luke 7:47 NLT

61: "Who is a God": Micah 7:18

61: "his anger": Psalm 30:5
64: "The Bible makes": See 2 Corinthians 7:8-11.
64: "If your brother": Luke 17:3
65: "Remember when": Matthew 6:15
65: "in wrath": Habakkuk 3:2
66: "turn justice": Amos 5:7
66: "You have turned": Amos 6:12
66: "Punishment must": James R. Lucas, *Walking through the Fire* (Nashville, Tenn.: Broadman and Holman, 1996), 187.
66: "His father had": 1 Kings 1:6
66: "Who ever heard": Hebrews 12:7 NLT
66: "Do you show": Romans 2:4
67: "a corrupt witness": Proverbs 19:28
67: "Nothing emboldens": As quoted in *The Most Brilliant Thoughts of All Time*, edited by John M. Shanahan (New York: HarperCollins, 1999), 183.
67: "mercy triumphs": James 2:13
68: "What does the Lord": Micah 6:8
68: "Whoever turns": James 5:20
68: "love each other": 1 Peter 4:8
68: "You neglect": Luke 11:42
68: "Administer true": Zechariah 7:9
69: "Maintain love": Hosea 12:6 (emphasis mine)
69: "Fiorello La Guardia": As told in *The Little, Brown Book of Anecdotes,* edited by Clifton Fadiman. (Boston: Little, Brown, and Company, 1985), 339–340.

Chapter 5: Master Parents Teach through Values and Teach through Results

71: "faith comes": Romans 10:17-18
72: "Their voice": Psalm 19:4
72: "The heavens": Psalm 19:1-2
72: "Don't be misled": Galatians 6:7 NLT
73: "made up only": Isaiah 29:13
73: "spiritual act": Romans 12:1
73: "strengthened in": Colossians 2:7
73: "Faith is being": Hebrews 11:1
73: "prayer and petition": Philippians 4:6
74: "have been taught": 1 Thessalonians 4:9
74: "You were taught": Ephesians 4:22-24
74: "the difference": Ezekiel 44:23
74: "man does not live": Deuteronomy 8:3
75: "Use worldly": Luke 16:9
75: "only to teach": Judges 3:2
75: "I . . . speak": John 8:28

75: "useful for teaching": 2 Timothy 3:16
76: "Talk about them": Deuteronomy 6:7-9
77: "also taught about": 1 Kings 4:33
77: "many things by": Mark 4:2
77: "Repeat them": Deuteronomy 6:7 NLT
82: "everyone who": Luke 6:40
82: "we who teach": James 3:1
82: "with authority": Matthew 7:29
82: "See, I have": Deuteronomy 4:5-6
82: "What you heard": 2 Timothy 1:13-14
82: "teach them to": Deuteronomy 4:9
84: "Those who plow": Job 4:8
84: "If the righteous": Proverbs 11:31
84: "the wages of": Proverbs 10:16
84: "what the righteous": Proverbs 10:24
84: "prosperity is": Proverbs 13:21
84: "a tree of life": Proverbs 11:30
84: "the righteous will": Proverbs 10:30
85: "The one who sows": Galatians 6:8
85: "Remember this": 2 Corinthians 9:6
85: "become weary": Galatians 6:9
85: "he who sows righteousness": Proverbs 11:18
86: "he who sows wickedness": Proverbs 22:8
88: "pure joy . . . ": James 1:2-3
89: "you may be": James 1:4
89: "He who loves": Proverbs 13:24
90: "later on, however": Hebrews 12:11
91: "The things we know": As quoted in *The Most Brilliant Thoughts of All Time*, edited by John M. Shanahan (New York: HarperCollins, 1999).
91: "no discipline seems": Hebrews 12:11
91: "Later on, however": Hebrews 12:11
92: "discipline is a dimension": James R. Lucas, *Walking through the Fire* (Nashville, Tenn.: Broadman and Holman, 1996), 184.
92: "The ultimate result": As quoted in *The Most Brilliant Thoughts of All Time*, edited by John M. Shanahan (New York: HarperCollins, 1999), 289.
92: "A servant cannot": Proverbs 29:19
93: "sow wheat but": Jeremiah 12:13
93: "break up your": Hosea 10:12
94: "Logical consequences": As quoted in *Word Lover's Book of Unfamiliar Quotations*, by Wesley D. Camp (Upper Saddle River, N.J.: Prentice Hall Press, 1990), 49.
94: "the wages of": Romans 6:23
96: "Though I taught": Jeremiah 32:33

96: "When a mocker": Proverbs 21:11
97: "Only be careful": Deuteronomy 4:9

Chapter 6: Master Parents Exercise Authority and Share Power
100: "founded the world": Psalm 89:11
100: "God is the King": Psalm 47:7
100: "the kings of the": Psalm 47:9
100: "The highest heavens": Psalm 115:16
101: "The earth is": Psalm 24:1
101: "Where can I": Psalm 139:7
101: "Obey your parents": Colossians 3:20
101: "If you are": Isaiah 1:19
101: "For the mouth": Isaiah 1:20
102: "Obey the Lord": Jeremiah 38:20
102: "obey him with": 1 Timothy 3:4
102: "rule by their": Jeremiah 5:31
102: "He who would": As quoted in *The Most Brilliant Thoughts of All Time*, edited by John M. Shanahan (New York: HarperCollins, 1999), 273.
103: "commands are": 1 John 5:3
103: "I am free": 1 Corinthians 9:19
103: "obey your parents": Ephesians 6:1
103: "Don't make your": Ephesians 6:4 NLT
104: "No one can": Matthew 6:24
105: "As obedient": 1 Peter 1:14
106: "Encourage and": Titus 2:15
106: "true son in": Titus 1:4
107: "To obey is": 1 Samuel 15:22
107: "If anyone loves": John 14:23-24
107: "Dear children": 1 John 3:18
109: "So do not": Matthew 6:31-33
109: "to obey everything": Matthew 28:20
110: "You are awesome": Psalm 68:35
110: "He gives strength": Isaiah 40:29
110: "I have given": Luke 10:19
110: "[He] gave them authority": Matthew 10:1
110: "he gave them power": Luke 9:1
110: "Ask whatever": John 15:7
110: "If we're wise": See 1 Kings 3:9-14
110: "at once Jesus": Mark 5:30
111: "Jesus knew that": John 13:3-4
111 "got up from": John 13:5
111: "You know": Matthew 20:25-26
112: "all the kingdoms": Luke 4:5-6

112: "Obey the government": Romans 13:1 NLT

112: "The authorities": Romans 13:3-4 NLT

113: "for building": 2 Corinthians 13:10

114: "Peter Drucker": Peter Drucker, *Managing in a Time of Great Change* (New York: Truman Talley Books/Dulton, 1995), 17.

115: "Power tends": As quoted in *Peter's Quotations,* by Lawrence J. Peter (New York: Bantam Books, 1979), 439.

115: "Everyone who": Matthew 25:29

117: "will be taken": Matthew 21:43

117: "Sibling rivalry": Nancy Samalin, "Sibling Rivalry Is Not Just for Kids," *Bottom Line* (15 September 2001).

118: "With the measure": Matthew 7:2

118: "A boy becomes": As quoted in *Word Lover's Book of Unfamiliar Quotations,* by Wesley D. Camp (Upper Saddle River, N.J.: Prentice Hall Press, 1990).

119: "O Lord, our": Psalm 8:6-9 NLT

119: "divine power": 2 Peter 1:3

119: "For [God] granted": John 17:2

119: "It is for freedom": Galatians 5:1

119: "God seeks comrades": As quoted in *Word Lover's Book of Unfamiliar Quotations,* by Wesley D. Camp (Upper Saddle River, N.J.: Prentice Hall Press, 1990). 69.

120: "Those who exercise": Luke 22:26

120: "the whole assembly": 1 Chronicles 13:4

121: "Now it is required": 1 Corinthians 4:2

121: "the kingdom of": 1 Corinthians 4:20

122: "those who follow": 2 Peter 2:10

122: "From everyone": Luke 12:48

123: "points his finger": "King Nothing," sung by Metallica, © 1996 by Creeping Death Music. Published by Elektra Entertainment Group. From the CD *Load* © 1996 by Elektra Entertainment Group.

123: "submit to one": Ephesians 5:21

124: "The spirit of": As quoted in *Word Lover's Book of Unfamiliar Quotations,* by Wesley D. Camp (Upper Saddle River, N.J.: Prentice Hall, 1990), 103.

124: "Give him some": Numbers 27:20

125: "Whoever wants": Matthew 20:26-28

Chapter 7: Master Parents Insist on "the Way" and Insist on Freedom

127: "I am the Lord": Isaiah 48:17

128: "It is for freedom": Galatians 5:1

128: "For you have": Galatians 5:13 NLT

128: "And now I will": 1 Corinthians 12:31

128: "Stand at the": Jeremiah 6:16

129: "Thomas said": John 14:5-6
129: "This day I call": Deuteronomy 30:19
129: "Anyone who": James 4:4
129: "Salvation is": Acts 4:12
130: "And a highway": Isaiah 35:8
131: "See, I am": Jeremiah 21:8
131: "I will instruct": Psalm 32:8
131: "Do not be like": Psalm 32:9
131: "My son, give": Proverbs 23:26
131: "The Son can": John 5:19
132: "Show them the way": Exodus 18:20
132: "who went ahead": Deuteronomy 1:33
133: "Then you will": Joshua 3:4
134: "run in such": 1 Corinthians 9:24
134: "the corrections": Proverbs 6:23
134: "he who heeds": Proverbs 10:17
135: "Who, then, is": Psalm 25:12 (emphasis mine)
135: "train up a": Proverbs 22:6 NKJV
135: "It is for freedom": Galatians 5:1
136: "where the Spirit": 2 Corinthians 3:17
136: "The greatest gift": As quoted in *Word Lover's Book of Unfamiliar Quotations,* by Wesley D. Camp (Upper Saddle River, N.J.: Prentice Hall, 1990), 107.
136: "I have chosen": Psalm 119:30
139: "See to it that": Colossians 2:8, 16, 20-23
139: "infiltrated our": Galatians 2:4
140: "There is a way": Proverbs 14:12
141: "Dogma does not": As quoted in *The Viking Book of Aphorisms,* by W. H. Auden and Louis Kronenberger (New York: Barnes and Noble Books, 1993).
141: "I no longer": John 15:15 (paraphrase)
141: "Freely you have": Matthew 10:8
142: "proclaim liberty": Leviticus 25:10
142: "All creation": Romans 8:21 NLT
142: "The Jerusalem": Galatians 4:26
143: "Then you will": John 8:32
143: "I will walk about": Psalm 119:45
143: "Too often": Dr. Rick and Jerilyn Fowler, "The Ground Rules," *Christian Parenting Today* (Summer 2002): 33.
144: "the boundary": Psalm 16:6
145: "Clear limits tend": Marianne Neifert, "Why Kids Need Rules," *Parenting* (March 2001).

147: "Never tell people": As quoted in *The Most Brilliant Thoughts of All Time*, edited by John M. Shanahan (New York: HarperCollins, 1999), 208.

148: "Everything is": 1 Corinthians 6:12

148: "Everything is": 1 Corinthians 10:23

148: "Be careful": 1 Corinthians 8:9

149: "The apprentice": Richard Rhodes, *The Making of the Atomic Bomb* (New York: Touchstone Books, 1986), 35.

150: "What you have": As quoted in *The Viking Book of Aphorisms*, by W. H. Auden and Louis Kronenberger (New York: Barnes and Noble Books, 1993), 354.

150: "Choose for yourselves": Joshua 24:15

150: "I have chosen": Psalm 119:30

151: "To lead the people": As quoted in *Up the Organization*, by Robert Townsend (New York: Fawcett Books, 1970), 80.

151: "Whether you": Isaiah 30:21

151: "what you have": Luke 12:3

Chapter 8: Master Parents Protect Their Kids' Innocence and Expose Their Kids to Reality

153: "In regard to": 1 Corinthians 14:20

154: "The Lord protects": Psalm 116:6

154: "He protected": Joshua 24:17

154: "I am sending": Matthew 10:16

154: "all have sinned": Romans 3:23

155: "[Jesus] called": Matthew 18:2-3

155: "sure of what": Hebrews 11:1

156: "do everything": Philippians 2:14

156: "In the shelter": Psalm 31:20

156: "You will keep": Psalm 12:7

156: "Protect me from": Psalm 140:1

157: "Your enemies will": Matthew 10:36 NLT

157: "richly provides": 1 Timothy 6:17

157: "have not learned": Revelation 2:24

158: "If anyone comes": 2 John 10-11

158: "wise about what": Romans 16:19

158: "whatever is true": Philippians 4:8

158: "Holy Father": John 17:11

158: "You are my": Psalm 32:7

158: "The Lord is": 2 Thessalonians 3:3

159: "And lead us": Matthew 6:13

159: "For God cannot": James 1:13

159: "Jesus was led": Matthew 4:1

159: "Watch and pray": Matthew 26:41

159: "Get up and pray": Luke 22:46
159: "If you had known": Matthew 12:7
160: "Christ Jesus came": 1 Timothy 1:15-16
160: "The conduct of": Proverbs 21:8
161: "always protects": 1 Corinthians 13:7
161: "They have not": Daniel 6:22
164: "There's a fine": Peggy Shecket, as quoted in "Raising a Street Smart Child," by Kathy Koontz, *Parenting* (September 2001): 125.
165: "A good scare": As quoted in *Word Lover's Book of Unfamiliar Quotations,* by Wesley D. Camp (Upper Saddle River, N.J.: Prentice Hall Press, 1990), 99.
165: "when those who": John 16:2 NLT
166: "A righteous": Proverbs 12:26
166: "Be courteous": As quoted in *The Manager's Book of Quotations,* by Lewis D. Eigen and Jonathan P. Siegel (New York: AMACOM, 1989).
167: "in danger from": 2 Corinthians 11:26
167: "There were also": 2 Peter 2:1
167: "Children need your": Henry Cloud, "The Friendship Factor," *Christian Parenting Today* (July/August 2001).
168: "speak up for": Proverbs 31:8
168: "Flee from sexual": 1 Corinthians 6:18
169: "You are slow": Hebrews 5:11-13
169: "solid food is": Hebrews 5:14
169: "Growth demands": As quoted in *The Most Brilliant Thoughts of All Time,* edited by John M. Shanahan (New York: HarperCollins, 1999), 225.
170: "I am sending": Matthew 10:16
170: "be on your guard": Matthew 10:17
170: "Jesus told a": Luke 16:1-15
171: "The master commended": Luke 16:8
171: "For the people": Luke 16:8
171: "I tell you": Luke 16:9
171: "will be welcomed": Luke 16:9
173: "Oh, that I had": Psalm 55:6, 8
174: "live as children": Ephesians 5:8, 11-13
175: "protects the way": Proverbs 2:8
175: "Dear friends, do": 1 Peter 4:12-13
176: "My prayer is": John 17:15, 18
176: "Be on your guard": Matthew 10:17
176: "Watch out for": Matthew 7:15-16
177: "Do people pick": Matthew 7:16-18, 20
177: "In regard to evil": 1 Corinthians 14:20
177: "Then we will": Ephesians 4:14
177: "I will walk": Psalm 101:2-3

178: "Consider carefully": Luke 8:18
179: "Doubting everything": As quoted in *Word Lover's Book of Unfamiliar Quotations*, by Wesley D. Camp (Upper Saddle River, N.J.: Prentice Hall Press, 1990), 73.

Chapter 9: Master Parents Keep Their Distance and Connect at the Soul

181: "Should you not": Jeremiah 5:22
181: "As the heavens": Isaiah 55:9
182: "You thought": Psalm 50:21
182: "O Jerusalem": Matthew 23:37
182: "I will bring": Jeremiah 30:21
183: "If a man curses": Proverbs 20:20
183: "The eye that": Proverbs 30:17
183: "Do not come": Exodus 3:5
183: "honor your father": Ephesians 6:2
183: "the first commandment": Ephesians 6:2-3
183: "Great is our": Psalm 147:5
184: "Parents are the": Proverbs 17:6
185: "When I have": Deuteronomy 31:20-21
185: "Indeed, God": Job 35:13
185: "If you remain": Leviticus 26:21
185: "to be content": Philippians 4:11
186: "If you, O Lord": Psalm 130:3
186: "too pure to look": Habakkuk 1:13
187: "The Lord is far": Proverbs 15:29
187: "I will go down": Genesis 18:21
187: "And the distance": Luke 15:11-32
188: "Jesus often": Luke 5:16
189: "Her children": Proverbs 31:28 NLT
189: "Who is this": Job 38:2
190: "The power [has]": Mari Lyn Gandner, "The Disappearing Generation Gap," *The Christian Science Monitor* (May 29, 2002).
191: "In him we live": Acts 17:28
192: "sets the lonely": Psalm 68:6
192: "It is not good": Genesis 2:18
194: "What other nation": Deuteronomy 4:7
194: "Yet I am always": Psalm 73:23, 28
194: "took the children": Mark 10:16
195: "gathers the lambs": Isaiah 40:11
195: "O Lord, do not": Psalm 38:21-22
195: "My soul clings": Psalm 63:8
195: "Your life is": Colossians 3:3

195: "close to the": Psalm 34:18
195: "Anyone who": 1 John 4:20
196: "triple-braided": Ecclesiastes 4:12 NLT
196: "You may have": Perri Klass, "Should You Be Friends with Your Child?" *Parenting* (June/July 2002): 106.
197: "Am I only": Jeremiah 23:23
197: "After his resurrection": Luke 24:36-38
197: "Instead, he visits": John 20:27
197: "Why, O Lord": Psalm 10:1
197: "Do not be far": Psalm 22:11
197: "Those who are": Psalm 73:27
198: "He determined": Acts 17:26-27
198: "perceive[s] my": Psalm 139:2
198: "Where can I go": Psalm 139:7
198: "I need to be": Crystal Kurgi, "I Wish You Knew," *Christian Parenting Today* (November 2001): 30.
199: "Peter followed": Matthew 26:58
199: "the tax collector": Luke 18:13
199: "They detest me": Job 30:10
200: "These people": Isaiah 29:13
200: "I hate all crooked": Psalm 101:3-4 NLT
200: "Don't you know": James 4:4
201: "is on high": Psalm 138:6
201: "who say, 'Keep away' ": Isaiah 65:5
201: "Now in Christ": Ephesians 2:13,17
202: "I took you": Isaiah 41:9-10, 13

Chapter 10: Master Parents Know That Love Is Conditional and Love Is Unfailing

203: " 'O Lord,' prayed": Daniel 9:4
204: "I trust in God's": Psalm 52:8
204: "It probably came": Luke 17:3
205: "You belong to": John 8:44
206: "Do not judge": Luke 6:37-38
206: "My conscience": 1 Corinthians 4:4
207: "Forgive us our": Matthew 6:12
207: "If you forgive": Matthew 6:14-15 NLT
208: "Be careful not": Matthew 6:1, 3-4
209: "If we claim": 1 John 1:6
209: "What upsets me": As quoted in *The Most Brilliant Thoughts of All Time*, edited by John M. Shanahan (New York: HarperCollins, 1999), 89.
210: "Continue your": Psalm 36:10
210: "He will give": Matthew 6:33 NLT

210: "But if anyone": 1 John 2:5
211: "If you obey": John 15:10
211: "Keep yourselves": Jude 21
211: "What a man": Proverbs 19:22
211: "Many a man": Proverbs 20:6
211: "Though the mountains": Isaiah 54:10
212: "Can a mother": Isaiah 49:15
212: "Though she may": Isaiah 49:15
213: "The earth is": Psalm 33:5
213: "Show us your": Psalm 85:7
213: "We meditate": Psalm 48:9
213: "How priceless": Psalm 36:7
213: "Save me because": Psalm 6:4
213: "Have mercy on me": Psalm 51:1
213: "But I trust": Psalm 13:5
214: "I will punish": Psalm 89:32-33
214: "Through the unfailing": Psalm 21:7
214: "May your unfailing": Psalm 119:76
214: "Satisfy us in": Psalm 90:14
214: "God demonstrates": Romans 5:8
214: "You go and show": Matthew 18:15
215: "leave your gift": Matthew 5:24
215: "Part of kindness": As quoted in *Word Lover's Book of Unfamiliar Quotations,* by Wesley D. Camp (Upper Saddle River, N.J.: Prentice Hall Press, 1990), 166.
215: "God has said": Hebrews 13:5
215: "Show me unfailing": 1 Samuel 20:14
215: "Sow for yourselves": Hosea 10:12
216: "though he brings": Lamentations 3:32-33
217: "The Lord's unfailing": Psalm 32:10
217: "Let the morning": Psalm 143:8
217: "But the eyes": Psalm 33:18
217: "The Lord delights": Psalm 147:11
217: "In your unfailing": Psalm 143:12
217: "May your unfailing": Psalm 33:22
218: "Let those who": Psalm 97:10
218: "Turn to me": Psalm 119:132
218: "For as high as": Psalm 103:11

Chapter 11: Parenting Your Child like God Parents You
221: "The Philadelphia yellow-fever": David McCullough, *The Path between the Seas* (New York: Simon and Schuster, 1977), 141.
231: "Assure them that": For a tool you can put in their hands, see my book

Am I the One? Clues to Finding and Becoming a Person Worth Marrying (Nashville, Tenn.: Broadman and Holman, 2003).

Epilogue

234: "Children are the": As quoted in *The Most Brilliant Thoughts of All Time,* edited by John M. Shanahan (New York: HarperCollins, 1999), 193.